SEXUALLY VICTIMIZED CHILDREN

DAVID FINKELHOR

THE FREE PRESS
A Division of Macmillan Publishing Co., Inc.
NEW YORK

Collier Macmillan Publishers
LONDON

The Free Press
A Division of Macmillan Publishing Co., Inc.
866 Third Avenue, New York, N.Y. 10022

Collier Macmillan Canada, Ltd.

First Free Press Paperback Edition 1981

Library of Congress Catalog Card Number: 79-7104

Printed in the United States of America

Hardcover printing number

  5 6 7 8 9 10

Paperback printing number

  2 3 4 5 6 7 8 9 10

Library of Congress Cataloging in Publication Data

Finkelhor, David.
  Sexually victimized children

  Bibliography: p.
  Includes index.
  1. Child molesting—United States. I. Title.
(DNLM: 1. Child abuse. 2. Sex offenses. 3. Sex
deviation. WM610.3 F499s)
HV6626.F56   616.8'583   79-7104
ISBN 0-02-910210-3
ISBN 0-02-910400-9 pbk.

For my parents

CONTENTS

LIST OF TABLES

Acknowledgments

This book owes an enormous amount to Murray Straus. He encouraged me to believe that research on this subject was feasible even as a dissertation. He helped shepherd the project through many of the unusual hurdles presented by work in such a sensitive area. His perceptive criticism and editorial work are reflected in virtually every page.

In my many years in higher education, he is the finest teacher I have met, one who still believes that graduate work can be an apprenticeship. I have benefited greatly from his generosity and his insight. He has made many outstanding contributions to the field of sociology and the study of the family, but many of the most important do not even bear his name. As in the case of this research, they are incorporated in the training, teaching, and work of his students and colleagues.

I also sincerely want to thank the subjects of this study for their candor and their time. Twenty-five respondents showed special courage and made a large commitment of time and emotional energy to the project by volunteering to be interviewed. Their testimony was poignant and has helped tremendously to advance my understanding of this problem.

Sue Leslie labored long and hard in the preparation of the data and the typing of the manuscript. Sue Loeser helped with the interviewing, shared in the excitement, and contributed a great deal of sensitivity and skill to our talks with respondents. She has been a pleasure to work with.

Sigi Fizz has come to the rescue on many occasions with her technical assistance, administrative skill, and foresight. She saved the project many times from disastrous errors, inefficiencies, and delays. Barbara Kenney, Judy Zandonella, and Kathy Bergstrom prepared the transcripts. Ruth Miller, Suzanne Smart, and Rebecca Reiss helped in data-coding and typing.

Kersti Yllo, Gerry Hotaling, Jean Giles-Sims, Roger Libby, Noel Cazenave, Martha Huggins, Pat Miller, Gilbert Geis and Judith Herman gave me useful comments at various times. Pam Hagan deserves a great deal of credit and respect for the help she has given.

I would also like to thank the members of my dissertation committee for their constructive criticism: Stuart Palmer, Betty Roberts, Howard Shapiro, and Paul Wright.

The following also helped at points along the way: The UNH Human Subjects Review Committee, James Cerny, Richard Gelles, Ron Mazer, Lucinda White. Many teachers and colleagues gave me access to their classes and thus made possible the gathering of data.

The National Institute of Mental Health contributed in an important way to the support of this research under grants T32-MH15161 and R01-MH30939.

Even the DEC-10 computer, ordinarily the source of so much exasperation, seemed to shine favorably upon this project.

1

INTRODUCTION
AND
BACKGROUND

CHILD PROTECTION WORKERS from all over the country say they are inundated with cases of sexual abuse. A mother calls to report that she thinks her husband is molesting her daughter and she does not know what to do. A seventh-grade boy tells his school guidance counselor that a neighbor down the street has been giving him money to pose naked for pictures; he wants the man to stop, but he is afraid to tell his parents. A three-year-old girl brought to the emergency room with stomach pains is discovered to have gonorrhea, and she tells the doctor her seventeen-year-old brother has been "making me lick him" while her mother is away at work. These are illustrative cases.

Public outrage, which has for several years focused on stories of bruised and tortured children, is shifting to a concern with sexual exploitation. Between 1977 and 1978 almost every national magazine had run a story highlighting the horrors of children's sexual abuse. A national campaign against the making and sale of child pornography exploded into political prominence in a matter of weeks; and in record-breaking time it obtained the passage of protective legislation nationally and in thirty-five states (Densen-Gerber, 1978), despite the qualms of some civil libertarians. From the point of view of public awareness, what we have been witnessing amounts to nothing less than the discovery of a "new" social problem.

It is the purpose of this introduction to try to situate this social problem, the sexual abuse of children, within a number of perspectives. It will describe the social movements responsible for the current publicity. It will try to distinguish sexual abuse from two other, closely related problems to which it is often compared: physical abuse and rape. It will try to explain why sexual abuse is emerging as a public issue at this particular historical moment. Finally, it will try to anticipate some of the important ideological controversies that may arise out of the new attention drawn to this problem.

1

Feminists and Child Protectors

New social problems tend to arise when they are promoted by consti-tuencies that have both political power and public credibility. If the sexual abuse of children has risen to prominence as a social problem rather quickly, it is because it has been championed by an alliance of two consti-tuencies by now rather experienced in the promotion of social problems. One of these groups is the child protection lobby, whose power has in-creased in recent years as physicians have swelled the ranks of what was originally composed largely of social workers. It has had a great deal of success in the last ten years in achieving public recognition for child abuse as a social problem (Pfohl, 1977).

The second experienced group that has taken an interest in children's sexual abuse is the women's movement. Despite some setbacks in recent years on questions requiring direct political clout, it has played a role in sponsoring a large number (perhaps the largest number) of the enduring public issues of the last ten years, such as equal employment, abortion, wife-battering, and rape. The coalition of these two influential groups has created a professional and moral legitimacy for the problem which has helped boost it into prominence.

Despite their alliance, these groups have not promoted the problem in exactly the same way. Each one has tried to assimilate this new problem in-to the framework of old problems around which it has successfully cam-paigned. Thus for the child protection lobby, sexual abuse is but another facet of the child-battering problem with which it is already familiar. In their publications, one often sees reference to "the physical and sexual abuse of children," both topics lumped together in the same phrase. The women's movement, on the other hand, sees sexual abuse as a subcategory of the general phenomenon of rape. For example, Brownmiller (1975), the feminist who did the most to raise public consciousness about rape, argues for replacing the term incest with that of father-rape.

In reality, sexual abuse of children does not belong in either category. It is not just another kind of rape, nor is it just another kind of child abuse. As a social phenomenon, it really does belong at the juncture between these two concerns. It shares aspects of both other problems, but it also has features unique to itself.

Sexual Abuse and Rape

THE SIMILARITIES

Some of the similarities of children's sexual abuse to rape are obvious. (1) It is a sex crime (although not necesarily a sex-motivated crime). That is, it involves the genitals and sexual regions of either the offender or victim. (2) The offenders are almost all men. (3) The victims experience a kind of trauma unique to sexual offenses. They feel humiliated and stigmatized. They wonder whether they are at fault for their own plight, and they often fail to tell anyone about the experience because of the shame and doubt. Both experiences can have serious consequences for a person's sexual adjustment (Burgess *et al.*, 1978; Hilberman, 1976). (4) Finally, society has in the past treated both offenses similarly, in effect, denying that they were important and blaming the victim for their occurrence (Brownmiller, 1975).

THE DIFFERENCES

On the other hand, some aspects of the sexual abuse of children make it very different from rape.

1. The victims are male as well as female. Although among reported cases, boys make up only a small portion of the total, the research reported here and other research show that boys are frequent victims. Rape does occur to men, most notably in prisons, but in the general population its incidence is infrequent: thus rape is almost entirely a crime against women.

2. People who sexually abuse children are more often friends and family members of their victims (Peters, 1976). Rape is not so entirely different as many people think. Unfortunately it has been stereotyped as a crime committed only by strangers in deserted alleys, which is misleading: much rape is committed by men known to their victims. Still, over 50 percent of reported rapists are strangers to their victims, and only a scant 7 percent are actual family members (Mulvihill and Tumin, 1969, Vol. 2, p. 217). By contrast the vast majority of reported sexual abusers of children are friends or family: 30 percent relatives and 45 percent acquaintances, according to one survey (De Francis, 1969). The pattern for sexual abuse is typically one of much closer relationship between offender and victim than is the case for rape.

3. Children's sexual abuse more often than rape consists of repeated incidents, a friend or relative taking advantage of a child on several occasions (DeFrancis, 1969). It is not uncommon for relationships to start for a child at an early age and to reoccur continuously or at intervals over a period of five to ten years without being discovered or broken off. Rape, in contrast, typically occurs only once. At least a woman is likely to be raped only once by a given offender. The exception to this, of course, is marital rape, where the offense can occur repeatedly because many women are legally and economically trapped in their marriages and because marital rape is not currently defined as a crime. However, we know fairly little about this

problem, so comparison is difficult. Perhaps to be cautious, we should only say that among reported cases at least, children's sexual abuse is much more often than rape an offense of multiple occurrences.

4. The sexual abuse of children involves less physical force and violence than rape (Peters, 1976), which is quite commonly accompanied by a physical assault. Rape victims are often threatened with lethal weapons, a kind of coercion much less common in sexual abuse. Children are small and compliant, and many of the same results can be achieved without violence. The authority and power of persuasion held by an adult are usually adequate to establish the sexual contact.

5. The sexual act that occurs in the sexual abuse of children is usually not intercourse, but rather fondling of the genitals, masturbation, and exhibition (Peters, 1976). In contrast, a rape almost always involves sexual intercourse or attempted intercourse. In a strict legal sense rape *means* sexual intercourse: and if intercourse fails to occur, some other charge, like attempted rape, is brought.

Other kinds of sexual offenses not involving intercourse do occur to adult women and with some frequency. If we consider sexual harassment rather than just rape, we would probably find that attempts at intercourse constitute only a small proportion of all the sexual coercion against adult women too. However, on the basis of the available, admittedly sketchy, evidence (Peters, 1976) it still appears likely that intercourse is more often the goal of sexual coercion directed against adult women than children. We can also say that rape, as it is currently defined, i.e., independent of sexual harassment, involves intercourse more often than does the sexual abuse of children.

6. Children's sexual abuse implicates more people than does rape, which typically involves one or two assailants and a victim. The fact that many rapes are group affairs has been emphasized by Amir (1971). Nonetheless, the main protagonists are only the victim and the offenders. By contrast, because the sexual abuse of children often takes place in the context of a family, many others are usually involved. Most research has shown that when these sexual abuses occur, even with persons outside the family, other family members are intimately implicated (De Francis, 1969, pp. 108-112).

7. Children's sexual abuse engages a different set of social agencies. Rape reports usually go to the police, or lately to rape hotlines. Responsibility for dealing with sexually abused children is more diffuse, but social agencies generally play an important role. There are serious questions about whether the criminal justice system has the tools to cope with children's sexual abuse (Zaphiris, 1978). On the other hand, advocates of rape prevention seem to believe that better police protection and more expeditious court action, items of little help in sexual abuse, can ameliorate the rape problem (Sheppard *et al.,* 1976).

Sexual Abuse and Physical Abuse

Curiously, some of the very features of children's sexual abuse that distinguish it from rape make it similar to physical abuse. It is in this sense that sexual abuse is situated at the juncture of both problems.

THE SIMILARITIES

(1) Both physical and sexual abuse take place between children and the adults who have responsibility for taking care of them: they are family problems. (2) They both involve patterns that go on over extended periods of time. In fact, there is some evidence that not only do abusive relationships continue for many years but also they can be transmitted in the process of socialization from generation to generation within the same families (Greene, 1977; Summit and Kryso, 1978). (3) Both physical and sexual abuse fall into the domain of the child protection worker, who must negotiate in the interests of the child among the family, community, and court system.

THE DIFFERENCES

There are also some striking differences between physical and sexual abuse which have been insufficiently acknowledged, particularly by child-care workers. The result is that many interventions made into cases of sexual abuse on the basis of experience with physical abuse have been mistaken.

1. Sexual and physical abuse of children do *not* tend to occur simultaneously. De Francis (1969) found only 11 percent of sexual abuse cases involved physical abuse. Gil (1973) found only 0.6 percent of the physical abuse cases involved sexual abuse. Very important differences exist in the family dynamics surrounding each phenomenon (Zaphiris, 1978).*

2. The trauma of children's sexual abuse is primarily psychological, not physical. Physical abuse by definition causes pain, and it also leaves

---

* This statement does not mean that force and violence are absent in families where sexual abuse occurs. In one type of sexually abusive family, abusing fathers are tyrannical and often use physical force against their children and wives. But there are many sexually abusive families where this force does not occur. Even where violence is present, apparently it is not severe enough in many cases to result in the physical injuries that constitute current criteria for diagnosing child abuse.

evidence in many cases. But most important, physical abuse is life-threatening. Children's sexual abuse does sometimes result in physical damage to the genital area, and there are increasing reports of childhood gonorrhea. However, the lives of such victims are rarely in danger, unless of course, the sexual is combined with physical abuse (Peters, 1976, p. 411).

3. The motivations behind the two kinds of abuses are different. Some sexual abuse of children is like rape and expresses a hostile, coercive, or sadistic impulse toward the child (Burgess *et al.*, 1978); other sexual abuse, although sometimes as destructive in its impact, is not so hostile in its impulse. It may emerge from a desire for sexual gratification or sexual assertion. Physical abuse, however, even though it may come from a parent who loves the child, expresses at the moment a desire to harm the child (Gil, 1973, p. 7).

4. Social attitudes toward the two kinds of abuses are different. In overt ideology, at least, our society is much more intolerant of behavior resembling sexual abuse. Sexual behavior of any sort is only approved in highly restricted contexts and sexual behavior with children not at all. An adult even talking to a child about sex is considered provocative, as is demonstrated by the enormous skittishness shown by schools and teachers around the question of providing sex information to young children.*

Violence, by contrast, is overtly approved in many more conventional situations, one of the most common being for use in disciplining children (Steinmetz and Straus, 1974). This approval is so widespread that many adults are only vaguely aware of what the difference is between so-called "strict discipline" (a code phrase for the liberal use of physical punishment) and abuse.

5. Finally, the children most vulnerable to sexual abuse are preadolescents (Queen's Bench, 1976), whereas those most vulnerable to physical abuse are young children and small infants under six (Maden and Wrench, 1977). Of course, vulnerability to both kinds of abuse extends over the whole range of childhood. Infants have been used for sexual purposes (Sgroi, 1975), and even adolescents may be beaten or killed. But the most frequently beaten and severely injured children are infants, whereas the peak vulnerability to sexual abuse occurs from ages eight to twelve.

In summary, sexual abuse is not a more serious or less serious problem than rape or physical abuse. It is a different problem, and it has its own characteristics. In some ways, it could be described as a conjunction between the two. However, because it is different from each, it needs to be studied from its own distinct vantage.

---

* Next to this overt condemnation, there is a covert approval of some kinds of sexually abusive behavior toward children, as in indicated by the popularity in some segments of the population of so-called "kiddie porn." Where this attitude exists it is at least hidden or repressed and subject to disapproval by most of the rest of society.

The Historical Context

There is an important difference between a social problem—a situation recognized by some not necessarily large segment of the population—and a public issue—one recognized by a broad section of society, particularly policy-making elements. Many social problems championed by specific groups never achieve the status of public issue. Sex education has, for example, foundered on the divide between social problem and public issue for many years, with some groups in society strongly advocating it, but with no real broad and sustained national mobilization behind it.

Sexual abuse of children had that same intermediate status for a long time. Although serious scholars from Kinsey to Freud to Havelock Ellis have devoted attention to it, dating back to the turn of the century and before, they all failed to express alarm about the problem. Nonetheless, sexual abuse, in a somewhat different guise, did become an issue of large public concern at a certain historical moment—although it did not last. To understand why sexual abuse is again becoming a public issue now, and how this issue is currently taking shape, requires an understanding of its history as a public issue in the past.

If sexual abuse has failed to become a sustained public issue, many observers would blame our Victorian heritage. In spite of the gradual sexual liberalization of the last century, it has still been extremely difficult for people to discuss openly many sexual topics. The vast majority of people who have had such sexual experiences in childhood have probably kept them secret even from their closest confidants (Armstrong, 1978; Landis, 1956), many living lives burdened by shame and guilt. This reticence has made it hard to document the problem.

Only in quite recent times have the moralistic attitudes about sex abated enough so that discussions of sexual anomalies of various sorts have become acceptable. This atmosphere has no doubt encouraged many people who were victimized as children to discuss their experiences, leading to a general increase in public awareness. Since many such people are middle class and sometimes in positions of power and responsibility, the problem has acquired a credibility which problems often do not have when they are widely thought to be isolated cases or restricted to the lower class.

FREUD'S CONTRIBUTION

There is more than just Victorianism behind the fact that sexual victimization has taken so long to surface as a public issue. The intellectual history of the problem has also played a role. It is important to consider the effect of the ambivalent attention given by scientists, who were in a position to have called more attention to sexual abuse but didn't.

One of these of course, was Freud, a figure who must be placed at the center of any account, critical or complimentary, of the history of children's sexual victimization as a social problem. It was Freud, whose theories of childhood sexuality, if nothing else, brought this subject out of the total darkness of the Victorian era into the arena of contemporary scientific discussion. But even if he did unveil the issue, there are many among the contemporary commentators who feel that Freud did much more to distract from and derail serious study of the problem than he did to further it (Herman and Hirschman, 1977; Rush, 1977).

Childhood sexual experiences played a key role in Freud's early theories of neurosis. Confronted by a large number of his patients—young, tormented Viennese women—who reported having been sexually approached at an early age by fathers and brothers, he at first suggested the idea that childhood sexual trauma was at the root of adult psychological problems.

He later changed his mind, however, and decided that the stories he had been hearing from his patients were fantasies, not true experiences. This belief led him to the formulation of the famous Oedipus complex, which postulated a strong impulse in the child for sexual union with the parent, leading to fantasies and sometimes overt acts by the child. Psychopathology stemmed now not from sexual trauma with adults but from failure to "resolve the Oedipal situation," to give up the fantasies and transfer sexual impulses to more socially acceptable people.

Rush (1977) has speculated that Freud abandoned his original theory because he was unwilling to face its implications: that the predatory acts of his own peers and colleagues in Viennese society (and even perhaps his own father) lay behind his patients' difficulties. He might challenge sexual Victorianism, but to challenge male sexual conceit was too much for even this iconoclast.

Whatever his motives, his revised theory sponsored or at least helped rationalize two very negative developments in the study and treatment of sexually abused children. It equipped the budding army of mind healers with an ideology that discounted patients' reports of childhood sexual victimization. Several generations of women who have brought up such experiences in psychotherapy have found them discounted and contradicted by their therapists (Herman and Hirschman, 1977).

Adding to whatever trauma such a denial might produce, Freud's revised theory also turned his original theory upside down by placing blame for whatever overt events might have irrefutably occurred on the child, not on the adult. Such experiences were now the result of the child's Oedipal impulses rather than the adult's predatory ones. It was an ironic development: Freud's revised theory took the moral opprobrium directed at the offender in such situations and placed it on the victim. In some people's view, this ideology of denial and blaming the victim has been the biggest obstacle to the serious study and promotion of the problem of children's sexual victimization.

KINSEY'S CONTRIBUTION

Kinsey was another central figure in the history of research on child sexuality, and he too had a rather ambivalent impact on the study of sexual victimization. On the one hand, Kinsey's studies broke new ground, establishing that childhood sexual experiences were virtually universal and thus giving assurance to many people that their previously imagined deviance was in fact shared by many others. However, in spite of evidence from his survey that child molesting, sexual abuse, and incest were far more widespread than anyone had previously been able to show, he gave these findings very little attention. He made pronouncements that he thought incest was more in the imaginations of psychotherapists than it was in the experiences of their patients (1948), and he wondered why any child should be so distraught at having its genitals fondled by a stranger (1953, p. 121). He chose to give great emphasis to the normality of homosexual experiences, masturbation, and extramarital affairs, but downplayed the commonness of sexual abuse.

Certainly Victorianism and sexism have played their parts in blocking recognition of the seriousness of children's sexual victimization. But a full understanding of the story requires us to remove ourselves from the vantage point of contemporary sexual discussion to the reality of sexual politics of the last several generations.

CHILD MOLESTING AND THE MORALISTS

Many people think sexual abuse is a discovery of the 1970s—which is far from the case. Concern about child molesting and the sexual corruption of children have been persistent themes of moralists for decades. If one can judge from the spokesmen on the subject, the people who are "discovering" sexual abuse today are the liberal professionals and academics. This theft by the liberals of a onetime conservative issue can happen today only because of a realignment of political forces on issues of public policy concerned with sexuality.

At several times in the recent past, sexual abuse has exploded into public awareness. In 1937 for example, four girls were murdered in connection with sexual attacks, and a wave of mass hysteria ran through New York City (McCormack, 1938). Again in 1949 a particularly gruesome sex murder of a child in California coincided with reports of sex crimes in other parts of the country, all of which sponsored a flurry of anxious magazine articles and calls for legislative action ("Horror Week," 1949; "Sex Rampage," 1950).

In fact, action was forthcoming. Commissions were set up in several states, notably New York, California, New Jersey, and Massachusetts, to study the problems and make legislative recommendations. In response to these commissions and sometimes independently, so-called "sexual psychopath" laws were hastily enacted in a dozen or more states. These laws, which are still on the books in many places, allow for the detainment for an indefinite period of anyone diagnosed by a psychiatrist to be a sexual psychopath (Sutherland, 1950).

Most of these actions were directed at a wide variety of sex crimes, not just child molesting, although it was usually seen as the most important and was often the one that sparked the legislation. Moreover, child molesting at the time was thought to be primarily a problem of disturbed strangers who accosted young children, whereas today it is realized that most sexual assaults on children take place at the hands of family and friends. Nonetheless, this period was one of widespread public concern about the sexual abuse of children, perhaps even greater in terms of its extent and the action it produced than the one we are witnessing today.

Where, during this period, were the professionals—researchers, for example, like Kinsey—who are today discovering sexual abuse? For the most part, they steered clear of the issue of child molesting. They were busy lobbying for sexual reform: greater availability of contraceptives, more and better sex education, more enlightened treatment of sex offenders, fewer restrictions on erotic literature, decriminalization of consensual sexual acts, permissiveness toward childhood sexual exploration, and so forth.

The liberal professionals feared, with some justification, that the concern over child molesting was likely to scuttle their reform efforts. The issue was being used by conservatives to oppose sexual reform. To each of the liberal endeavors, conservatives painted a grim picture of the widespread immorality, promiscuity, degeneracy, and criminality that would take place if they were implemented. A no less prominent guardian of the conservative cause than J. Edgar Hoover described the situation in an article, "How Safe Is Your Daughter?" in the popular *American* magazine in 1947: "Depraved human beings more savage than beasts are permitted to roam America almost at will," he bemoaned. If liberal reforms were to be achieved, the children would be the ones to suffer.

In the face of this paranoia, liberal professionals tried to downplay concern about child molesting. They insisted that it was rather infrequent and certainly not on the increase ("Crime in California," 1953), and they pointed out that the children were often the ones at fault because they had been "seductive" (Bender and Grugett, 1952). The liberal psychiatrists who took charge of many of the commissions tried to defuse the anxiety being generated by moralists and the press. They emphasized that child molesters were not sex fiends and hardened criminals, that the problem was not one of decaying moral standards and sexual permissiveness, and that the arena for dealing with it lay in the mental-health field rather than with new, repressive legal measures ("Sex Rampage," 1950).

Such a concern helps explain some of the paradoxical positions taken by Kinsey, for example, who downplayed sexual abuse in flat contradiction to the results of his own surveys. Although Kinsey has often been portrayed as a detached "orgasm counter," in fact he had a strong reformist zeal (Pomeroy, 1972). He was in the forefront of those trying to assuage the public's anxiety about child molesting ("Sex Rampage," 1950).

Thus, concern over children's sexual abuse bloomed for a period, but in the face of concerted resistance from the professional and research community, people who are ironically now the most perturbed by the problem, interest waned and the problem went into eclipse for twenty years.

REALIGNMENT OF SEXUAL POLITICS

Now, of course, it appears that there has been a dramatic realignment of forces in sexual politics. The liberal-moralist battle remains, but on many issues the moralists have been defeated, and initiative has passed to the liberals. No one familiar with battles over abortion, sex education, homosexual rights, etc. would dare proclaim a victory for sexual reformers, but the successes of recent times and the sexual liberalization of large segments of the population have created a very different climate.

The result is that the liberal position, no longer monolithic and consolidated by adversity, has broken into component parts—advocates for women, advocates for homosexuals, sex educators, libertarians, and so forth. Sexual abuse is emerging as an issue at this historical moment because that earlier coalition is fragmenting. The women's movement, which was once in almost total alliance with the sexual reform movement, has gained in strength and autonomy and has formulated its own priority issues, some of which were not priority issues of the earlier coalition. Sexual abuse is one of these new issues which has emerged from a recasting of the sexual reform agenda from the point of view of women.

Interestingly, there appears to be very little concern (at least publicly expressed) that the current publicity about child molesting will foster a conservative backlash against sexual liberalism, the backlash that was feared by reformers in an earlier period. This attitude may be in part because those concerned about protecting children do not identify so strongly with other reform causes any more; but more likely, it is because they believe that the climate of sexual liberalism is well enough established that it cannot be reversed. The very success of sexual liberalism has created conditions under which this potentially more troublesome issue (from the liberal point of view) could have its day.

SEXUAL ABUSE AND SEXUAL REFORM

However, the sexual abuse of children still promises to be a controversial social problem. It is possible that some serious clashes over public policy will result from the development of this new concern. The clashes are likely to occur not between those who want to keep and those who want to roll back the sexual revolution. Rather, they will divide those who want to give priority to alternative programs of sexual reform. Those who are most concerned about protecting children from abuse may find themselves at odds with those in favor of creating a freer sexual environment, particularly in the family.

The following discussion is speculative and inferential. Very little has appeared in print arguing the ideological positions that will be outlined here. Yet it seems highly likely that a public policy debate about family sexuality is in the offing, fueled to some extent by the recent concern about sexually abused children. In the next few paragraphs we will try to anticipate some of the positions in this discussion, based on the available literature. This speculation is important and worthwhile because it points out what may become some of the important theoretical and empirical questions about family sexuality.

We have described so far some of the social, historical, and ideological developments that have permitted a new awareness of the sexual exploitation of children. This awareness carries with it an outlook on the nature of sexuality in family life—an outlook conditioned by two important facts: (1) The sexual exploitation of children is common. (2) It often takes place in the family. These facts convey an image of the family as a place in American society where children are sexually vulnerable.

It is important to recognize that there have been ideological developments from other quarters, also within the sexual reform tradition, that have been urging a different kind of outlook on family sexuality—one arguing, in effect, for more rather than less sexuality in family life. These points of view are not necessarily in conflict, but they could be.

Those arguing for more sex are not in favor of sexual abuse. Rather, they are interested in combatting a climate of sexual repressiveness in which they believe the culture is trapped. They believe people in our society are sexually inhibited and guilt-ridden as a result, primarily, of childhood sexual repression, which causes among other things sexual perversion, sexual maladjustment, marital problems, and the inability to express affection

(Martinson, 1973; Pomeroy, 1974). If there is any opportunity to unlock this vicious cycle, they believe, it is in the family. In this view, in order to counteract sexual repressiveness, families must become more sexually open environments. To do so, children must be encouraged to take much more positive attitudes toward sex and sexual curiousity, and parents and children need to talk candidly about sexual matters. The secretiveness, anxiety, and taboo which dominate the topic of sex in most families must be abolished (Pomeroy, 1978).

Those who would create more sexual openness think it crucial, as a key to this process, to eliminate some of the myths that create sexual anxiety within the family (Currier, 1977). For example, there is the myth that children are not sexual, that they should not be permitted to masturbate, show sexual curiousity, or engage in sex play with other children. This myth has been well-enough demolished that it is now ritually disproven in most child-rearing manuals.

However, there are still new frontiers. For example, many of those in favor of sexual reform in the family have begun to promote the idea of family nudity (Pomeroy, 1978). They have mounted an assault in recent years against the psychoanalytic convention that adult nudity is harmful to a child because it is overstimulating or arouses oedipal anxieties. On the contrary, say the reformers, nudity fosters sexual comfort and positive gender identification (Oremland and Oremland, 1977).

A certain wing of this movement has developed even more radical proposals. Some have argued that intercourse in a child's presence (the classic Freudian nightmare) or mild forms of sex play between parents and children need not be traumatic, and if they are handled the right way, can have educative functions (Oremland and Oremland, 1977).

A few have been willing to suggest that the whole cornerstone of family sexual anxiety—the incest taboo—needs to be re-examined (Constantine and Constantine, 1973; Pomeroy, 1978). Currently, there is research underway to uncover "positive" incest experiences, ones indicating that sexual contact among family members need not be so extraordinarily antisocial nor so highly traumatic as has been stereotyped (Nobile, 1978).

This train of thought is disturbing to those concerned about sexual abuse (Goldsen, 1978; Steinem, 1977). It poses the obvious question of whether the logic of family sexual liberation results in making children more vulnerable to sexual victimization. Will it promote the fantasy of sex with children, and in men with weak control of their sexual impulses, lead to overt exploitative activity?

The criticism by those concerned with sexual abuse has been primarily directed at those more extreme proponents of the sexualized family. But it might easily encompass some of the more moderate proponents, too. Given the large number of children sexually abused by family members, they may ask, should the family become any more sexualized than it already is? Do children need to be protected from rather than subjected to the sexuality of their elders?

On the other side, those who are advocating a change in family sexual values and behavior may come to see the child protectors as obstacles to their cause. Won't focusing so intently on the threat of sexual exploitation within the family, they may ask, only increase family sexual anxiety and lead to increased sexual repressiveness? Won't it promote a climate where fathers continue to be self-conscious about even hugging their daughters, let alone treating sex in a casual and open way? Despite its laudable intentions, won't the preoccupation with sexual abuse in the family have a chilling effect on openness about sex?

The Debate on Family Sexuality

Thus there is clearly the potential for conflict between those who are pressing for more open sexuality within the family and those trying to protect children from sexual exploitation. Drawing out the elements of each position, in anticipation of a public confrontation and perhaps even in exaggerated form, is useful because it allows us to analyze the assumptions of each point of view. There are four important theoretical issues about which the two camps appear to disagree, all of which can be addressed with empirical findings.

1. Is sexual abuse a result of too much sexual repression or not enough? On this issue, those most concerned about sexual abuse (Rosenfeld, 1977) tend to be arguing from a Freudian perspective, even though they are often critical of Freud and his treatment of abuse victims. Freudian doctrine has maintained that the family was an environment rife with incestuous impulses which always threatened to get out of control. Evidence in recent years that there is a great deal of sexual abuse and incest has supported the Freudian intuition that such sexual impulses are the norm and not the exception.

These unruly impulses are kept in check primarily by taboo and repression (Freud, 1962). Such constraints perhaps do not need to be as rigid as in Victorian times, nor do they need to apply to so many aspects of sexuality. But some basic ones must exist, such as the taboo on incest and sex with children. When these constraints are too weak, behavior that is uncontrolled, antisocial, and exploitative can easily occur. Sexual abuse, this point of view would predict, should occur in families with weak normative controls.

However, those concerned about freeing the family from sexual repression would probably say exactly the opposite. Their view implies that sexual repression is the cause of, not solution to sexual exploitation. Sexual repression breeds people who have twisted and hostile forms of sexual expression, who feel intensely sexually deprived and thus exploit other, defenseless people. They would probably predict that sexual abuse would be more common in highly repressive environments.

2. Is childhood sexual expression really related to any social benefits? Those favoring more open sexuality in the family may be particularly willing to run risks involved in the increasing sexualization of children because they believe the benefits will be so positive. They believe we can eradicate many social ills by allowing children and families freer expression of sexual impulses. In such a society, would there really be fewer sexual problems, less social exploitation, and even less violence? There is evidence from research in child development that sexually anxious parents breed passivity (Sears, 1965, p. 152), and from anthropology that sexually open societies have less killing (Prescott, 1975), but more evidence is needed.

3. What are the long-term consequences, for the child, of sex with an adult? Those believing in more open sexuality in family life might take a position of cultural relativism, arguing that sexual experiences between adults and children are only harmful because our society makes such a fuss about them. The main damage occurs not from the experience itself but from the social reaction a child encounters. Even in this society, there may be many instances of children who had positive or at least innocuous experiences (Pomeroy, 1978). If family sex is not really that harmful and what harm there is comes from societal reaction, then it may be more important to change societal reaction than to focus so exclusively on the dangers of family sex.

Those concerned about sexual abuse are likely to be skeptical about this reasoning. Through personal exposure, they are acutely aware of the enormously traumatic experiences many children have had and the disruption they caused in their later lives. In support, the weight of Freudian opinion is that the great disparity between the physical size and social sophistication of adults and children makes child-adult sexual encounters inherently traumatic (Oremland and Oremland, 1977). Anthropological evidence suggests, too, that although adult-child sexual contact does occur in some cultures, it is not common (Ford and Beach, 1951), and that the taboo on incest, one important form of adult-child sex, is universal (Murdock, 1949).

4. Do changes in the sexual culture of families benefit males and females equally? Feminists in particular among those concerned about sexual abuse may charge that much of the pressure for sexual liberation comes from a male point of view. It has tended to emphasize more sex and better sex with more people. These have not necessarily been the sexual priorities of the women's movement. Feminists may wonder whether the sexual liberation of the family would have benefits for women that are more clear cut. Or would it tend primarily to benefit men, while the women carried

most of the burden of risk because of their greater vulnerability to sexual exploitation?

From this discussion, we can see that sexual abuse is not just a problem for social workers. It is also a problem for social theorists since it poses some key questions about the nature of the family and human sexuality. Unfortunately these are not questions we can address fully in this study. Rather they are part of a research agenda for a whole generation.

What this study can do is set the stage for a serious scientific investigation of the problem, by asking some questions preliminary to any deeper probing. For example, how widespread is the phenomenon of sexual encounter between adults and children, and between family members? What are the main descriptive features of these experiences? Beyond these general questions, findings from this study do cast light on some of the controversial issues raised here. For example, is sexual abuse the result of too much or too little repression? In Chapter 9, there are some clues to an answer in the discussion of some of the family factors that are statistically correlated with experiences of sexual victimization. In Chapter 10, we try to assess whether the general historical trend toward sexual liberalization has been associated with an increase or decrease in the incidence of sexual abuse. Both of these matters reflect on the connection between sexual repression and sexual abuse.

Other elements of the controversy are addressed throughout the study. In almost every chapter, for example, comparison is made between the experiences of boys and girls. This is crucial to an assessment of whether changes in family sexuality will have a differential impact on the sexes. Another continuing concern is identifying the important sources of trauma. Are they intrinsic to the experience of adult-child sex or do they stem from social reaction? The implications of our findings for some of these controversial issues will be summarized in the conclusion of this work.

The Scope of This Study

THE EXPERIENCE OF INTEREST

To address some of the issues raised here, this study could have investigated a variety of subjects: sexual development, childhood sexual experiences, sexual exploitation, family sexuality, to give some examples. Even the topic we have been so confidently referring to as sexual abuse is not just one topic. It has been used to mean incest, sexual assault, sexual exploitation, and more. But what this study is interested in are sexual experiences that occur between children and older persons. All the experiences we wish to study have the following characteristics: (1) They occur to children. (2) They are considered inappropriate by society. (3) They involve persons who by virtue of being older have a substantial advantage in authority and sexual sophistication over their child partners.

We excluded sexual experiences that occur among peers, no matter what the age of the child. This exclusion eliminates what is often called sex play among preadolescent children and adult-style sex as it occurs among preadolescents and young adolescents. Who is a peer and who is an older person is not always easy to define. Our method of using a strict age difference allows for some ambiguity, unfortunately, but we feel it is the best of the alternatives that were practical for this study. We think it has been successful, but that is something the readers will have to judge for themselves. Further discussion of our methods is provided in Chapter 3.

We considered defining our subject matter in other ways, for example, sexual overtures toward children where force was used, or sexual experiences of children that the child reported as negative. However, rather than trying to define it in terms of the experience of the child, we decided to use the social inappropriateness of the age of the partners involved.

NAMING THE PROBLEM

What to call this kind of experience poses another problem. Various terms have been proposed in the last few years: sexual abuse, child molestation, sexual victimization, sexual harrassment, sexual assault, child rape, and sexual misuse. Each appears to emphasize a slightly different aspect of the phenomenon. The differences are not great, but a choice must be made.

Sexual assault is not a good term because many of the experiences we will be discussing do not involve physical violence. Similarly, child rape is not accurate because of many of the differences from rape which we described earlier. Child molestation is a classic term, but it is too closely associated with the stereotype of the stranger in the schoolyard and does not appear to encompass the many family members who are involved. Sexual harrassment is too weak, and sexual misuse makes the child sound like a thing, not a person.

So far in this chapter, we have used the term sexual abuse, which is probably the most widespread. We have used it because it has been adopted most consistently by the movements we have been describing. But we have not chosen it for our title, and we will de-emphasize its use in the remainder of this work for a reason mentioned earlier: Sexual abuse is a concept based on a parallel with physical abuse, emphasizing its aggressive and hostile motivation. But sexual abuse is not necessarily aggressive and hostile.

We favor the term sexual victimization, which emphasizes that the child is victimized by age, naivete, and relationship to the older person rather than by the aggressive intent of the abusive behavior. However, we do not wish to be doctrinaire about this terminology. The term sexual abuse, because of its currency, will appear from time to time in the rest of the text.

Some researchers might reject any of these terms. All of them are highly charged and have pejorative connotations that may be distracting to an unbiased examination of the problem. This is not our position, however. We recognize that these terms are political and moral ones, but we do not feel that this disqualifies them from use in scientific investigation.

For one thing, it is the intention of this work to support the renewed social and political concern over the problem of sexual victimization. As this research will show, children are sexually victimized by adults far more often than is generally realized. This is a serious social problem, and in the effort to raise public consciousness, a term that arouses, like sexual victimization or even sexual abuse, is a good one.

Second, merely choosing another, "sanitary" term like "childhood sexual experiences with older persons"—a term that we will use extensively, incidentally—does not solve any problems. It is still obvious to anyone but the most gullible that what the researcher is interested in is the phenomenon that is being called sexual abuse by people in the social and political arena.

The better course of action, and the one adopted here, is to use the value-laden term but to carefully caution readers about perceptual biases that it may introduce.

In addition to the major theme of sexual victimization of children, this work has a secondary interest: incest. For purposes of the study, incest means sexual contact between family members and relatives, including those of the immediate and extended family. Much sexual victimization is incestuous and much incest is sexual victimization as we have defined it; but they are not identical. In particular, sexual contact between family members of the same age is a kind of incest that is not victimization, and sexual contact between an unrelated adult and child is victimization that is not incest. However, because the two are so closely related, we felt we could not address one issue without the other; thus findings on incest are discussed in Chapter 6 and continued to some extent in Chapters 7, 8, 9.

The Plan of the Book

Chapter 2 is devoted to theories about why sexual abuse occurs: the motives of the offender, the vulnerability of the child, the dynamics of the families, and the function sexual abuse plays in the larger society.

Chapter 3 explains the justification for and strategy adopted by this study. It outlines some of its limitations, as well, and assesses, to the extent possible, its validity.

Chapters 4 through 9 present the actual findings of the study, embedded in a discussion of the issues raised by them. Chapter 4 gives an inventory of the sexual victimization experiences. Chapter 5 looks at the older partners: who they are, how old, what sex. Chapter 6 introduces the subtopic of incest, distinguishes it from the larger subject of sexual victimization, and reports some of the findings about it. Chapter 7 tries to answer the question, "Why were some experiences more traumatic than others?" Chapters 8 and 9 try to find out whether there were any features in their backgrounds that distinguished the sexual victims from the other people in the sample. Chapter 8 looks specifically at social and demographic features, and Chapter 9 at family structure and composition.

Chapter 10 compares selected findings from this study with those from other studies in an attempt to answer two questions: (1) Has the incidence of sexual victimization been increasing or decreasing? (2) Are there differences between the kind of cases that are reported to agencies and those that are not.

Finally, Chapter 11 gives a short overview of the findings, some suggestions for future research, and some commentary on how the findings of this study reflect on the social policy questions posed earlier in this chapter.

The reader's attention is also drawn to Appendix C, which contains the personal account of an incest victim interviewed by the author and an interpretive commentary on her experience. The account graphically illustrates the family dynamics and personal impact of one of the most severe kinds of sexual victimization.

2

WHY ARE
CHILDREN
SEXUALLY VICTIMIZED?

THIS CHAPTER PRESENTS THIRTEEN THEORIES about why children are sexually victimized. These theories are concerned with why offenders do it, why it happens to some particular children and in some particular families, and why it is apparently so common in our society. Altogether, however, they do not add up to an inspiring panorama of insight. Knowledge on this neglected subject is still in a primitive state, as is almost any topic related to sex.

Actually, a deeper flaw is the fact that we know more about sexual deviance than we do about sexual normality or ordinariness—to choose a less value-laden word—and this topic is a good case in point. Here we are inquiring how children come to have sexual experiences with adults when we hardly know how they come to have sexual experiences at all. Thus all theories about children's sexual victimization must be viewed against their true backdrop: a vast ignorance of the forces governing the development and expression of sexual behavior in general.

Theories about the Offender

Early theorizing on this subject was heavily moralistic and medical as the following view illustrates:

(1) ABUSER AS DEGENERATE

In this theory sexual abusers of children were seen as psychopathic, feeble-minded, physical and moral degenerates (Krafft-Ebing, 1935), but such preconceptions did not long withstand the light of evidence.

20

The early efforts to study sex offenders had a kind of heroic quality to them; long-suffering interviewers made meticulous studies of the dregs of humanity in dismal prisons as they tried to get beyond the myths of the sex fiend. Their research on this subject revealed that most of the stereotypes were false. Only a small portion of such sex offenders were psychotic, senile or mentally retarded (Cohen and Boucher, 1972; Glueck, 1954; Gebhard *et al.*, 1965). They painted a rather more human, sometimes even sympathetic, portrait of the child molester, one which in many cases made him sound more attractive than the run-of-the-mill criminal.

They were not primarily strange men who lured away their victims in parks, playgrounds, and alleyways. More often they were friends, neighbors, or relatives of the children they victimized. They were not brutal and sadistic, for the most part, but used their authority or charm to gain children's confidence, cooperation, or at least, passive assent. And unlike rapists, they did not try to have intercourse with their victims. Rather their penchant was for genital fondling, exhibition, and masturbation.

Since many of these researchers were psychoanalytically oriented, their theorizing focused on the developmental experiences of these offenders.

(2) Seductive Mothers

An offender's sexual interest in children resulted from a disturbance in his relationship to his parents. Many child molesters were viewed as men who had overly seductive mothers, whose overtures aroused their incest anxiety. The incest anxiety in turn spawned a fear of adult women and adult sexuality and a turning toward children, who did not present such a threat (Glueck, 1954).

Other theories followed the early Freudian model and focused on early childhood sexual trauma as the source of deviant behavior.

(3) Sexual Fixation

Sexual preoccupation with children resulted from an unusually pleasurable childhood sexual experience, so that the offender, like Lolita's notorious Humbert Humbert, becomes fixated at an early developmental stage or conditioned to respond to that early childhood stimulus (McGuire *et al.*, 1965; Nabokov, 1955). A negative sexual experience could have a similar effect by either deterring the individual from normal sexual maturation or driving him into a compulsive repetition of the original situation in an effort to change the outcome.

Imaginative as these psychoanalytic theories are, they have not received a great deal of empirical confirmation. Subsequent studies on larger samples have failed to find regular patterns. Only a minority of offenders show the childhood traumas and the warped parental relationships that the psychoanalytic approach would predict. Men who become sexually involved with children seem to be a much more heterogeneous group than was originally thought (Swanson, 1968). Researchers have more and more had to turn away from an overarching theory toward typologies that take account of the variety of personalities, situations, and behaviors.

The following five propositions are not theories in the sense previously cited. Rather they are empirical generalizations about sex offenders against children based on the most current research. For the most part, they explain some of the difficulty in establishing a theory of sexual victimization.

(4) DIVERSITY OF SEXUAL OFFENDERS AGAINST CHILDREN

(4a) Only a minority of incarcerated child molesters (25 to 33 percent) have a primary and relatively permanent sexual interest in children, something that would be described as a personality characteristic (pedophilia). The rest became involved for what seem more transient reasons: an unusual opportunity, stress, the frustration of other sexual outlets, etc. (Gebhard, *et al.* 1965; Groth, 1978).

(4b) A sexual involvement with children has very different motivational roots in different men. In some it is an act of sexual gratification, but for others it expresses a need for closeness or for aggression.

(4c) Sexual interest in children, particularly on an enduring basis, does seem to be connected to a fear of adults and adult sexuality. Children are often attractive to such men because they are naive, undemanding, and do not have adult physical characteristics (Hammer and Glueck, 1957).

(4d) The motivation for involvement with children depends a great deal on the age of the offender, the age of the child, and the activity involved. Adolescents molest children for different reasons than do adults. Men who are sexually interested in very young children differ from those interested in older ones. And the motivational roots of exhibitionism, for example, contrast strongly with those of incest (Gebhard *et al.*, 1965; Mohr *et al.*, 1964).

(4e) Alcohol shows a consistent connection with patterns of sexual abuse of children (Browning and Boatman,1977;Gebhard *et al.*,1965; Virkkunnen, 1974). Nonetheless, many social scientists doubt that this large number of sexual offenses means that alcohol causes or releases a sexual interest in children (or other deviant interests). Drinking may be more of a way in which the activity is excused or rationalized by the offender than a causative factor (Gebhard *et al.*, 1965; McCaghy, 1968).

Of course, even these generalizations must be taken with an appropriate dose of caution. What these men have in common may be more the fact that they have been caught than that they had sex with children. The vast majority of offenders against children, the undetected ones, may be of an entirely different breed.

Thus, although simple profiles of the typical sexual abusers have not been forthcoming from research on incarcerated offenders, the findings have at least influenced the direction of future efforts. It is acknowledged that they are not generally impulsive, raving, sex maniacs or psychopaths. This knowledge, combined with the frustration of efforts to account for their behavior psychologically, has led to a new focus for research—on the family situation where sexual abuse arises.

Theories about the Victim

Since it has been easier, on the whole, to talk to victims than to offenders, a great deal of therorizing has taken place about the children who are involved in child-adult sex. Many attempts have been made to relate its occurrence to something about the psychology of the victim.

From the time this question was first taken up, the idea that children might be the instigators, not the passive victims, of the offense has had a great deal of currency. For many years, the one myth researchers took the most relish in exploding was that children were helpless prey to adult offenders. It has been pointed out repeatedly in the literature that children do things that contribute to their victimization: they act suggestively, they go along with the offender's proposition, they allow the situation to continue, and they fail to report it to anyone who could take action to stop it. All these seem to indicate varying degrees of complicity in the offense (Ramer, 1973).

Freud, as we pointed out earlier, laid the groundwork for this orientation with his theory that every child in his or her fantasy life wishes for sex with his parents, and by extension, other adults and that this fantasy sometimes spills over into reality. Lauretta Bender, a famous American child psychiatrist and one of the earliest to research adult-child sexual encounters, found that all the victims she interviewed were unusually attractive children who made seductive overtures to the psychiatrists (Bender and Blau, 1937). The theory based on these kinds of observations usually is articulated as follows.

(5a) THE SEXUALLY ACTING-OUT CHILD

Some children act in ways that actively encourage adults to approach them sexually. These are children who have poor relationships with their parents, who are needy in other ways, and who have discovered that they can obtain attention and affection from an adult by arousing his sexual impulses (Burton, 1968).

A related theory which holds the child less fully responsible for the sex offense emphasizes the following:

(5b) THE SEXUALLY DEFENSELESS CHILD

When approached by offenders, many children seem to collaborate in their victimization by failing to take self-protective actions. They accept the adult overtures, they agree to accompany the adult somewhere, they allow the situation to continue, and they do not take action to stop the molestation. Such children are believed to be disturbed, have sexual conflicts, few friends, or a passive outlook, all of which make them especially vulnerable (De Francis, 1969; Weiss *et al.*, 1955).

In the field known as "victimology," there is a tradition of theories like these that try to understand the ways in which victims contribute to their own victimization. The process is usually called "victim precipitation," and it highlights the fact that victims frequently contribute to their own murders — by striking a first blow or hurling an insult — or to their own robberies — by leaving doors unlocked and valuable possessions in plain sight.

What is unusual in the case of sexual abuse of children is the degree of importance that the victim precipitation analysis has assumed. The idea that murder victims bring on their own demise developed fairly late in the field and had a moderate effect on our understanding of homicide. In contrast, the idea that children are responsible for their own seduction has been at the center of almost all writing on sexual abuse since the topic was first broached.

Victim precipitation in sexual abuse is also unique because it is so poorly defined. In homicide cases, it has been given the very precise meaning that the victim was the one to strike the first blow (Curtis, 1976). In discussions of rape, it was defined as an actual offer of sexual intercourse that was later withdrawn. But in the case of sexual abuse, anything a child might do that does not conform to the standards of an "ideal" victim is liable to get the child called an accomplice.

Some critics have said this kind of preoccupation really reflects the fantasies the researchers have about the children and also the defense a male-dominated society erects to avoid recognizing a particularly seamy side of male sexuality (Rush, 1974). In addition, it also reflects the fact that researchers who have studied only the victim are likely to try to use what they know about his or her psychology to account for the experience. (In homicide cases, by contrast, victims are not usually available for study.) All these factors may account for an overemphasis on victim precipitation.

This theory has some important logical defects that should also be noted (Silverman, 1974). To an extent that has not been adequately recognized, the idea that victims contribute to their own victimization is a tautology. By the mere fact of acting and making choices, people have control over things that bring them to fateful junctures, an existential truth illustrated in Thornton Wilder's *Bridge of San Luis Rey*. It is too easy and incorrect to conclude from this truth that a victim had a desire or predisposition for the misfortune that befell him or her.

In addition, the whole notion of victim precipitation depends very much on whose point of view is taken. What may have seemed like a precipitating gesture from the point of view of the offender (or more likely the researcher)—such as rubbing up against someone — may not have been for the victim. Children most certainly do not share adult meanings of sexual gestures, but since researchers are also usually adults, they are more likely to identify with the offender's view. For some offenders, the mere fact of a child's physical beauty may be enough to precipitate sexual overtures. Is the victim responsible for this occurrence? Fortunately, in the last few years, largely as a result of consciousness raising by the women's movement on the subject of rape, investigators have become somewhat more circumspect about blaming the victim.

Theories about Family Context

Some of the earliest research discovered that much sexual abuse of children took place among family members, but it has been only recently that families, rather than family members, have been implicated in this problem. This new awareness required a willingness to talk to all the family members, instead of just the ones most handy. The discovery of family therapy as a method of clinical treatment, and also an increasing interest by sociologists in the problem, have also helped advance a family approach to sexual abuse, in contrast to the earlier psychodynamic approaches.

Family dynamics have been easiest to identify in the case of incest. Father-daughter incest has been the kind most theorized about, since it is the kind most frequently observed. Here the sexual abuse takes place in the heart of the nuclear family, and the group process is most readily analyzed. Thus we will review some theories about incestuous families and show how in some cases these theories can be generalized to include sexual abuse outside the family. (The personal account of father-daughter incest appearing in Appendix C illustrates well the operation of these theories.)

(6) SOCIAL ISOLATION

Incest occurs in families characterized by a high degree of social isolation (Bagley, 1969; Riemer, 1940; Weinberg, 1955). In the stereotype, such families come from backwoods Appalachia: they are poor and interbred. But similarly isolated families can be found in cities and suburbs too. The isolation appears to reflect and reinforce several forces that promote incest. These families shy away from social interaction and draw in upon themselves. As a natural part of this process, sexual attachments that would ordinarily develop with people outside the family occur in the family. The external outlets are not available, nor are they sought. Riemer (1940) shows how incest may develop in such families because they turn inward in response to family crises and life changes, whereas other families might turn to help from the outside.

Social isolation creates a climate in which deviance is freer to emerge. Also, such families are insulated from the scrutiny of public view, which must enforce the incest taboo in less isolated families, and without available models, incestuous behavior may come to be accepted as normal. It has been suggested that some of these isolated families are part of subcultures where incest is not regarded with the same kind of disapproval as in the culture at large. In fairly self-contained communities, the tolerance of incest can be transmitted from generation to generation, relatively unchanged.

(7) ROLE CONFUSION

Incest and other kinds of adult-child sex are forms of role confusion (Summit and Kryso, 1978; Zaphiris, 1978), and as such are eminently problems of sociopathology rather than psychopathology. In adult-child sex, adults place children in adult sexual roles. A father acts toward his daughter as he would toward his wife. Brothers and sisters treat each other as lovers rather than relatives. Ironically, this very sociological point of view on family pathology — that incest is a problem of role confusion in a family—has been elaborated most by psychiatrists, not sociologists (Minuchin, 1974).

In this theory, father-daughter incest is a kind of functional adaptation by a family to severe role strain (Henderson, 1972; Lustig et al., 1966; Machotka et al., 1966). Parents in these families usually have unhappy marriages, and sex between spouses is unpleasant or nonexistent (Molnar and Cameron, 1975). Fathers are often authoritarian and physically abusive within the family (Weiner, 1962) but incompetent as providers (Cormier et al., 1962). Mothers, for their part, are either unwilling or unable to fulfill parental functions (Browning and Boatman, 1977). They are ill, still heavily under the sway of their own families, or uncomfortable with the responsibilities of motherhood. In addition to tension with their husbands, they have strained and alienated relationships with their daughters.

In this situation, incest is a possible outcome and sometimes even a solution to the family dilemma. Depressed, incapacitated, and subservient, many of these mothers are unable to provide any protection for their daughters. They are peripheral family members. In a situation where the father-daughter bond is the strongest emotional axis in the family, it eventually leads to sex. In cases where the mother is incapacitated, alcoholic, or absent, a daughter often assumes many of her housekeeping and child-caring responsibilities and displaces her sexually as a natural extension. Some mothers are even said to feel content at being relieved of these family and sexual obligations. What this all amounts to is a mother-daughter role reversal brought about by a strain and breakdown of the normal family relationships.

(8) THE MILIEU OF ABANDONMENT

According to still another theory, incest may occur in response to a pervasive kind of emotional climate, one dominated by the fear of abandonment. In such families where each member fears he or she may be abandoned by the others, sexuality may be the final resource used to stave off this trauma (Henderson, 1972; Kaufman *et al.*, 1954).

There are two themes that seem to characterize families in which this kind of crisis leads to incest. First, they have a record of abandonment that dominates family history. Second, the cast of characters seems to be constantly changing. Stepparents and foster children shuffle in and out of the family circle, and the family boundary seems to be diffuse and poorly maintained. Very frequently the fathers in such families have nomadic life styles and are away from the family for extended periods as a result of military service, job requirements or marital incompatibilities. Incest has often been noted to occur when the fathers return from such an extended absence. It is a desperate attempt to give some substance to tenuous family ties that can't seem to be sustained in any other way.

To explain why daughters tolerate and in some cases encourage incestuous relationships that extend over periods of months and years, one frequently cited factor is that daughters may be receiving a kind of attention and affection that was otherwise unavailable to them. Also daughters may harbor the perhaps accurate notion that without the incestuous relationship there would be no family at all (Lustig *et al.*, 1966). Of course, once the incest begins this fantasy becomes all the more real, since revelation and termination of the relationship are virtually certain to bring about the crisis of family dissolution that was feared all along, when authorities often move in to put the offender in jail or the victim in a foster home.

Sexual Victimization: The More General Case

The foregoing three theories have been formulated to explain father-daughter incest and not children's sexual victimization in general. One of the hypothesized mechanisms, mother-daughter role reversal, primarily applies specifically to the nuclear family. But the other theories, fear of abandonment and social isolation, can apply to sexual abuse in general.

Quite a bit of the reported sexual abuse takes place between members of the extended family: grandfathers, uncles, cousins, and other peripheral relatives. It is quite readily seen how both social isolation and its subculture, more tolerant of intrafamily sex, could explain these cases of sexual abuse outside the nuclear family. Fear of abandonment also can draw members of an extended family into a forbidden sexual relationship.

Other theories using family factors have emerged from the study of the more general case of sexual victimization both inside and outside the family.

(9) MARITAL CONFLICT

Marital conflict can make children vulnerable to sexual victimization by anybody, in two ways. First, it often subjects them to contradictory messages about sex, and the resulting sexual confusion hampers their ability to handle potential sexual abuse. Second, the conflict is hard on the child and leaves him or her insecure about where to turn for protection. When a child feels unprotected, he or she is more apt to become entangled in a sexual situation with an adult in which he or she feels helpless (Weiss *et al.,* 1955).

(10) OVERSEXUALIZATION

It has been suggested that some families are oversexualized, and children from these families are more vulnerable to sexual abuse, even outside the family (Litin *et al.,* 1956). Children in such families have inappropriate sexual models and an unusual kind of sexual socialization. Moreover, they are sexually stimulated by their own parents, perhaps not directly, but as a result of talk or exposure to unusual sexual behavior. These two factors make them vulnerable to sexual involvements with adults.

(11) POOR SUPERVISION

Children are vulnerable to sexual abuse when they are poorly supervised (De Francis, 1969). This theory echoes ideas expressed in the two preceding theories, except that it is more general. Not just family conflict or oversexualization, but any situation resulting in neglect of a child can lead to vulnerability to sexual abuse.

Social and Cultural Sources

Sexual victimization of children is not universal. There are societies where it is not known to occur (Mead, 1968), and there are undoubtedly parts of our own society where it is less common. Unfortunately, we know little about the demography of sexual abuse. Although anthropology has taken a lively interest in why incest is almost universally tabooed, it has devoted little attention to the related question: why is the violation of the incest taboo more common in some societies than in others?

It is understandable that anthropology would have a difficult time addressing our question: what are the causes of sexual victimization? The concept itself is so culturally relative. In some societies sexual contact takes place on a regularly sanctioned basis between adults and children (Ford and Beach, 1951). It is not a deviant act and no victimization would be said to take place. For example, in some societies homosexual acts between men and boys play a part in tribal ritual. Among the Keraki of new Guinea, each prepubescent boy passes through an initiation in which he is introduced to anal intercourse by one of the tribe's older men (Ford and Beach, 1951). The same source cites several other such instances in other societies.

However, all societies prohibit most adult-child sexual contact, and the incest taboo, one form of this restriction, is virtually universal (Weinberg, 1955). Where adult-child sex is permitted, it is either in highly ritualized and structured circumstances or not considered sexual. What is important about sexual victimization in our own society is that this rather important taboo is violated fairly often. There are two major theories that account for the frequency of this violation from a social and cultural point of view.

(12) Male Supremacy

Sexual victimization may be as common as it is in our society because of its degree of male supremacy. It is one way in which men, the dominant status group, control women. To maintain control, men need a vehicle by which women can be punished, brought into line, and socialized to a subordinate status. Sexual victimization and the threat of it are useful in keeping women intimidated (Brownmiller, 1975). Inevitably the process starts in childhood with the victimization of girl children.

Whether or not it functions to maintain male dominance as Brownmiller argues, in a male-dominated society the sexual exploitation of women and children by men is certainly easier. Sex in any society is a valuable commodity, and a dominant group—such as men—will try to rig things to maximize their access to it. The cultural beliefs that underpin the male-dominated system contribute to making women and children sexually vulnerable. For example, to the extent that family members are regarded as possessions, men can take unusual and usually undetected liberties with them. The fact that the male sexual urge is viewed as overpowering and in need of satisfaction allows men to rationalize escapades of antisocial behavior, such as sexual abuse. In a system of severe sexual and generational inequality, women and children lack the resources to defend themselves against such sexual victimization.

The theory is fairly effective in explaining the sexual abuse of women by men and the preponderance of male offenders and girl victims. Children, however, are a subordinate group in almost every society, and probably have more power in our society than most. What the theory does less well at explaining is why, given their universal powerlessness, children are often sexually exploited in some societies and in others they are not.

(13) SOCIAL FRAGMENTATION

Sexual abuse is common in this society, according to another theory, because of the increasing isolation of individuals and families. Although no one yet has formally articulated this theory to account for sexual abuse (but see Frederick Cuber of Odessey Institute quoted in Dudar, 1977), it can be used to explain many kinds of family and sexual pathology and is readily adaptable to sexual abuse as well.

We discussed earlier the theory that incest tends to occur among isolated families and in isolated subcultures. Some theorists have alleged that isolation is, in fact, the dominant feature of our society. The isolation encompasses not just families but also individuals and results from increased mobility and the disintegration of neighborhoods, communities, and kin networks (Lasch, 1977; Parsons, 1949; Slater, 1968).

As mentioned earlier, isolation facilitates sexual abuse in two ways. It reduces the intensity of general social supervision, so that all kinds of deviance can increase. Second, it deprives people of socially sanctioned forms of support and intimacy, so that they may turn to forms that are taboo. Sexual abuse is thus a symptom of pervasive loneliness.

Although both these theories leave certain aspects of the problem undiscussed, they highlight a need to analyze sexual victimization from the point of view of the organization of society as a whole, and not just as the outcome of the idiosyncrasies of certain individuals, families, and subgroups.

The Consequences to the Victims

There are still two more theories we need to review. These are theories not about causes but about consequences, and they have generated more furor than most of the previous theories combined.

Among those who study the problem, an intense dispute has raged for more than forty years over how serious a problem sexual abuse really is. On the one hand, there are those who argue that although generally unpleasant, the vast majority of sexual offenses against children are rather innocuous affairs best treated as one of the minor and transient hazards of childhood. Meanwhile, others point out the many case histories of children who have been permanently scarred by the experience, alleging that we have not yet begun to recognize the true toll of this widespread problem.

The first group tends to argue things as follows. The innocence of childhood, they say, is a form of natural protection against the long-term effects of sexual abuse. A great many ordinary things are frightening to children—a trip to the doctor, a ride on an airplane—but by the same token the pain passes quickly. The same is true of sexual abuse.

Moreover, children have only a dim sense of adult sexuality. What may seem like a horrible violation of social taboos from an adult perspective need not be so to a child. A sexual experience with an adult may be something unusual, vaguely unpleasant, even traumatic at the moment, but not a horror story. Most children's sexual experiences involve encounters with fondlers and exhibitionists, Kinsey pointed out, and "it is difficult to understand why a child, except for its cultural conditioning, should be disturbed at having its genitals touched, or disturbed at seeing the genitalia of other persons." (Kinsey, 1953, p. 121). Most of the women who reported such contacts in Kinsey's sample did not appear to suffer any long-term consequences (Gagnon, 1965). One other survey (Landis, 1956) and several other case studies (Bender and Grugett, 1952; Burton, 1968; Yorukoclu and Kemph, 1969) have also found children to be relatively unscathed.

On the other hand, there is no lack of reports of traumatic outcomes of such sexual experiences. Hospital emergency rooms, for example, are regularly visited by child victims of sex offenses, and the children seem to suffer many of the same severe consequences as do adult women who have been raped (Burgess and Holmstrom, 1974). There is confusion, crying, depression, and subsequently a sense of shame, guilt, and awareness of stigma. These emotions endure for some time.

It has been noted that child victims fare better to some extent than adult rape victims because they are less likely to have suffered massive physical coercion or threat (Peters, 1976), but not because they are so quick to forget. The fact that so many child victims fail to report their experiences to anyone, even parents, is powerful evidence that the experience is surrounded by conflict.

The picture from clinical records on adults who were former child victims also tends to support this view. Psychotherapists report an unusually large number of child sex victims among their clients (Herman and Hirschman, 1977; Swift, 1977), and note that women with such experiences are often suffering from depression (Henderson, 1972; Molnar and

Cameron, 1975; Sloane and Karpinsky, 1942) and difficulty in relating to men (Herman and Hirschman, 1977).

Studies of specific deviant groups also reveal frequent experiences of sexual abuse in the histories of these people. A large proportion of female drug addicts (Benward and Densen-Gerber, 1975) and prostitutes (James and Meyerding, 1977) were found to have incest in their backgrounds. Adolescent runaways also commonly appear to be child sex victims (Weber, 1977). The trauma of these experiences does not easily fade away, say these observers. Sexual abuse victims are often doubly and triply victimized over an extended period of time, once by the offender and then again by parents, relatives, and the social agencies appointed to handle the problem. Parents often blame the child for getting into trouble. Finally, the police, social workers, and courts often subject the victims to brutal and insensitive interrogation, publicity, and exposure, which compounds the trauma (Burgess *et al.,* 1978; Schultz, 1975).

Many comments have been and will be made about this controversy before it is settled. Only three very elementary observations will be made here.

1. Obviously *some* people have been traumatized by early childhood sexual experiences (even this is conceded by the antialarmists), but the argument appears to be over whether such trauma is typical or occurs only in isolated cases. Actually, the real dispute is more of a political one: is this a social problem worthy, because of its serious harmful consequences, of a massive mobilization. It seems to me that even if only a small number of children are harmed by these experiences, it is still worthy of mobilization. So the real question to be answered is not whether or not children are harmed, but how are they harmed, in what instances, and how it can be avoided.

2. In favor of the antialarmists, it must be mentioned that the reports of trauma are subject to the clinical fallacy. Therapists, clinics, and drug treatment facilities are by definition dealing with traumatized individuals. It is not clear whether, for each person who seems to be badly affected by the childhood sexual experience, there are many others who were not affected.

Moreover, there is the additional difficulty of identifying the exact trauma-inducing factor. Many of the people reporting childhood sexual experiences also come from environments containing plenty of other trauma-inducing experiences (Geiser and Norberta, 1976). Are their current problems caused by the highly visible sexual experience or by some of the other environmental factors, the family disorganization, for example? These are strands of the puzzle that need to be disentangled.

3. In criticism of the antialarmists, however, it must be said that they have often demanded proof of unreasonably serious difficulties before accepting that any trauma occurred. If a person avoids mental hospitaliza-

tion, manages to marry, and becomes a parent, antialarmist researchers have often concluded that no serious damage took place. This view seems overly optimistic. Even if the result were something so "comparatively" minor and subjective as an inability to feel comfortable in the presence of older men, it needs to be taken seriously as evidence of deleterious long-term effects.

Fortunately, this question of trauma and the consequences of sexual victimization is one most amenable to empirical examination, which we will do briefly in Chapter 7. It is certain to become one of the focal points of future research on the subject.

3

A SURVEY ON CHILDREN'S SEXUAL VICTIMIZATION

THE STUDY OF THE SEXUAL VICTIMIZATION of children has taken place almost entirely through the agency of police, courts, jails, child protection agencies, or psychiatrists' offices. One researcher will study the histories of convicted sex offenders. Another will scrutinize police records of complaints filed about incidents of sexual abuse. A third will interview families who report an incident to a social agency. Still a fourth will analyze the accounts of victims who, many years later, tell their stories to psychotherapists. There are serious questions about how much can be learned in these ways about a problem, which like the proverbial iceberg, is 90 percent hidden from public attention of any sort.

For one thing, there are many reasons to think that cases coming to the attention of these agencies are special in some way. Convicted offenders, as the cliché goes, are the failures of the world of deviant behavior. They are the ones who carried on their activity so blatantly or brutally or stupidly that they got caught (wanted to get caught, the Freudian might add). Families who report incidents are likely to be either the ones so wracked by family conflict they could not contain the humiliating secret or the ones who had no other recourse. And the people who end up in the psychiatrist's office are often the ones having the hardest time coping with life.

A second limitation on these studies is that they are usually based on a very small number of cases. Theoretical papers based on four incidents or less are not at all uncommon in the literature. A final problem is that the histories are usually collected under circumstances not really conducive to accuracy and objectivity (Lester, 1972), such as in a police investigation.

Of course, it is easy to be critical of all that has gone before, to discount years of work and hundreds of pages with a few sharp words. So while there is truth in the idea that our knowledge about the sexual victimization of children has been drastically limited because we have studied it through the vehicle of psychotherapy and the criminal justice system, it must be borne in mind that this is not an easy area to study by any method.

Rationale for a Survey

Is a survey the solution? Survey advocates—who are also usually sociologists, rather than psychologists or psychiatrists—often see this tool as the way to supplant unruly subjectivity with real science in the study of a new social problem. They see swarms of clinical fallacies, preconceptions, and the researchers' own projections dispersing in the face of survey data.

True, surveys of a social problem of this sort do have some important contributions. (1) They provide a large number of cases for categorizing the range of possibilities. (2) They provide the possibility of a control on the thing being studied, so that situations in which it occurs can be distinguished from those in which it does not. (3) They provide an opportunity to generalize to a larger population.

Surveys also have their drawbacks. They can introduce their own kind of selection factors, so that their respondents may be hardly more representative than a group of psychotherapy patients or jailed convicts. They can cramp complex experiences, feelings and human phenomena into categories and fixed responses that completely distort the meaning and import of an experience. In the hands of the unscrupulous or careless, they can be every bit as much of a vehicle for preconception and prejudice as the case history.

However, the time appears ripe for surveys on children's sexual victimization. Aside from the fact that it has scarcely been done before (the "because it's there" motivation of the world of social scientists), there are a number of reasons for doing such a survey that have only arisen in the recent past. For one thing, only recently have people realized that this experience is widespread enough to be amenable to survey analysis. When an event occurs too infrequently, a survey is an inefficient way of gathering information about it. Case studies in such instances are a better road to knowledge. Second, sex research and public discussions of sexual matters have a new legitimacy. This development has made such a survey on the sexual victimization of children more acceptable both to potential respondents and to other authorities whose cooperation would be essential in any such undertaking.

Third, our sophistication in doing research on such sensitive topics has increased dramatically in recent times. Other sensitive topics—sexual intercourse, family violence, contraceptive practices—have now been extensively studied, and many techniques have been developed for improving validity, participation, and confidentiality. The most recent addition to this technology, which gives both encouragement and technical assistance to a study of this sort, is the victimization survey which has now been conducted for several years at a great deal of government expense.

Fourth, there is now a burgeoning government concern about this subject and related matters—family violence, victimization, and child abuse—which creates the need for new and different kinds of information. At the time of earlier clinical and court studies, the main pressure for new knowledge came from psychotherapists and judges. Now government officials have become more involved in the problem, trying to formulate strategies requiring the creation of new services, the reorganization of existing services, and the outlay of larger sums of money. They need data on social and demographic factors—information useful in the prevention of victimization or the identification of vulnerable children. This last requirement also puts a premium on the kind of information available by survey rather than by case study.

AN EXPLORATORY STUDY

Despite new incentives to do research in this area and opportunities created by new knowledge and techniques, there are still some serious obstacles to surveys that can be of recognized scientific value. Childhood sex and incest are still highly tabooed topics among many segments of the population, and there is no assurance that a high degree of candor can be obtained. Moreover, ignorance of the subject so heavily outweighs knowledge that surveys probably will make many mistakes before learning how to approach the subject accurately and impartially.

For these reasons, this study was conceptualized as exploratory, which in essence means that one of the purposes of the research was to find out whether research was possible. Exploratory means some other things too: that instead of testing hypotheses, the purpose of the study would be to develop them; that the research would cast a wide net over the subject matter to find out which avenues of approach were most fruitful; and that there would be less emphasis on scientific proof and more on scientific inquiry.

To counterbalance the shallowness of a survey approach, it was decided to try to combine it with a small-scale interview study. First a survey would be conducted to answer questions about incidence, about social and demographic factors, and about the range of experiences. Subsequently interviews would be conducted to find out more about the details of the experience, its meaning and impact, and how it fit together with family background and other developmental experiences.

Combining these two approaches solved an important problem of the interview approach alone: how to recruit people who had had childhood sexual experiences for personal interviews. Word of mouth, bulletin boards, and newspaper ads are biased and ineffective procedures of recruitment on such a sensitive topic. However, if interviewees were recruited from the survey, there was a chance of getting a large group, by distributing enough surveys, and a representative group, by providing enough motivation to attract otherwise reluctant volunteers.

Although the interviews are a crucial part of the whole study, this report is based primarily on an analysis of the results of the questionnaire. Administrative problems and the need for elaborate procedures to protect human subjects have created some delay in the completion of the interview portion of the research. Moreover, once collected, the interviews require lengthy preparation before they are amenable to analysis. For these reasons, a systematic study of the results of the interviews has been deferred for another publication.

Designing the Survey

In designing the study, there were four main goals: (1) Representativeness—the survey had to touch on some population more heterogeneous than case loads from social welfare agencies or incarcerated criminals. (2) Validity—the responses needed to be as truthful as possible. (3) Protection of subjects—we needed to find ways not to embarrass or endanger the people who participated in our survey. (4) Feasibility—the study had to fit within some fairly narrow constraints on time and budget.

Unfortunately, we could not maximally achieve all four of these objectives at once. The ideal in representativeness, for example, would have been some kind of scientifically selected nationwide sample allowing generalization to the population of the whole country: the dream of every survey researcher. Obviously such a study was not currently feasible. Even if expense and time were not considerations, such a national sample still might not be the best for our purposes. For example, knocking on scientifically selected—but totally unfamiliar—doors might lead to an unacceptably high refusal rate. Also, if interviewing people in their households posed a serious threat of compromising their confidentiality and exposing them to the questions of friends and relatives, then this method would clash with the objective of protecting our subjects. Thus many priorities had to be juggled.

Ultimately, we decided on a sample of college students in social science classes in a variety of New England colleges and universities. This is a rather conventional choice for research of this sort, but in this case, the sample provided some distinct advantages for the subject matter, over and above the conventional reasons that college students are handy and available.

College students, for example, are particularly attractive in dealing with the validity problem of this kind of research. For maximum validity, a study needs subjects who are well motivated, not threatened by the subject matter, not inconvenienced by the research, and able to provide the needed information. As a group, college students are probably more suited to these needs than any other. For one thing, they are among those most comfortable with sexual topics. For another, because the survey could be presented in classes where it related to the subjects under study and had the endorsement of a familiar professor, respondents were much more likely to want to participate than if they had been approached by a stranger in their households or in public.

Third, taken as part of class time, the survey would not inconvenience students much, and thus we were assured of a higher participation rate. Perhaps most importantly, college students are still fairly close in time to their childhood experiences and would suffer from less memory distortion than would an older person questioned about a comparable event. In fact, given that children and adolescents are virtually inaccessible to research on such topics because of rules for their protection, college students are the youngest subjects available and thus the best from the point of view of memory.

College students have some other distinct advantages in the matter of protecting against the violation of privacy and confidentiality. Although researchers routinely use anonymous questionnaires to deal with this danger, they are not always conscious of other ways in which they make their subjects vulnerable. One of the most common is when attention is drawn to a person's participation in such a study. Even when a respondent's answers are confidential, the person is still liable to be interrogated by others about his or her responses, making it difficult for a participant who does not like to lie.

It is particularly difficult, for example, to question people who are living in family units without it being conspicuous to other family members. However, because many students live autonomously, and because filling out the survey would be part of ordinary class time—not distorting their routine in any way—it is unlikely that a student's participation would be noticed by any of his family or intimates. This seems a distinct advantage.

LIMITATIONS OF SAMPLE

However, student samples also present other distinct disadvantages which have been catalogued many times before. The main ones are their homogeneity and lack of representativeness. Student surveys are most homogeneous, of course, in age. The vast majority of college students fall between the ages of seventeen to twenty-two. Even surveys that try to recruit older college students, as this one did, rarely can manage more than a few students over age twenty-four. In this study, we were able to recruit 18 percent of the sample from this age.

However, homogeneity in age is the less serious problem. After all, by age eighteen, all those respondents who will have childhood sexual experiences have already had them. Living longer will not give them any more or any different kinds of childhood experiences. This homogeneity only means that we can find out little about the experience of any age group besides this one, and thus we will not know whether the incidence of such sexual experiences is increasing or decreasing and whether their nature is changing. However, this is not an enormous limitation.

The more serious problem comes from the fact that colleges are selective. Only about 40 percent of an age group currently attends college in this country, and this 40 percent contains the brightest, the most motivated, the most upwardly mobile, the mentally healthiest, and of course, the most well-to-do. This group is distinctly different in their life experiences from those who do not attend college.

Most attention is usually paid to the bias of social class in student samples. In our sample, for example, the median family income was around $14,000—well above the $10,236 national figure for 1970, the time period for which most of the respondents were estimating their family income, but about the norm for families of college students (Astin *et al.,* n.d.). Although the income distribution deviates significantly from that of the population at large, it does include a fairly large number of individuals from lower-income backgrounds. Twenty percent of the sample reported family incomes of under $7,000. Thus there was still a good income range in this sample.

For our purposes, the more serious bias of this sample is that it excludes many people who may be troubled, disorganized, of below average intelligence, or from deviant subcultures. Such people are the least likely to make it through the various educational filters that tend to reward intelligence, self-discipline, and conformity. However, these may be the very people who have had, or who are the most vulnerable to having experiences of sexual victimization and incest.

We can try to adjust figures on incidence to offset the exclusion of these people by assuming the rates are too low, but it is much harder to assess what kinds of knowledge about the experiences we are missing. Unfortunately, we cannot assume that their experiences are similar to those included in the sample. They were probably more damaging, and hence may have emerged from very different personal, family, and social circumstances.

Another limitation of the survey is the fact that it was conducted almost entirely in social science classes, raising the question of whether some additional biases were introduced. For example, there is a popular belief among college teachers that students take social science courses to work out personal problems. Is it possible that students with upsetting childhood sexual experiences were more likely to take these courses to get help for problems related to the experience? This factor, if true, might result in an inflated number of reports of sexual victimization in the survey.

However, we are skeptical that this bias is operating on any large scale in the survey. Most of the courses surveyed were large introductory courses, taken by students from a wide variety of disciplines. Because of distribution requirements, almost all college students take one or two social science courses. We suspect only a minority of these students, if that many, take these courses specifically because of personal problems. Moreover, we doubt whether the popular belief has any validity, and we do not know of any empirical evidence to support it. Even if social science students feel more troubled, it is still questionable that they actually have more negative life experiences.

In summary, this student sample probably excludes some crucial segments of the relevant population for the phenomenon we are studying. However, it is a good sample from the point of view of motivation, recall, and confidentiality. It is easily a much more normal and representative group than any of those that have been previously studied—court cases, therapy clients, and volunteers.

Survey Procedure

The survey was taken at six New England colleges and universities, chosen to give a diverse sample. One school was small, private, expensive, and elite. Two others were large residential state universities, one from a primarily rural state, the other from a more urban industrialized state. A fourth was an urban state university branch campus, about 50 percent of whose enrollment consists of commuters. A fifth was a community college (no residential students) in a New England industrial town. The last was a recently formed community college without any physical plant, which delivers evening courses in high school facilities to a primarily adult population.

Surveys were conducted in classes whose subject matter ranged from sociology to psychology to social work to human sexuality and included both introductory and upper-level courses. The classes were chosen on the assumption that the most highly motivated respondents would be ones who could see the connection between the research and the subject they were studying and whose professors could give the research and the researcher a positive endorsement. Thus classes were not sampled systematically but rather according to the subject matter and the receptivity of the professor.

The questionnaires were completed by students during class time. The research was first presented to the class, including discussion of its importance, its sensitivity, and the precautions that were being taken. Questionnaires were distributed, and students were told that participation was completely voluntary. Respondents took forty-five minutes on the average to complete the questionnaire, and they were free to leave when finished, or before if they did not wish to finish. A key dilemma was how to recruit volunteers for personal interviews without compromising their anonymity or the anonymity of their questionnaire. The problem was solved by including a separate flyer in each questionnaire on which students could volunteer for a personal interview. Instructions indicated that we wanted to interview only those who had had some kind of sexual experience with family members. The flyer asked volunteers only for a first name or a nickname, and a phone number for contacting them. All students, whether volunteering or not, were asked to fold up the flyers and hand them in separately. Thus we obtained information for reaching interviewees without making them conspicuous to the class and without having to learn their names or use their anonymous questionnaire.

Data Analysis

The questionnaire used in the survey (see Appendix B) took between forty-five minutes and an hour to complete. It contained questions about childhood sexual experiences with adults and children, incestuous sexual experiences, and coercive sexual experiences at any age. It also asked about sources of the respondent's sex information, attitudes and practices about sex and discipline in his or her family of origin, and current sexual behavior. Questions also probed family background, the nature of family relationships, family composition, and various social and demographic features. In all, over six hundred items of information were gathered.

Because of the large amount of data and the large sample, it was necessary to place limitations on the data that would be analyzed and reported in this book. Only two kinds of sexual experiences will be analyzed here: (1) childhood sexual experiences with older persons, and (2) sexual experiences with relatives. Other childhood experiences and coercive adult sexual experiences will be reported on at a later time. A selection has also been made from among information available in the survey on family, sexual development, and current behavior. This report will limit itself to matters of family composition, social and demographic background, and parental role adequacy. Questions relating to sex education, family sexual norms, family violence, and current sexual behavior will be taken up elsewhere.

The data analysis was also streamlined to permit a reduction in the number of questionnaires that had to be coded for our current purposes. All 796 questionnaires received were first analyzed for the sexual experiences reported, and those that contained either a childhood sexual experience with an older person or one with a family member were selected. The analysis of the 350 experiences of these 264 individuals provides the data for Chapters 4 through 8.

It was also important to compare how those with relevant experiences differed from those without such experiences in terms of their family background and social and cultural origin. The group without relevant experiences is made up of 532 individuals whose questionnaires were not selected in the first analysis. Instead of comparing the "experience" group with the whole "nonexperience" group, however, a 50 percent systematic sample (every other case) was taken from the latter, and only these were coded. Then in any analysis involving both groups, each response in the nonexperience group is given a weight of two in order to give correct estimates of incidence for the sample as a whole. Thus, if there were thirty low-income families in the nonexperience group, this figure was doubled and added to the number of low-income families in the experience group to get the total number of low-income families represented in the whole sample. This sampling and weighting procedure is a convenient technique to simplify data analysis and does not introduce any biases into the study.

Description of the Sample

The sample used for the data analysis consisted of 796 students, 530 females and 266 males. The surveyed classes contained a disproportionate number of women—which was treated as an advantage to and not as a defect in the sample, since it was expected that women would report more sexual victimization. The extra proportion of women boosted the number of experiences from the number that would have been reported in a sample with an equal number of men and women. In an exploratory study like this, more experiences gave us more information.

The sample had the expected college-age distribution, 75 percent being twenty-one years of age or under. Our efforts at diversification, however, did result in a limited group of older students. About 18 percent of the sample was over twenty-four, ranging all the way to seventy-four years old for the oldest participant. As for marital status, about 15 per cent were currently or had been married, but the vast majority was single and had never been married.

The composition of the sample reflects the fact that just one of the campuses surveyed was in a large city. Only 12 percent of the respondents had grown up in cities of over 100,000 in population. The largest proportion (43 percent) came from towns of between 5,000 and 25,000, which makes it primarily a small-town sample.

The ethnic and religious breakdown mirrors this regional and small-town composition. First, there were almost no blacks in the sample, since blacks live almost entirely in the metropolitian areas in New England, and in addition, are grossly underrepresented among residential college populations.

The fact that there are so few non-whites in this sample needs to be strongly emphasized. In some of the research on sexual victimization (De Francis, 1969; Peters, 1976), non-whites make up a large percentage of the victims studied. The findings of this study can obviously not be generalized to them.

The largest ethnic representations were Irish, English, and French-Canadian, around two hundred students reporting each of those groups in their ancestry. There was also a scattering of Scots, Italians, Germans, and Eastern Europeans.

Fifty-three percent said they had grown up as Catholics, 34 percent as Protestants, and 6 percent as Jews. Five percent claimed no religious background.

The sample came largely from intact, middle-class family backgrounds. Only 11 percent reported that their parents had been divorced or separated. The median income, mentioned earlier, was very close to $14,000.

Volunteer Bias

The modern world has come to accept the sex survey as it has the airplane, but few people need to entrust their lives to the former's reliability. So although they have provided much food for thought, there are few definitive proofs that such surveys tell the ultimate truth about the sexual practices of the whole population.

The kinds of distortions that are alleged to invalidate the surveys can be conveniently divided into two types. One is caused by the inability or refusal of certain kinds of people to participate. Thus there may be a certain segment of the population whose behavior we never learn about. A second kind of distortion is caused by the inability or refusal of people who do participate to report accurately. The first is called volunteer bias, and the second, response invalidity.

We mentioned earlier ways in which our sampling procedure might underrepresent certain kinds of cases of sexual victimization because of the exclusionary bias of college attendance. There are other biasing possiblities in our process of data collection. Not everyone enrolled in the classes we approached actually completed a questionnaire. From the hypothetical population of all the students in all the classes surveyed, subjects were excluded in one of two ways: (1) they may have been absent from the classes on the days when the questionnaire was administered, or (2) they may have declined to fill out the questionnaire once it was presented to them. In addition they may have skipped relevant questions in the surveys they did fill out.

We obtained from the professors the theoretical enrollments of the classes and compared them to actual attendance on the days the survey was given. Approximately one-third of the eligible population was excluded as a result of nonattendance. Although nonattenders may be less serious students, may be ones more vulnerable to illness, or may have some other distinguishing features, we suspect that on the whole nonattendance does not introduce large systematic biases in such samples. Factors relating to nonattendance may be fairly random or only tangentially associated with an experience of sexual victimization.

However, a second bias may be introduced because participation in the survey was necessarily voluntary. Of the students to whom the questionnaire was presented approximately 8 percent chose not to participate. The reasons for not participating may be related to the experience under investigation. Some may have refused because they found the subject matter offensive. Some may have had experiences they did not want to discuss. Others, no doubt, merely left because they were not being required to stay and they had other more pressing things to do. And an unknown percentage of the nonparticipants left because they had already filled out the survey in another class. Note that 92 percent is a good participation rate, compared to the 75 percent which is now typical of door-to-door surveys. It is also somewhat higher than that found in other sex research on college students (Kanin and Parcell, 1977; Delameter and MacCorquodale, 1975; Reiss, 1967). Thus the volunteer bias in this study is less than is standard for research of this sort.

There is no consensus among researchers on just how this volunteer bias may distort the findings of sex surveys. In some instances it may inflate the reports of a certain kind of sexual behavior; in other cases it may depress them. Kinsey found in his 100 percent group samples (groups with no volunteer bias) fewer reports of homosexuality and other sexual activities than among samples that were only portions of whole groups, suggesting that those with more and more varied experiences were more eager to be interviewed (Kinsey, 1948, p. 99). However, it is just as easy to imagine that people with certain kinds of deviant experiences may prefer to keep them private and thus decline participation in research like this.

Barker and Perlman (1975) sent sex and nonsex surveys on a random basis to subjects who had previously taken personality tests. Curiously, response rates were identical for both surveys. Moreover, there were no differences on 108 personality measures between those who did and did not respond to either survey. This result suggests that volunteer bias does not affect findings at all, and also that contrary to stereotype, sex surveys are not more vulnerable to this kind of effect than any other kind of survey.

A third source of volunteer bias occurs in our survey because some of the actual repondents chose, as they were instructed, to skip certain questions they found too personal or did not wish to answer. Thus 78 or 10 percent of the sample refused to answer about childhood sexual experiences, perhaps because they had something to hide or perhaps because they simply found such questions disturbing or too intimate.

Fortunately, we have some other information on who these particular nonrespondents were because they did fill out other sections of the questionnaire. There is nothing noticeable about this group to distinguish them from the others. There is a slight preponderance of Catholics among them, but not enough to be statistically significant.

The only other trend among nonrespondents is that they seemed particularly numerous at one of the schools. This is a reflection of either the student culture at that school or the conditions under which the survey was administered there. Because it is not associated with any demographic or family differences, the disproportion at this school can probably be discounted as unlikely to have had any effect on issues we are concerned about. Thus from evidence that we can marshall from our own study, we are fairly confident that no large bias has been introduced by the procedure by which respondents chose to participate or not participate in the survey.

Validity of Responses

The second perennial question about sex research is whether the responses we do receive can be trusted. Aren't people likely to misrepresent experiences that they imagine are deviant? And beyond that, aren't many experiences, even if not consciously misrepresented, subject to the great distorting influence of time, memory, and unconscious processes?

Once again, the history of research on sex gives both alarming and reassuring counsel to those concerned about response validity. Kinsey and his colleagues were confident that very few of their respondents lied. Their checks on validity showed their data to be remarkably accurate. The reports of husbands tallied with those of wives, and retrospective accounts of events like the age of onset of puberty corresponded well with medical findings based on direct observation.

Other researchers have not been so sanguine. It has been a generally accepted principle in the field that validity declines with increases in the threatening nature of the subject matter, and sexual topics have been shown to be among the most threatening. Clark and Tifft (1966) tried to validate data with lie detector tests performed on respondents after they had filled out questionnaires. They found that all items in their survey were subject to some over- or underreporting, and on the whole, the more sensitive items, like homosexuality and masturbation, were subject to the most.

Similarly, Bradburn *et al.* (1978) showed that people who say they are most ill at ease about discussing a certain behavior tend to give lower reports of engaging in such behavior and refuse to answer such questions more often. This finding suggests to these researchers that there is a fair amount of underreporting and misrepresentation in most surveys, and the largest amount occurs in those whose subject matter makes people the most uncomfortable. They speculate that real incidence rates are between 8 percent higher than reported for topics like intercourse to 27 percent higher for topics like smoking marijuana.

Presumably a topic such as ours, involving reports of childhood sexual experiences and incest, would be among the most threatening imaginable and thus liable to great distortion—probably underreporting, if we followed the conclusion of the Bradburn research. Unfortunately, there is no way to obtain direct validity checks on the experiences reported by our subjects. We too suspect that they are underreported, but we cannot prove it.

It is possible to provide some indirect validation of certain other experiences of a moderately threatening sort that are reported in the survey. Validation comes from comparing our findings with the findings of other surveys of comparable populations on the same topics. For example, in our study 66 percent of the women reported a childhood sexual experience. This figure compares to the 48 percent in the Kinsey study who said they had such an experience. We also asked respondents whether they had engaged in sexual intercourse. For unmarried college women, the percent of nonvirgins ranged from 55 percent for freshmen to 85 percent for seniors. These rates are double the rates reported by Simon and Gagnon in a 1967 national college student survey (Gagnon, 1977, p. 182), but they are almost exactly the same as those in one of the most recent of such surveys, this one in Colorado (Jessor and Jessor, 1975). It would appear doubtful from these comparisons that there was substantial underreporting of either premarital intercourse or childhood sex experiences. Both of these findings convey the impression that the group of respondents with which we are dealing was being quite candid about reporting sexual behavior.

Defining a Childhood Sexual Experience

Probably the most difficult problem of the whole study was how to define sexual victimization. Although many clear-cut cases come to mind at the mention of the term—e.g., the child who is forced to fondle an adult—there are also vast hazy areas. As we pointed out in our introduction, because child sexuality is currently an ideological battleground, what one defines as sexual victimization depends in part on philosophical and moral issues as well as empirical ones.

There were two somewhat separate issues that the research needed to confront. What was sexual and what was victimization? We will take them up in that order.

A sexual experience is an unfortunately vague term that can be used, depending on the person, to refer to both a very wide or a very narrow range of things. For some, nothing less than genital arousal culminating in orgasm is a sexual experience; others might consider sexual something like sucking a thumb or awaking in the morning with an erection from a full bladder.

CAN CHILDREN RECOGNIZE SEXUAL GESTURES?

Defining what is sexual is additionally complicated by the fact that we are referring to childhood experiences, and most children have even a more amorphous idea, if they have any at all, of what is sexual than have most adults. Some observers feel that in his or her naivete a child is likely to label things as sexual that would not be considered so by most adults, for example, a fond caress from a relative. The implication is that there would be many false reports of childhood sexual experiences (Trankell, 1958).

It is our belief, however, that the distortion occurs in the other direction. If anything, the child, as a newcomer to the vocabulary of sexual gestures, is likely to fail to recognize sexual actions and intentions on the part of others or to interpret them as something else. Children, viewed in this light, may be the victims of many sexual acts they don't even notice.

However, our interviews with adults about their childhood sexual experiences have persuaded us that this is mostly a hypothetical concern. It is true that if an experience was not labeled sexual by a child, it is not likely that as an adult that person would spontaneously remember the event. But since our interviews covered a wide range of childhood and family experiences, we anticipated that instances of such unlabeled sex might emerge in the course of our talks. None did.

Instead, what was much more common was for an interviewee to suddenly recall in the course of the discussion a childhood sexual experience that he or she had forgotten about, forgotten not because it was not seen as sexual but because that awareness was painful, shameful, or frightening.

HOW CHILDREN RECOGNIZE A SEXUAL ACT

We were impressed at how accurately children perceived sexual experiences as sexual. In most cases, even very young children spontaneously recognized a sexual activity. Obviously, they did not understand "sexual" in the full sense that adults understand the term. But they knew the activity was different, it was taboo, it involved visceral sensations, and it should be done covertly and not mentioned. One thing that makes these experiences stand out is the feeling the children had about the peculiar way in which the adults were acting:

> **R:** I can't remember the exact age I was when things started to happen, but it was somewhere around four or five. The first big incident was one night when my mother went to my grandmother's for the night. My father put his penis between my thighs and began pushing it back and forth and told me that "Mommy likes it when I do this."
>
> I just lay there. I didn't have any idea what it was he was doing. I knew that what he had done was not right, I guess, because of the sneaky way he was acting.
>
> The way I interpreted the above occurrences was just that I had a vague idea it was something bad. I didn't know what sex was. I only knew that the way he acted was something I didn't want to be part of (Armstrong, 1978, pp. 56-57).

Another thing that made the activities so clearly definable to these children was that they involved the genitals. Most children learn very early the special nature of their own and others' genitals, and after that, all social activity pertaining to them is clearly unusual. Parents and caretakers have genital contact with the child up until toilet training, but after that it ends abruptly. We encountered no instance of an adult having contact with a child's genitals in which the child was unclear about whether the activity was sexual or part of normal caretaking.

In a few rare instances, an adult did begin to have sexual contact with a child before the child had any inkling that something unusual was happening. Following is the experience of one interviewee whose father began to fondle her at age three:

> **R:** I can remember as young as three years old sitting in front of the TV watching TV on a little TV stool. My father was always comforting and warming to me. . . . So I would scoot my chair back and he would put his arm around me and then he would put his hand in my underwear. And fondle me—at three years old. I can hardly believe it. I thought nothing of it except he did it. . . . So that went on from like three until, gee, I would say five, six, or seven.
>
> My father would always take me places with him too. And we would be riding in the car and he would do the same thing or he would put his hand on my chest. There was nothing there, but he did it anyway. I was always getting poison oak. He used to always come and doctor the poison oak and then he'd always check the places where I didn't have it to make sure I didn't have it, which were the places which were covered. "Oh, we'll check here." Of course, there was never anything there, but he'd always check.

REMEMBERING EARLY EXPERIENCES

In this instance, as in other similar ones, the child upon reaching age seven, eight, or nine suddenly realized that this behavior was inappropriate. Either the children learned more about sex, or they found out that such things did not happen in their friends' families, or most often, they sensed an inappropriate quality in the parent's attentions. At that point the sexual meaning of all the previous activity became clear to them.

Thus it is our impression that even when a young child at first fails to recognize the inappropriate sexual content of some family behavior, the meaning of that behavior does become clear at some subsequent point in most cases. It is true, however, that in the histories we have taken, the inappropriate sexual activity continued up through the time when the realization took place. If the fondling had ended when our respondent was four, would she still have "discovered" at age eight that she had had a sexual experience with her father? Our guess is yes, but we have no specific cases to illustrate it.

It is fairly common, however, for children to suddenly "remember," when they learn about sexual intercourse as preadolescents, that at an earlier age they interrupted their parents in an activity that seemed peculiar at the time but which did not have a clear meaning until later. It is in a similar way that children recognize a sexual event that has happened to themselves, even if they had no sexual label to apply to it at the time. When children do learn to understand the meaning of sexual gestures, that understanding seems to include the past as well as the present, and in a fairly accurate fashion. The sex is not forgotten.

HOW THE QUESTIONNAIRE DEFINED SEXUAL

Nonetheless, this discussion does illustrate one of the important limitations of our method (and perhaps any method) of investigating childhood sexual experiences: we are dealing with subjectively defined material. That the experience was sexual is something decided by the respondent in the survey, not by the researcher.

The instructions to the respondents read as follows: "We would like you to try to remember the sexual experiences you had while growing up. By 'sexual' we mean a broad range of things, anything from playing 'doctor' to sexual intercourse—in fact, anything that might have seemed 'sexual' to you." The "might have seemed" was included as a deliberate attempt to see if respondents would volunteer some amorphously defined experiences. A list of conventional kinds of sexual activities was then given for the respondent to choose from, plus an open category marked "other."

However, only a handful of respondents used this category, and most of these were for oral-genital contacts—clearly sexual in nature.

Ultimately, we have no sure way of knowing if, in many of the cases, respondents were doubtful about whether the experience they recorded (or one they didn't) was really sexual. But on the basis of interviews with respondents who had earlier filled out surveys, we believe that this situation was extremely rare.

Although it is possible some people's childhood sexual experiences are not even in conscious awareness, because of repression or because they were not labeled as sexual by the child, we think such instances are relatively few. This would be a fascinating study in its own right, but one that will have to wait for another time.

Defining Victimization

Victimization is also a slippery concept, subject to various definitions according to one's values. Has a child been victimized who eagerly accepts an invitation for a sexual experience with an adult? If parents fail to give a child proper sex information, has the child also been victimized? (For the broadest conceptualization of sexual abuse, including things like circumcision, see Van Stolk, 1977.) The question of "whose point of view?" comes into play here, as it did in trying to define what is sexual. Is victimization judged from the point of view of the victim or of an outside observer?

There seemed to us three possible ways of defining sexual victimization. We will say a bit about each possibility and explain how we arrived at our final choice.

THE CONSENT STANDARD

Among adults, a person is usually thought of as sexually victimized when something is done to that person that he or she did not consent to. In the case of children, however, consent is much more problematic. When a child agrees to take off her clothes for her uncle, is this a form of consent?

There seem to be two major difficulties with the consent standard when applied to children. (1) Children are less aware of the meaning and consequences of various, particularly sexual, behavior. Most children, for example, have no way of realizing the strong community censure of adult-child sexual contact. Can a child consent to an activity of whose implications she is only dimly aware? (2) Children, because they are under the physical and legal control of adults, are rarely in the position to be able to consent freely or not consent freely. Thus when a powerful and authoritative person in a child's life, like an uncle, asks her to do something she has never done before, can a child be said to have consented in any adult sense of the word when she does what he asks? Here is an example of just such a situation:

> **R:** It was with my uncle and I'd say I had to be about five. It started off as a silly game. In French (Canadian), a bug is called a *"bébête,"* and he would say, "the *bébête* is going to get you," and he'd go up my leg, which was all right. But then he went all the way up my leg and under my underpants and he would touch me. I just didn't like it. He made me very uncomfortable. I didn't know what he was doing. I just knew I didn't like it.

> **I:** Did you ever say to him, "I don't want to play *bébête"?*

> **R:** I wasn't a very outspoken child when I was young. Very timid. He was my uncle, he was my elder, and you don't tell your uncle what to do. That's how I was brought up. If I had it to live again now [laughs] it would be different.

In this case, the child found the activity unpleasant. But even if she had enjoyed it, it is still impossible to see how she could have truly consented to sexual activity with such a powerful authority in her life.

Thus for research, it seemed inadequate to use the consent standard of victimization. If we only counted experiences in which force was used, for example, we felt we would be excluding many kinds of sexual victimization caused by the juxtaposition of an adult's authority with a child's naivete.

FEELING VICTIMIZED

Another method would have been to consider victimization any experience in which the respondent felt victimized. This plan would solve two problems. (1) We would not be telling someone who did not feel victimized that, yes indeed, he or she was a victim. (2) Respondents could view the experience in light of subsequent events and decide whether they had eventually suffered from it, even though at the time they had willingly participated.

The one drawback here is that self-perception as a victim is just too subjective a standard. Many people, we have found in our interviewing, react strongly against the idea of seeing themselves as victims under any circumstances. Others readily embrace the label. Whether they do or not seems related to how they like to view themselves in general, and not to the objective circumstances of their childhood sexual experiences. We preferred to make our own judgments about the respondents' experiences based on the descriptions they gave us.

Ultimately, we even included under our definition of victimization some respondents who said their experiences had in fact been positive (9 percent of the girls and 19 percent of the boys). We believe that given the difference in authority and knowledge between adults and children in this society, it is not possible for a child to truly consent to a sexual relationship with an adult. We would make the same argument for the situation of sex between psychotherapist and patient. Even if a patient said his or her experience had been positive, we would say that he or she had been victimized by the sexual advance of the therapist. In other words, victimization can take place even if the victim does not necessarily feel victimized and damaged, if and when conditions of genuine consent are not possible at the outset.

THE COMMUNITY STANDARD

The third method for defining victimization, and the one we decided to use, refers to community standards about what is an exploitative sexual relationship. The standard is based on the age of the child and the age of the child's partner. This method has several advantages: (1) It is objective and easy to use. (2) It is the method used by the law in some states to assess the legality or illegality of sexual acts involving children. (3) It is a method that has also been used in other research on the subject, and therefore, will allow us to compare results more easily with those of other studies.

Thus our definition of victimization is based on age discrepancy. The determination of the exact age criteria are explained in the following chapter.

4

THE
EXPERIENCES
DESCRIBED

How many children are sexually victimized? Many people want to know the answer to this question. When a social problem is of fairly recent (in this case renewed) concern, it is common for there to be a preoccupation with discovering the true prevalence. People newly concerned with the problem hope that a prevalence rate will give it moral and political credibility. A rate provides a kind of scientific banner to wave to justify their concern, especially when it is suspected, as in the case of sexual victimization, that the true prevalence is much higher than people have commonly thought.

However, the importance of a true prevalence rate can be vastly exaggerated. Although intrinsically interesting, it is really not a statistic of great practical use. Once we know that a problem is significantly large, discovering exactly how large can be a pointless search, one that does not necessarily add any information about what causes the problem or what to do about it. But it is hard to deny curiosity, and so little is currently known even approximately about the prevalence of sexual victimization that we are still far removed from the point where such a pursuit becomes trivial.

Prevalence

In this study, 19.2 percent of the women and 8.6 percent of the men had been sexually victimized as children. This statistic is close to one-fifth of the women and one-eleventh of the men. These figures, which are impressively large, do seem to justify a search for at least a rough estimate of the true prevalence of sexual victimization.

Nonetheless, these figures should be accepted with some caution. As indicated earlier, because this is not a random sample, it is not fair to generalize about the general population or even about college students. We can only say that within this sample, where no obvious factors indicated a rate that would be artificially high, the prevalence of sexual victimization was substantial.

If anything, in fact, there are reasons to think this rate might be artificially low. As we mentioned in Chapter 3, college students are more middle class and more psychologically healthy, and so perhaps less likely to have been sexually victimized. In addition, there were certainly some students in the sample who failed to report their experiences because of embarrassment or memory loss. So we might want to regard these figures as low estimates for the prevalence of sexual victimization in the population at large.

Another important caution should be observed. The exact figures we obtain about the prevalence of sexual victimization depend on how we define it. There is not yet in this field any generally accepted definition of sexual victimization. Our definition is one that may include too much from some people's point of view and too little from others'.

KINDS OF SEXUAL ACTIVITY

A sexual experience between a child and an older person can include many kinds of things, and we decided to include in our count all of the following: (1) intercourse, simulated intercourse, or attempted intercourse between the child and the older person; (2) any instance in which the older person fondled the child's genitals or vice versa; (3) any instance where a child was subjected to an exhibitionistic display of genitals by an older person; (4) any instance in which the child was kissed, hugged, or fondled in a sexual way; (5) four cases in which adults made overt and frightening sexual overtures to young children (such as asking them to show their genitals) but no actual contact took place.

Some people may wish to argue with this definition. For example, concerning number (4) above, children are frequently kissed and hugged by adults. How could we be sure that these experiences were sexual? We accepted the experience as sexual if the respondent said it was. It was our impression from the interviews and from the responses to the survey itself that children were fairly accurate judges of when a touch from an older person was affectionate and when it was sexual. But it is possible that there is some inaccuracy here. Only 6 percent of the sexual experiences reported by girls and none of those reported by boys involved a sexual kind of hugging and kissing and that alone.

Another area of possible question is category number (3). Twenty percent of the girls' and 14 percent of the boys' experiences fell into this category, which were encounters with exhibitionists. Some people are reluctant to treat such encounters as examples of victimization. We decided to include them nonetheless for two important reasons. First, exhibitionism is really a kind of assault. It is not consented to, and the intention of the exhibitionist is usually to surprise, shock, or frighten his victim (MacDonald, 1973). Second, the exhibitionist often achieves his aim. Many of the respondents in our survey reported that their encounters with exhibitionists had been highly unpleasant affairs.

The most common kind of sexual activity between children and older partners was some kind of genital fondling. Thirty-eight percent of the girls' experiences and 55 percent of the boys' had been of this sort. Instances in which children were asked to touch or play with the adult's genitals with their hands or mouths are included here, as were the frequent instances in which adults fingered or mouthed a child's genitals. When one speaks of sexual victimization, this is most often the kind of activity referred to. More will be added to this discussion later in the chapter.

DEFINING OLDER PARTNER

The definition of victimization also requires an age range. To some extent, the exact ages chosen are arbitrary and are certain to include or exclude some questionable cases. The prevalence rate one finds depends on which age criteria are chosen. In our definition of victimization, we included three categories of relationship based on age criteria: The first is immature children who have sexual encounters with legally defined adults. This category includes all experiences between a *child twelve or under* with an *adult eighteen or over*. Well over half of the sexual experiences for girls and not quite half for boys fell into this category (see Tables 4–1 and 4–2).

T A B L E 4 – 1. Girls' Childhood Sexual Experiences with Much Older Persons

Age Relationship	Percent of Sample (N = 530)
Child with adult partner	11.3
Child with adolescent* partner (min. 5 yrs. older)	5.7
Young adolescent with adult partner (min. 10 yrs. older)	3.8
Total	19.2†

* This category includes a few cases where older partner was not yet an adolescent but still five or more years older.

† Column does not add because some persons had experiences in two or more categories.

TABLE 4-2. **Boys' Childhood Sexual Experiences with Much Older Persons**

AGE RELATIONSHIP	PERCENT OF SAMPLE (N = 266)
Child with adult partner	4.1
Child with adolescent* partner (min. 5 yrs. older)	2.3
Young adolescent with adult partner (min. 10 yrs. older)	2.3
Total	8.6

* This category includes a few cases where older partner was not yet an adolescent but still five or more years older.

These are the most classic and generally recognized instances of sexual victimization. The following is an example taken from an interview with one of our respondents:

When this boy was eight and until he was ten, he used to go visit his uncle by the seashore for the summer. The uncle's next-door neighbor, also considered an "uncle" by the family, drove a truck for a candy and potato chip distributor. He would invite the boy into his truck for candy and potato chips and in return would play with the boy's penis and ask the boy to rub his penis. This activity continued weekly throughout three summers, until the respondent, uncomfortable about it, unable to escape from the man, and afraid to tell anyone, simply refused one summer to return to his uncle's house for vacation.

A second category includes immature children who have sexual encounters with adolescents or much older children. This category includes all experiences between a *child twelve and under* and another person who is *under eighteen but at least five or more years older than the child.* Much sexual victimization, we know, takes place at the hands of older children. Cases are commonly reported, for example, of adolescent babysitters who take sexual advantage of the children for whom they have been given responsibility. We wished to make sure such cases were included in the tally.

Some sexual victimization of children also takes place at the hands of older siblings. One of our respondents remembered that at age four she had been twice cornered in her bedroom by her sixteen-year-old brother who made her stroke and lick his penis. Another respondent talked about an experience at age eight during the depression, in which her thirteen-year-old brother and his friend bribed her and her younger sister to let the boys try to have sexual intercourse with them. Both girls (5.7 percent) and boys (2.3 percent) had such experiences with older children (see Tables 4–1 and 4–2).

The third category, early adolescents who have sexual encounters with much older adults, includes all experiences between *adolescents thirteen to sixteen* and legally defined *adults at least ten or more years older than the adolescent*. Some of the most classic sexual victimization experiences occur in early adolescence. Three of the father-daughter incest cases reported in our sample occurred after the daughter was twelve, two of them not until she was sixteen. It first happened to one of our interviewees when she was fourteen and asleep one afternoon on the couch next to her father who was watching TV. Her mother was out working. She awoke to find her father had unbuttoned her blouse and was fondling her breasts. This petting activity continued for six months and got more serious, until the father finally pressured her to have intercourse, but she refused and avoided him successfully after that.

Nonetheless, adolescents are sexually mature and have many consensual sexual experiences, sometimes with older partners. In order to exclude experiences that might be considered normal adolescent sexual experimentation, only experiences with partners who were ten or more years older were included in this category. We felt that a ten-year difference in the case of a young adolescent was substantial enough to indicate the presence of victimization.

These adolescent sexual experiences with partners ten or more years older were clearly not consensual, romantic liaisons. Close to 70 percent of both the girls' and boys' experiences involved force. About three-quarters of the experiences were related as negative by both sexes. In every case but four, these relationships either involved force, were experienced negatively, or involved a family member. They can be confidently labeled as victimization. A small number, 2.8 percent of the girls and 2.3 percent of the boys had such experiences (see Tables 4–1 and 4–2).

PREVALENCE SUMMARIZED

All told then, sexual experiences with substantially older partners are surprisingly common: They happened to at least one out of every five girls. Note, too, the large number of boys who reported such experiences—less than half as often as girls, but still almost one boy in every eleven. This group of boys' and girls' experiences will be the subject of this and the next chapter.

Relationship to Partner

Almost half of the girls' experiences were with family members (Table 4-3), including fathers, stepfathers, brothers, uncles, cousins, and grandparents. An experience with at least one of each of these relatives is represented in the sample. (Only brothers and cousins who conformed to our criterion in age difference are discussed here.)

Boys' experiences are also primarily with older people they know, but to a much lesser extent with actual relatives. Only 17 percent of the boys' experiences were with family members, but still 70 percent were with relatives and acquaintances combined.

These figures are additional confirmation of the now well-established fact that sexual victimization occurs to a large extent within a child's intimate social network (see studies cited in Appendix A-2).

The experiences with relatives are particularly striking because they often involved relationships in which there was a great deal of trust and affection. One woman related that she had been particularly close to her maternal grandfather while growing up. She often went to spend weekends at his house, where he would take her fishing, tell her stories, and give her a lot of special attention. The grandfather had his own room, and he would usually ask his granddaughter to come and cuddle with him at bedtime. At first she enjoyed the cuddling, but the grandfather's caresses became progressively more sexual until he began to fondle her vagina and press up against her. When this behavior began to happen she realized that something was wrong and started to feel very uncomfortable about the bedtime cuddling. She declined his invitations after that, and although the experience did not destroy the relationship, she was left with a disturbing childhood memory and a secret she never dared to share with anyone.

Childhood sexual experiences with relatives are especially upsetting because in so many cases the child's confidence in a particularly important person is destroyed. Moreover, the experience usually introduces a secret or a tension, not just between the child and the older partner, but between the

TABLE 4-3. **Relationship of Older Partners to Victims**

RELATIONSHIP	GIRLS (N = 119) PERCENT	BOYS (N = 23) PERCENT
Family member	43	17
Acquaintance	33	53
Stranger	24	30

child and other close relatives, too. In this case, our respondent did not dare to confide in her mother. Not only was she afraid of her mother's reaction—would her mother even believe her?—but she felt an obligation to protect her mother from this terrible revelation about the mother's father. The destructive power of these kinds of terrible secrets is very great and is a common theme in many of the stories of sexual victimization by family members. (More details on family ties between children and their adult sexual partners appear in Chapter 6 under the heading of Incest.)

Duration of the Experiences

One respondent gave an account of sexual contact with her father that started when she was four and lasted until she was fifteen—which was an unusually long experience. Others reported experiences that lasted a few weeks, a few months, or a few years. Some encounters were episodic, spanning many years but only occurring two or three times. For example, one women was molested as a child by her brother-in-law when she spent a week at his house while her mother was delivering a baby. Nothing more happened for over a year until he came to visit at their house, at which time the genital fondling reoccurred.

There was a great variety in the patterns, but the majority of experiences reported (60 percent) were single occurrences. A child has an encounter with an adult; it is unpleasant, and the child avoids the adult afterwards. Or the child tells a parent what has happened, and the parent takes some action to make sure it does not recur. Some experiences happen only once because they were with strangers whom the child has never seen before and never sees again.

About 40 percent of the experiences occur more than once, and about 40 percent last more than one week. In other words, if the experience happens more than once, it usually goes on for longer than a week. The long relationships usually continue for a long time, which is illustrated by the fact that the *average* duration of relationships for girls is thirty-one weeks. With so many single experiences, there are a few very enduring experiences that pull up the average.

Age at Time of Experience

At what age are children most liable to encounter sexual experiences with older persons? Perhaps this figure will cast some light on just what it is that makes children vulnerable.

Most studies, including this one (Table 4-4), have shown that children are vulnerable at all ages (see studies cited in Appendix A-1). Experiences at age three or four are not at all rare, and reports have appeared of children even as young as three months being treated in emergency rooms as the result of molestation (Sgroi, 1976). At the other end of the spectrum, children encounter such experiences until they stop being children: and then sexual abuse may continue, although it is called something else.

In spite of the wide range in age at which experiences occur, it has often been assumed that among girls it is particularly the onset of puberty that enhances their attractiveness to adults. In the analysis of incest, for example, much has been made of how hard it is for some fathers and other male relatives to cope with the sexual fantasies provoked when their daughters, sisters, and nieces begin to develop. In other words, it is assumed that a girl's vulnerability to sexual overtures increases as she acquires adult sexual characteristics (Schechter and Roberge, 1976).

This assumption appears to be wrong, however. Data on the age distribution of the sexual experiences of subjects in this study are presented in Table 4-4. Overall, experiences for both girls and boys cluster around the preadolescent period. The mean age for girls is a fairly young 10.2. When broken down into single-year intervals (not presented in the table), there is one peak at 8 years old and a set of peaks in the 10- to 12-year-old bracket. These findings are confirmed in many other studies of both reported and unreported cases, which show mean ages of this young or younger (Appendix A-1).

This evidence undermines the idea that pubescence is the crucial factor in girls' vulnerability to sexual abuse. Certainly at age ten or twelve, some girls are beginning to develop secondary sexual characteristics. But at age eleven, for example, only about 40 percent of American girls have started breast development, and in no more than 15 percent would the development be noticed if the child were clothed (Marshall, 1975). Thus a majority of the experiences with adults take place before signs of puberty appear.

Also damaging to the idea that pubescence creates vulnerability is the

TABLE 4-4.   Age of Children at Time of Sexual Experience with Older Partner

AGE GROUP	GIRLS (N = 119)	BOYS (N = 23)
Mean Age	10.2	11.2
	Percent	
4–6	14	18
7–9	23	9
10–12	47	41
13–16	16	32

finding in Table 4–4 that the number of experiences actually drop somewhat after puberty.* Other studies have indicated a similar drop (Queen's Bench, 1976). This finding does not mean that adolescents have fewer total sexual experiences—on the contrary. But it does mean that young adolescents have fewer experiences with adults and substantially older partners. If puberty really made girls more vulnerable we would expect a substantial increase in experiences in the age category thirteen to sixteen.

How do we explain this special vulnerability in the preadolescent years? Lolita's Humbert Humbert believed that a certain type of man was fatally attracted to little girls in that twilight age between childhood and adolescence, and the allure faded with the onset of puberty. Such a pattern was intrinsic to the urge (Nabokov, 1955).

However some more mundane features of child development also might explain the vulnerability. Preadolescence is a period when children begin to operate more independently. They begin to go places on their own, and they are not so closely supervised. In this independence they may become more vulnerable.

Children also start to become aware of adult sexual meanings in this period, but they are still naive in that the full implication of sexual gestures is not yet apparent to them. Thus while they may provoke sexual reactions by their appearance and behavior, they are not yet skilled in avoiding and discouraging sexual maneuvers from adults. One reason for the drop in abuse in the early adolescent period is that once girls reach puberty, they quickly acquire those skills.

This explanation provides support to a theory of symbolic interaction rather than a physiological view of sexual experience (Gagnon and Simon, 1973). The physiological approach has always tended to emphasize the sexual triggering mechanisms inherent in physical aspects of sexuality—homones, secondary sex characteristics, nudity, and so forth. Symbolic interaction analysis has pointed instead to gestures and role playing as the key components of sexual behavior. In terms of such a contrast, children's vulnerability to sexual abuse is more related to their vocabulary of sexual knowledge and skills than to physiological factors such as breast development.

---

* Part of this decrease may be an artifact of data collection and definition. Respondents were asked to describe all kinds of sexual experiences before age twelve, but only the nonconsensual ones after age twelve, so they may have left out some early adolescent experiences that we would have classified as victimization. Secondly, victimization was defined as a ten-year age gap for the over-twelve group but as only a five-year gap for the younger children. However, the difference in number of experiences between the group aged ten to twelve and the group aged thirteen to sixteen is large, even though the former group spans only three years while the latter spans four. Moreover, the difference remains large even if a ten-year gap is used as the criterion for both groups. This and the fact that other studies have also found a decrease in victimization after age twelve prompts us to trust this finding.

Kinds of Sexual Activity

Sexual activity between adults and children cannot always be evaluated by the standards ordinarily used to evaluate sexual activity between adults. Too many things are different. In an ordinary consensual adult sexual experience, we know that certain agreed-upon scripts govern behavior, and certain gestures mean certain things to both participants. In the case of a sexual experience between children and adults, however, the scripts and meanings are much less apparent to those of us looking in from the outside. Thus great caution must be taken in jumping to conclusions on the basis of conventional sexual stereotypes.

For example, a great deal of misunderstanding exists about the role of intercourse in adult-child sexual encounters. Since intercourse is the goal of much adult sexual activity, many people are surprised to discover that intercourse is not that frequent in sexual contacts between adults and children. In this study only 4 percent of the experiences reported by girls involved intercourse.

The physiology of sexual relations must be considered. It is difficult, and sometimes impossible, for grown men to have intercourse with most young girls. Their vaginas are too small. When intercourse is attempted, it is usually accompanied by intense pain and injury to the girl's genital area.

But more important, many of the adult men seeking sexual contact with children are not looking for sexual intercourse. This fact obviously pertains to exhibitionists, who seem to derive their satisfaction from the shock and surprise their behavior produces in their victims. Contact with exhibitionists makes up about 20 percent of the sexual experiences girls have with adults.

The avoidance of intercourse is also true with other kinds of adult-child sexual activity, the most common of which involves the touching and fondling of genitals (38 percent in this survey). Adults will ask children to fondle their genitals, or adults will want to finger and sometimes have oral contact with the child's genitals. Fleeting one-time occurrences of child molesting often involve a man who tries to rub a child's genitals. But even in those sexual relations that last a long time, often the activity will consist primarily of masturbation and genital fondling with no intercourse.

Such men may have the opportunity to try intercourse, but they do not take it. This was the experience of one of our interviewees, who was sexually involved with her father for eleven years, starting at age four:

> **R** (experience at age eight): I remember this the most—that he went to my room, picked me up, brought me to his bed and I remember that he masturbated on my chest. I thought he urinated all over me. To me that was the vilest and

most horrible thing that could be done. But he never tried to insert himself. That was the nearest that he ever would have come to that point. . . .

Later he didn't do any more of the masturbating on my chest, nothing else. Mostly it was just him putting his hands in my pants and stimulating me. . . . I can remember there was a time when I used to put like four or five pair of underwear on under my pajamas hoping that he would get discouraged. And then he set down ground rules that we couldn't wear underwear to bed. . . .

It wouldn't be every night. Two, three times a week, but it was so bad that every night you'd lie awake wondering if this was going to be the night. Lots of times he'd be out very late in the morning and I would fall asleep and wouldn't hear him come in and I would wake up and he'd be there and I'd be horrified. . . .

So things went on like that for just a long, long time. It was even worse when I started developing, you know around twelve, thirteen, fourteen.

Is it that such men are using masturbation and genital fondling as a substitute for intercourse, which they really desire? Are they afraid to try intercourse either because the child is too small or because actual intercourse with a child is a more severe taboo than they want to violate? These may be two valid reasons for the low frequency of intercourse in children's sexual victimization.

However, work with adults who sexually molest children suggests that for many of them sexual intercourse is not their goal. The sexual contact they are seeking with children is of a more childish sort (Gebhard *et al.,* 1965; Mohr *et al.,* 1964). Their interest in children may represent a flight or escape from more adult forms of sexuality.

From the point of view of the adult then, it is probably wrong to interpret masturbation or genital fondling as a "lesser" form of sexual contact. This mistake is made, for example, when the definition of incest is limited to sexual intercourse between family members. Many long-term, emotionally charged intrafamily sexual relations do not involve intercourse, but they may be quite similar in intensity and duration to ones that do.

Initiation and Force

As mentioned in Chapter 2, there has been a long-standing concern with establishing how much the child participated in the sexual experience. We have tried to point out, and we agree with others who have pointed out (Armstrong, 1978; Rosenfeld, 1978; Rush, 1974), that this is not a fruitful, and is in fact a destructive, preoccupation in the field.

Our data show the children to be the recipients of sexual actions, not the initiators, and also the victims of force and coercion. Only in a tiny minority of cases did the respondents say that they had initiated the sexual activity. Ninety-eight percent of the girls and 91 percent of the boys said it was the older partner who started the sexual behavior.

Force was present more often than not in these experiences. Fifty-five percent of the girls and almost an equal percentage of boys reported that the partners used some kind of force to gain their participation. The force ranged from actual physical constraint, such as holding the children down, to the threat that they would be punished if they did not cooperate.

However, even where respondents did not report overt force, it is hard not to see elements of coercion in the differences in age or authority of the parties involved. In an incident mentioned previously, an eight-year-old girl was bribed by her brother and friend to allow them to try intercourse with her. This act took place in the midst of the depression, in an impoverished family. Our respondent described herself as an extremely shy and compliant child to whom the sum of twenty-five cents seemed like a fortune. Her brother had always been a kind of a hero to her, and he had been given substantial authority over his younger siblings by the parents. There was coercion implicit in the whole situation.

It is true that children often did not take actions that might have, from an adult point of view, protected them or prevented a recurrence of the experience. But in many cases, children were confused about the situation, did not perceive their options, or were deliberately misled by their partners. The respondent, described earlier, who was victimized by the potato chip salesman, was not forced into sexual activity; but when he became uncomfortable with it, he did not know how to terminate it. He doubted that faced with a choice between his story and the neighbor's denial, his real uncle would believe and protect him. Here again, there was a kind of coercion present in the very structure of the situation.

> **R:** He was accepted by everyone else around me and no one else knew. Everybody within the cluster, around the house, accepted him as being a friend and he could come into the house. . . . So if they were accepting him, then I really had to be careful. . . . Especially when you're a small kid they have such a physical intimidation over you. Now I can see that he's a very short, fat old man and I'd like to kick him down the stairs. Now I've got no problem, but at the time, just the fact that he told me not to tell. . . . You know, he said please, don't tell anybody. But the way he said it, it was like if you do, I'm gonna. . . . He never directly threatened me, but I just figured that he probably would. . . .

> **I:** Did you think that your uncle or that the family was capable of protecting you if you had asked them to protect you?

> **R:** See that's weird because they accepted him and they had known him for a long time. And I often wondered, if it's me against him, who are they gonna choose.

I: Because you were not really part of their family either?

R: No, I was just a guest. He's the next door neighbor. He's there all the time.

I: So you really doubted whether they would be willing to defend you?

R: Yeah.

The uncle did finally find out about his neighbor when the uncle's own son became a victim. The uncle forced the neighbor to move away.

Reaction to the Experience

Children were frightened by these experiences, as one might expect. Over half of the girls (58 percent) said they reacted to the experience with fear. An older person, someone in authority, someone they may or may not have known, made them do something that at the very least was unusual and probably also painful or coercive. That person was acting strange, furtive, and maybe even frightened. The children knew that what was happening was not right (De Francis, 1969). Not only was the adult acting strangely, but most children knew that such sexual behavior was wrong. Children learn at an early age that the genitals have a special connotation. The taboo and the naughtiness added to the fright.

Another common reaction was shock: 26 percent of the girls said they felt shock at the time of the experience. About one-fifth said they were surprised. A few said their reaction was more of a neutral sort, and a few (8 percent) actually remembered experiencing some pleasure as a result.*

The fact that any of the children experienced pleasure may surprise some people. Unfortunately the nature of the enjoyment has been seriously misunderstood and has led to an almost prosecutorial attitude in the past by some therapists, an attitude that has disturbed many victims.

Contrary to the stereotype, most victims in our study readily acknowledged the positive as well as the negative elements of their experience. They talked about the times the physical sensations felt good, or they remembered how their sexual experience with an adult or family member satisfied a longing for affection and closeness that was rarely met at any other time.

These were not expressions of adult kinds of sexual passions and longings. On the whole, they were part of a confusing flood of feelings and sen-

---

* Respondents could choose more than one response, so reactions are not mutually exclusive.

sations, usually dwarfed by an overwhelming sense of helplessness, guilt, anger, or fear. In fact, the pleasure often only intensified the guilt or the helplessness, since it added to the child's confusion and left the child feeling out of control of even his or her own emotions.

R: He would usually corner me somewhere and he would ply me with compliments. Between the compliments and because he was so nice and like a father figure, I was confused about what to do or how to handle it.

I was the last one to wear a bra in my sixth grade class. So I was very pleased at this situation, also. I think it really pleased me that he'd feel me up and say, "See, this is how it makes them grow." I would even check to see if they were growing. They never did.

I can remember getting pleasure out of our experience. However, for the most part, after a while I began to hate him, but I think for maybe just a few days or hours even there was a time when it thrilled me to think about it. When it actually happened, I didn't like it at all.

R: I would pretend that I was asleep. Why I did it I'm not sure. I think partly because there was still that need for that affection or whatever. Partly because it felt good. Usually I would just lie there and accept his advances and feel bad about it. I can remember lying in bed at night awake, just waiting for him to come, afraid to go to sleep, petrified.

R: Sometimes I hated it. You would sort of put your head down and march, hands in pockets, to the basement knowing that he would be waiting down the basement steps and around the corner with his zipper down and his penis hanging out for a blow job. And it was like, "Oh my God. I don't want to do this. I wish I could jump out the window."

But sometimes—there was a different side of my dad that I normally didn't see. There was a seductive quality to it. A total relaxation. He was not as gruff. He was not as stern. There would be some caressing from him which, I guess, I can look at it now and say—there were times and there are times—I know myself well enough to know that there are definitely times when I want to be caressed . . . [Armstrong, 1978, p. 185].

These ambivalent feelings were part and parcel of some of the most nightmarish experiences. They did not stop respondents from rating them as highly traumatic. Thus in spite of the pleasurable moments, most of the female respondents (66 percent) remembered the experiences as having been negative. None of our interviewees were glad that the experiences had happened. In the sample as a whole, only a small percentage of women (7 percent) rated the experience as positive. The mean rating for experiences based on a scale from 1 (positive) to 5 (negative) was 4.0.

To Tell or Not to Tell

Given that these experiences seemed to inspire mostly negative reactions, why were so few reported? Sixty-three percent of the girls and 73 percent of the boys did not tell *anyone* about the experience. It is understandable why many crimes of a personal sort are not reported to the police (Landis 1955; Gagnon 1965). Police involvement often brings down public exposure, humiliation, and bureaucracy on the head of the victim. But the children in this survey did not even report their experiences to their own parents, to their brothers and sisters, or to their friends. For a great number, our survey was the first mention they had made of it since it had occurred.

This finding is a sad commentary on the state of sexual anxiety in most families and communities. Undoubtedly in a large number of cases children made an accurate assessment that it would be a mistake to mention the experience to anyone. In all likelihood the reaction to their revelation would have been anger or hysteria. Since even adults commonly feel somehow responsible when they have been sexually abused, it is the extraordinary child who could tell a parent without being fearful—usually legitimately so—of being blamed. Moreover, most families give children very little practice in the discussion of sexual matters, so in many cases, the channels for bringing up the event or even the vocabulary for talking about it to parents was probably missing. One child who finally did tell her mother recalls,

> **R:** I expected to be scolded. I really did. That's why I remember the expression on her face. I expected to really get it for saying this, expected them to stick up for him and not for me because I was a child. And I was saying something bad about the adult, you know. That's what amazes me. Nothing was ever said. I wasn't accused of lying. Nothing. The whole thing stopped. He never touched me again.

Another child never said anything:

> **I:** Why don't you think you ever told your parents?

> **R:** Well, it was a mixture of thinking that they wouldn't believe me and being afraid that they would turn it around and blame it all on me. I wasn't going to say something and get blamed for everything, so forget it. Up until the time I put my mouth on his penis, it didn't seem like anything that serious anyway—just looking. And after I put my mouth on his penis, that seemed really incriminating, so I wasn't going to tell.

That these childish fears are often well grounded is illustrated in an interview with a women whose daughter came to tell her one day that her stepfather had been making sexual advances to her:

> **R:** I'm a nurse and I used to work nights. When she was fourteen, she told me that my husband had come into her room one night when I was working and tried to have sex with her. Well, I wouldn't believe it. As you can imagine, at the time I'd only been married a couple of years. I wasn't going to believe any such thing about my husband. I think it was sort of a self-protective mechanism. But I've learned a lot since then.

Many people who have had childhood sexual experiences, just like many adults who have been raped, say subsequently that the pain of silence and internally felt stigma was often worse than the pain of the experience itself. On the other hand, there are also a large number of victims who remember that the reaction of parents and other authorities caused a havoc in their lives that also dwarfed the pain of the experience itself. Caught in the dilemma of such a no-win situation, who is really to say that the child who chooses silence—apparently the most common response—is not making the most rational choice.

Experience of Boys

Women are the main targets of sexual assault. But an important discovery of our survey is that a substantial number of boys also have been sexually victimized (Table 4–2). Not as many boys (9 percent) have such experiences as girls (19 percent), to be sure. However, the number is higher than would be expected, boys reporting almost half as many experiences as girls.

Sexual abuse of boys is a phenomenon well known to child protection workers and has often received lurid coverage in news reports about pedophiles and other sex offenders. Stories have appeared in recent years describing rings of child prostitution, mostly involving young boys and often implicating community stalwarts (Lloyd, 1976).

However, among reported cases of sexual abuse, girls have always predominated by a wide margin. The American Humane Association study in New York (De Francis, 1969) found girl victims outnumbered boys ten to one. Many other clinical studies of sexual abuse report on girls alone, instances of male victims being so uncommon. Our finding would suggest that a great deal of sexual abuse against boys is going unreported. It is occurring but not reaching the attention of agencies.

A kind of double standard exists which may have hindered the recognition of sexual abuse against boys. As a result of our cultural stereotype, which casts men as sexually active and women as sexually passive, it has been possible to read more consent and less exploitation into the adult-child liaisons of young boys than in the comparable experiences of young girls.

Is there any truth to this picture? Our study reveals some interesting similarities and differences in the sexual experiences of boys and girls with older persons.

Boys appear to be older than girls on the average when they have their sexual experiences with older persons (11.2 years for boys, compared to 10.2 for girls). This difference of about a year, although small, is consistent with the findings of other studies (Appendix A–1). Other researchers usually attribute it to the fact that puberty occurs later in boys. However, since we have seen earlier that the onset of physiological puberty is not what triggers sexual victimization for girls, this may not be the best explanation. In fact, we are not certain about what this difference means.

Another age difference relates to the age of the older partners. Boys' partners are on the average younger (26.9 years old) than girls' partners (31.7 years old). This is because more of the boys' older partners are teenagers, and none of them was over 50.

A more striking difference is the extent to which boys' and girls' experiences occur within or outside the family. Girls' experiences are with older family members 44 percent of the time, compared to only 17 percent of the time for boys.

This difference may be due to the tendency of preadolescent and adolescent boys to be more independent and less family-centered than girls. Partly as a result of parental concern over sexual victimization, which parents usually think takes place outside the family, girls are often held in tighter rein. They may also be given more explicit and detailed warnings about sexual encounters with adults. Boys tend to explore the outside world with less caution. Thus boys may be in more situations outside the family where they would encounter a sexual approach.

Whatever the reason, this finding may indeed be taken as evidence that girls' experiences are more serious than boys'. To the extent that family sexual abuse is more disturbing and involves the violation of more taboos and trust, one would have to say that girls are more seriously victimized by adults than are boys. In this sense, the idea of girls being more vulnerable, not just in terms of numbers but in terms of the nature of the experience, is quite true.

As we mentioned, men are seen as more active parties in sexual encounters. From the data in the survey, however, this stereotype does not appear to describe the behavior of boys in adult-child relationships. Ninety-one percent of the boys reported that it was the older person who initiated the experience, which is only slightly less than the comparable figure for girls (98 percent). Although there are many stories about aggressive young teenage boys actively seducing older men, in our sample this was a relatively rare source of adult-child sexual involvement.

In addition, boys are likely to be coerced in their sexual encounters with older persons, just as likely to be coerced as girls, in fact. Both groups reported that over half of their partners used force in initiating the encounter. This finding suggests that boys are not more consenting than girls in most cases.

However a crucial difference between the experiences of boys and girls lies in their reactions to what happened. In their overall evaluation, girls rate their experiences more negatively than do boys: 66 percent compared to 38 percent. Boys report feeling more interest and pleasure at the time, and girls remember more fear and shock. This finding certainly confirms the impression that the experiences were more traumatic for the girls, but it does not mean that the boys' experiences were never traumatic. Indeed, some were extremely so:

I: Could you compare this to some other experience in your life?

R: Much more traumatic at the time. Very anxiety-producing. Probably there wasn't anything in my life as anxiety-producing.

I: So this was the biggest trauma of your life?

R: Oh, without a doubt. Mostly because I went through like two months of avoidance. I was always very conscious of where I was, who I was with, and was the group large enough so he couldn't single me out, and, you know, it was pretty terrifying. "Can I go outside? Is it safe to go outside?" Nothing really as traumatic as that.

Following is the testimony of another man whose childhood experience had an impact very similar to the kinds of traumatic effects described by many women:

I: Was the sexual experience just another one of those incredible things that happened to you? Or was there something special to it?

R: There was something more attached to it or I wouldn't have had what I consider an impeded development. I always wondered why I was so shy and inhibited. And not interested in dating or getting to know women. Only within the last two years, and I'm almost thirty-one, have I ever really enjoyed having sex with someone. I always figured it was something I had to do. When I was married and my former wife wanted to make love, I was always finding excuses not to. I didn't like it. It didn't turn me on. It wasn't exciting. It didn't feel good.

On the whole, however, such experiences were more numerous for girls. As mentioned earlier, their experiences occur more often with family members and with men who are of an older age than those who approach boys. Both these features of the girls' experiences (and especially the greater age of the adults, as we will see in Chapter 7) could account for part of the greater negativity in the girls' responses. Also, girls just may be more vulnerable to experiencing childhood sex as traumatic. Boys, for example, generally learn about sex at an earlier age, incorporate it more into childhood camaraderie, and have a less fearful outlook on it (Elias and Gebhard, 1969). This vulnerability no doubt stems in part from the fact that parents and other adults are very anxious about girls' sexuality.

Part of the anxiety is indeed justified, since as we have seen, girls do tend to be frequently victimized. Another part of the anxiety, however, relates to the cultural conception of girls as sexual merchandise that can be ruined or devalued. There is undoubtedly a self-fulfilling prophecy in the anxiety, which intensifies the reaction a parent makes or that a child anticipates a parent making and thus increases the traumatic potential of any incident.

In summary, boys' experiences occur at an older age with generally younger partners. They less frequently involve family members and are felt to be less frightening and shocking. Still, there is no strong evidence that boys are willing victims. Their experiences are typically initiated by the older person and occur under circumstances of some duress and coercion.

Because of the differences between them, we have treated boys' and girls' experiences separately in the rest of the data analysis. This procedure always produced much more meaningful results, particularly insofar as the girls were concerned. The findings about the boys' experiences appeared much less coherent, and there were many fewer significant correlations. More attention must be given to boys' experiences using a larger sample than this one.

Conclusion

This chapter has outlined some of the major descriptive features of the sexual experiences with adults reported by the boys and girls in our sample. In brief they are as follows:

1. Such experiences occur to about one in every five girls and one in every eleven boys.
2. Especially for the girls, the experiences often occur with family members.
3. Peak vulnerability for the child falls prior to puberty, ages ten to twelve.

4. Intercourse is not the major sexual activity. Rather most child-adult sex is touching and fondling of the genitals.
5. Coercion is present in over half of the experiences, and only a tiny fraction are initiated by the children themselves.
6. Only a minority of the experiences are ever reported, even to parents and friends, let alone police.
7. The girls had particularly strong and consistently negative reactions to the experiences; the boys less so.

5

OLDER PARTNERS

Myths of the Child Molester

CHILD MOLESTERS WERE ONCE PICTURED as sexually frustrated old men who loitered in public parks or outside of schoolyards in hopes of luring naive youngsters into their clutches with offers of candy or money (McDonald, 1952). Study after study has punctured this stereotype, so that if any vestige of it remains—as it certainly does—it is because the truth is more unpalatable than the myth.

The first unpalatable truth is, as we have already indicated, that most sexual abusers are well known to their victims. They are for the most part family members, friends, and neighbors, especially in the case of girls. In our survey, 76 percent of the older persons who had sexual experiences with the girls were known to them; 43 percent were actually family members. A roughly similar number of partners were known to the boys (70 percent), but there were many fewer family members among them (only 17 percent).

The myth of the child molester as a stranger is just part of a larger mythologizing process that surrounds all kinds of antisocial behavior. People worried about assault think their greatest danger comes from the anonymous mugger in a darkened alleyway. Many women stereotype the rapist as an unfamiliar black man who grabs them on the street or breaks into their house. In fact, most assault occurs among family and friends in people's own houses, and most rapes occur between people of the same race, many of whom are known to one another. In a familiar psychological process, people project the dangers they fear as far away as possible, onto pariahs, outcast groups, those they cannot identify with, convenient sociological receptacles. In fact, the greatest danger is often closest to home, even, as in the case of sexual victimization, right *in* the home.

The stereotype of the child molester stigmatizes not just strangers but also old men. Once again it is mistaken. Every bit of evidence indicates that sexual abusers are all ages, but if they predominate anywhere, it is among the young. Of course, figures for the ages of adult partners in this study, as

73

well as in others, come from estimates made by victims and are subject to the distortion caused by memory loss and the young age of some of them. As estimates, the accounts can be believed. In this study they show older partners of the children ranging from adolescents to age seventy. The average age for partners of girls is 31.7 and for boys 26.9.

The actual age distribution of partners is the exact opposite of what the stereotype might suggest (Table 5-1). The largest group is teenagers, then young adults, tapering down with age into an almost perfect inverted pyramid. The over-fifty group, the alleged "dirty old men," contribute only a tiny fraction to the sample.

No one factor explains this particular age distribution. Because of the way that male sexuality develops over the life cycle, different kinds of sexual motives must come into play at different times. Adolescents are experimenting with sex, often confused about sexual values and often impulsive. Young adults tend to be the most sexually active in all varieties of sex, including rape and homosexuality. Men in their thirties may be experiencing the anxiety of aging and the disappointment and conflict of the middle married years, which may fuel a sexual involvement with children.

Another factor to consider is accessibility, the simple question of who has the most opportunity for sexual contact with children. Adolescents have younger brothers, sisters, cousins, and family friends within easy reach, and adults in their thirties are likely to have their own children or the children of relatives and friends. They are also most likely to be engaged in activities that mix adults and children. As far as we know, senior citizens may have the motives to approach children, but they may just not have the opportunity. Nonetheless, the "dirty old man" stereotype is inaccurate.

A final part of the stereotype needs debunking: parks, schoolyards, and automobiles are not the sites where sexual abuse primarily takes place. The most frequent location is the home of the victim or the home of the offender—which would follow naturally from the fact that most of the abusers are known to the victims. Strangers would be more likely to need

TABLE 5-1. Age of Older Partners

AGE OF PARTNER	GIRLS (N = 119)	BOYS (N = 23)
Mean Age	31.7	26.9
	Percent	
10–19	33.6	39.1
20–29	23.5	21.8
30–39	17.7	21.7
40–49	16.8	17.4
50–59	5.1	—
60+	2.5	—

public places to perform their deeds, but familiar persons can operate in homes where their natural contact with children occurs. Although we do not have data in our own study on this question, this finding has been confirmed in other studies (De Francis, 1969; Landis, 1956).

The Male Monopoly

The most obvious characteristic of sexual abusers has been one of the least analyzed: they are almost all men. It is older males who initiate sexual contact with younger children in the vast majority of cases. This finding is just as true for boys as girls, meaning that most such sexual experiences for boys are homosexual (84 percent), and for girls heterosexual (94 percent). Women just do not make many sexual advances toward children.

The fact that men are sexual offenders is not often analyzed because it is so taken for granted. It is men who rape; it is men who are responsible for most sexual "deviations." It is so firmly entrenched in our image of male sexuality that we are not surprised to learn that men predominate in making sexual advances toward children.

THEORIES ABOUT THE MALE MONOPOLY

Various kinds of speculations have been offered to understand this phenomenon. Some see it rooted in the nature of male sexuality. For example, recent endocrinological research has revealed what Money (Money and Tucker, 1975) calls the Eve principle—that human sexual development, at least on a biological level, is biased toward the female, that only by "adding something" does male development take place. As a result, incomplete and faulty biological development occurs much more often in males.

This theory meshes neatly with the canons of some psychoanalytic thought that also sees male sexual development as more vulnerable to aberration (Stoller, 1975). According to Stoller, males, like females, start life in total symbiotic identification with their mothers. But in order to develop appropriate masculinity they, unlike females, must thrust aside this symbiosis, break off the identification with their mothers, and develop a new positive identification with their fathers. This transition is treacherous, and in many males the process is not completed. They are left anxious about masculinity, fearful of again becoming fused in the primal symbiosis with mother, and hostile toward women and the male-female sexual complementarity. Out of these conflicts emerge the homosexual, fetishistic, and pedophilic deviations.

In their analysis feminists connect this highly incriminating feature of male sexuality to the nature of a male-dominated society. They have argued that rules about incest and other sexual taboos are male-instituted regulations concerning the ownership and control of women (Herman and Hirshman, 1977). Because men make the rules and enforce them, they also assume the right to violate them. Having the power, both in the society and in the family, they can maintain a double standard: harsh sanction and taboos on female sexual delinquency, and more leniency and covert toleration for themselves.

ON WOMAN'S INCAPACITY TO RAPE

Still another popular opinion is that women do not rape, and by extension sexually abuse, because of the physiology of the sexual situation. Women do not rape because of their inferiority in strength, weight, and body size, and more importantly, because men must play a physiologically active role in the sexual act. "Man's structural capacity to rape and woman's corresponding structural vulnerability are as basic to the physiology of both sexes as the primal act of sex itself. Had it not been for this accident of biology, an accommodation requiring the locking together of two separate parts, penis and vagina, there would be neither copulation nor rape as we know it. . . . This single factor may have been sufficient to have caused the creation of a male ideology of rape" (Brownmiller, 1975, p. 4).

In other words, a woman cannot have intercourse with a man unless his penis is erect, and that is not a faculty under a woman's control (Walters, 1975, p. 127). Threat and coercion are certainly not incentives to sexual arousal, in fact they are deterrents, so it would seem hard if not impossible for a woman to take what she wants by force.

However, neither of these physical factors explains why so few women sexually abuse children. First of all, women do have physical and social authority over children, so differentials in size and power cannot be deterrents to female sexual aggression in this case. Women could as easily take advantage of children as men.

Second, in the sexual abuse of children, the problem of the "limp penis" is revealed to be not really important. For one thing, many adult males lure children into sexual activity with the implicit trust of the child and without the coercion and threat that inhibit sexual arousal. Women could do the same. But much more importantly, a great deal of adult-child sexual contact is masturbatory. The man fingers the girls' genitals to arouse himself, or he asks his partner to stimulate him; or he wants to photograph the naked child or expose himself to the child, for the child's horrified reaction. All of these activities in principle could be equally gratifying to a woman. A woman could just as easily as a man use a child's genitals or hand to masturbate with; but women don't. Although it is feasible for women to get sexual gratification from children in many of the same ways that men do, it rarely happens.

Thus, the fact that women do not rape or sexually abuse children suggests that the important difference lies somewhere else, not in the physiology of the act, but in the psychology of the actor and the sociology of the situation.

RELEVANT MALE-FEMALE DIFFERENCES

Women are so different from men in their relationships with children in our society that it is hard not to look for an explanation here. Several facets of this relationship are possible explanations for the female reticence about sex with children. First, women have more physical contact with children, which is freer and more total because it is more sanctioned. Physical contact with children is harder for men. They do not get much practice in it before parenthood and, even when they do, it is more inhibited and nervous because of the suspicions surrounding it. Women have more involvement with genital and excretory functions of children, and their greater comfort with these areas may defuse some of the sexual tension between women and children. Men, being more excluded from such activities, may develop a stronger fascination and a fantasy about them that can motivate a sexual approach.

Second, women also have more direct responsibility for children. They supervise their activities, watch out for their safety, and may come to identify more with their sense of well being. Thus women may better understand the trauma of a sexual intrusion on a child, and therefore be deterred.

However, one could easily exaggerate these differences. After all, in spite of women's greater responsibility for children and their greater closeness, they end up physically abusing children more often than men (Maden and Wrench, 1977). Thus it is wrong to overromanticize the bond between women and children. Closeness and responsibility could easily be cause for more rather than less abuse, if sexual abuse operated like physical abuse.

Moreover, not all women are mothers. There are sisters, cousins, friends, and strangers who may not have had all this supposedly prophylactic involvement. Comparable male relatives, friends, and strangers make sexual advances toward children. Why not female?

Third, the socially conditioned channels of sexual attraction draw women away from children, but men toward them.* In our society, women

* I am indebted to Kersti Yllo for this insight.

choose their sexual partners from men older than themselves, whereas men choose partners from younger women. Thus, for a man's sexual interest to attach itself to a child conforms to his general tendency to seek out a sexual partner of inferior size and age. This is not a natural tendency for a woman and may mean that it is more of a psychological contortion to see a child as a sexual object.

In a similar fashion, other themes in the process of sexual socialization make children more likely partners for men. For women, there is a greater emphasis on mutuality as a foundation for sexual involvement. Men tend to emphasize gratification as an end in itself and adopt an orientation encouraging them to see the other person as an object (De Beauvoir, 1953). Thus it is easier for them to view children as possible objects for their gratification.

The Female Minority

The foregoing may have given the mistaken impression that women never sexually abuse children. Actually, there are instances when they do, although it is uncommon. Probably the most notorious of these are the cases of mother-son incest that have been reported—although very infrequently—some of which have actually been prosecuted (Weinberg, 1955). When they do occur, instances of sexual abuse perpetrated by women seem to be taken less seriously and are not investigated or prosecuted with the same zeal as cases involving men. When brought to court, charges are often reduced to misdemeanor offenses, like impairing the morals of a child.

Women's sexual offenses against children may in fact be less serious, but it is certainly true that lenient treatment of female offenders is also abetted by myths about such experiences. For one thing, in heterosexual incidents, many men are titillated by the idea of an older woman initiating a boy into the ways of the world, so that when a woman has a sexual experience with a boy, they find it hard to consider it victimization. Moreover, the idea that males are the sexual aggressors is so strong that even when the male is a child and the female an adult, the assumption is that the boy must have taken an active part in the liaison. Thus instances of adult females interacting sexually with boys, are seen as less exploitative and less abusive than in the case of male offenders.

Fifteen instances of sexual experiences with substantially older women were reported in our survey. Although this is a small group for a statistical analysis, the comparisons, regarded with healthy caution, can give us a better idea of the kinds of sexual involvement women have with children.

The older female partners in the sample are not greatly different from the older male partners. They range in age from twelve to forty-five; they include a mother, an aunt, several sisters, and some strangers; and their activities range from exhibition to intercourse.

The two main differences are that the women are somewhat younger (averaging 22.1 years old as opposed to 29.4 for men) and they are substantially more homosexual; that is, their approaches are more often directed toward girls than boys. Advances from older women were homosexually oriented in 67 percent of the cases, whereas from the older men only in 14 percent.

Aside from these differences, the female partners are remarkable in their similarity to the male. They approach children whose average age is about the same. They both are members of the children's family in about the same proportions. There is little difference in the kinds of sexual activities they engage in. They both are the initiators of the activity in an overwhelming number of the experiences. They use force, when they do so, equally often, and the relationships with male and female older partners last about the same length of time.

These similarities are surprising. After all we have said about the fact that men are much more likely to sexually approach children, we might naturally expect that the instances when women did so would be quite distinctive.

However, in spite of the similarity in the form of the experience, they do not at all elicit the same kind of reactions from the children, and this is a key difference. Women provoked much less fear in the children they approached than the men did (20 percent for women compared to 62 percent for men). The children were more likely to be interested by the experience (40 percent compared to 13 percent), and they also reported fewer negative feelings about it in retrospect (40 percent versus 68 percent).

The fewer negative reactions among this group is partly explained by the fact that sexual advances by women are less intimidating. But one confounding factor is present here as well. A larger proportion of the children who had experiences with women were boys, and we know that boys report fewer negative experiences than girls. This fact in itself may be part of the explanation.

The tenor of these sexual experiences with older women is better illustrated with some examples. Ten of the experiences were with little girls, and several of these seemed to be fairly offensive. A seventeen-year-old girl, for example, started manipulating her nine-year-old sister's genitals, and this activity went on many times over a three-year period. The elder sister used some threat or coercion in her approaches, and the respondent recalled it as a negative experience. Another respondent reported that when she was ten a strange woman in her twenties exhibited her sexual organs to her. A number of these offenses involved force, and more often than not they were regarded negatively.

The boys reported a more mixed set of encounters with older women.

One reported that when he was twelve he had intercourse once with a twenty-three-year-old woman which he felt quite positive about. But a sixteen-year-old boy nearly had intercourse with a twenty-eight-year-old female stranger about which he felt the opposite. A six-year-old boy had his penis manipulated many times by an aunt in her thirties who sometimes used threats or coercion. However, he said he felt neither positively or negatively about the experience. Consistent with boys' experiences in general, they reacted less negatively than the girls, even when the major outlines of the experience were similar.

Thus the scanty evidence we have indicates that a few women are sexually involved with children, both boys and girls. Some of the boys' experiences with adult women are so-called "initiation" rites, which the boys view fairly positively—but not the bulk of them. For many children, the experiences with older women are like the experiences with older men: that is, they are often perceived negatively, especially by the girls, and involve some force. They would appear to qualify for the term sexual victimization.

Adolescent and Adult Partners

In Chapter 3 we posed some questions about who to include as sexual abusers. Many adolescents, we pointed out, take sexual advantage of children, so it seemed appropriate to include adolescent-child encounters in our statistical tabulations and not limit ourselves to strictly child-adult experiences. We proposed the five-year-age differential to try to separate the experiences with adolescents that would be abusive from those that would tend to be consensual.

Although we have lumped adolescents and adults together in several of our analyses, many people would wonder how equivalent such partners really are. In sex of all matters, teenagers are in their own way naive and inexperienced, in spite of their mature appetites and capacities. Their curiousity about sex is overwhelming. Yet they are unclear about sexual meanings and codes of sexual appropriateness. They are less in control of their impulses, less clear about their own sexual orientations, and vague about sexual responsibility. One might expect their sexual advances to children to reflect this naivete.

To the child partner of an adolescent, such naivete might be felt in different ways. Because the adolescent partner is in some respects still another child himself, the younger child might find herself somewhat less shocked, less scared, or less traumatized by the whole event. On the other hand, in the teenager's impulsiveness and irresponsibility, there might be elements of a brutality that could be very traumatic indeed. As anyone familiar with high schools knows, adolescents can display an inhumanity to one another and other children rarely matched in the adult world.

Thus it is not intuitively apparent how sexual victimization by adolescents might compare with that by adults. It might be more traumatic or less traumatic; it might involve different kinds of sexual activities; it might be more or less intense. To better understand such comparisons, we broke down the experiences of boys and girls according to whether their older partners were adolescents or adults.

The conclusion to be drawn is interesting. Experiences with adolescents and with adults are very similar for the girls. The immaturity of adolescents does not make much difference in what happens and how the experiences are perceived. However, for boys the differences are quite pronounced.

First we will take up the comparison in the case of girls. Adolescents and adults approach female children sexually in remarkably similar fashion. They both initiate the interaction all the time. They both use about the same amount of force. They both shy away from actual intercourse with the children, and although the adults are more often exhibitionists and the adolescents do more touching, they both actually fondle and touch the children in about the same proportions.

These similarities in approach are particularly striking in light of two big differences. The adolescents are much more likely to be family members—brothers and cousins primarily—and the partners of the adolescents are apt to be younger. Apparently neither the family connection nor the younger age of the children affects force or sexual activity.

Not surprisingly, the reaction of the female victims to the two kinds of partners is also similar. Respondents who had experiences with adolescents found them as traumatic as those who had experiences with adults. The former were somewhat less frightened and shocked at the time and less likely to tell anyone, but in retrospect they found the experience just as negative. This finding gives strong support to our decision to group adolescents together with adults. The experiences with teenagers look as victimizing as those with adults, at least insofar as the girls are concerned.

When it comes to the boys, we are faced with a different matter. The experiences boys had with adolescent partners were a different type from those they had with adults. The differences are striking in many ways. With adolescents, they involve more family members; they go on much, much longer; they involve less touching and more exhibition or oral sex; they are not so often coercive; and most important they are evaluated fairly positively. Eighty-six percent say they were interested, and over half felt pleasure (only 13 percent of the boys reported any pleasure with adult partners).

There are a scant seven of these cases, so true generalization is difficult. Still the tendencies seem quite clear. There appears to be quite a bit more consent and positive result when adolescents approach younger boys than when they approach younger girls, even in spite of the homosexuality taboo which is being violated in most of these cases.

Conclusion

Unfortunately, studying the older partners in children's sexual victimization is a tough research problem. Convicted sex offenders are available, but they are an unusual minority. From our survey, it is clear that few unapprehended older partners step forward to report their experiences, even on an anonymous questionnaire, although we know from our reports that such experiences are widespread and there must be many such offenders in our population. For theories about older partners we have to rely on the reports of their victims, an unreliable technique at best.

From these reports, we have been able to confirm much of what past research on sexual victimization has shown. The older partners are almost all men and of various ages: adolescents, young adults, and middle-aged. A few women do engage in such activities, and the experiences the victims have with some of them resemble the kind of experiences children have with men. On the whole, however, sexual victimization is a problem in the relations between men and children. The vicissitudes of male psychosexual development, the nature of male authority in society, and the kinds of experiences males have and do not have with children can all partly explain this problem.

6

ALL IN THE FAMILY

INCEST AND SEXUAL ABUSE are sometimes confused, but they are not the same. Sexual abuse normally refers to sexual relations between an adult and a child. Incest refers to sexual relations between two family members whose marriage would be proscribed by law or custom.

According to our survey, there are more incidents of incest than of sexual abuse. Twenty-eight percent of the women and 23 percent of the men admitted a sexual experience with a family member. Only 19 percent of the women and 9 percent of the men said they had been sexually abused.

Much sexual abuse is also incestuous, however. As we saw in Chapter 4, 44 percent of the experiences of sexual abuse reported by girls were actually with family members. In other words, about 9 percent of the women in the sample had an experience that was both incestuous and victimizing. Thus there is a good deal of overlap.

An experience is both incestuous and victimizing, in the terms we are using here, when a child's partner is both much older and a member of that child's family. Of course, cases can be one or the other without being both. When a child has an experience with an adult stranger or neighbor, for example, it is an instance of sexual victimization that is not incestuous. The majority of the sexual experiences with older persons reported in this survey by boys is of this sort. When a child has an experience with a family member who is essentially the same age (for our purposes within five years if the child is twelve or under and within ten years if the child is thirteen to sixteen), this is an instance of incest that is not sexual victimization. There were many such relationships between siblings and cousins.

Defining Incest

In addition to having a lively existence in popular mythology, incest is also an important topic to two divergent disciplines: anthropology and

83

psychoanalysis. Bandied about in these different contexts it is no wonder that the exact meaning of the term has been blurred rather than clarified.

One ambiguity concerns the kind of sexual activity implied. Often incest means simply sexual intercourse between family members, but in some discussions it has come to mean other kinds of sexual contact, such as mutual masturbation or genital fondling. In the writings of some psychoanalysts, incestuous involvement can even mean interaction with fairly little explicit sexual content, such as when a mother is unduly preoccupied with a child's body, his physical well being or cleanliness.

On the other hand, sometimes incest refers, not to sexual activity at all, but rather to marriage. Particularly when anthropologists discuss the relation between the incest taboo and exogamy, incest is used to mean the marriage of two family members of a proscribed proximity. Within jurisprudence too, incest can mean the marriage of two family members, and although sexual intercourse between the two is usually implied, the law forbids the marriage whether it includes intercourse or not.

For our purposes, we will use incest to mean sexual contact between family members, including not just intercourse but also mutual masturbation, hand-genital or oral-genital contact, sexual fondling, exhibition, and even sexual propositioning. It will not include unconscious sexual gestures, however, such as accidental exposure or a mother's concern about a child's body.

The rationale for this definition is based on the following two considerations. The taboo on incest in our culture applies to all sexual contact between proscribed parties, not just intercourse. Those members of society who know that having intercourse with their sister or brother is wrong also know that propositioning him or her is wrong. Any person who engages in conscious and overt activity that violates this taboo should be considered as committing incest. There may be more or less serious incestuous acts, but they are incest nonetheless.

Second, much incest involves children. As we have seen, for physiological and psychological reasons much intense sexual activity with children does not include intercourse. Yet it clearly involves the kind of behavior and motivation that are generally considered incest.

Another source of confusion concerns the precise partners who come under the umbrella of the incest taboo. There is general agreement, codified in law, that mothers, fathers, sister and brothers, grandparents, aunts and uncles are off limits in our society (Weinberg, 1955). But what about cousins, what about step-relations, and what about in-laws?

In earlier generations, first-cousin marriages were relatively common, and there are several states today where this kind of liaison is still permitted. Even where it is not, many people believe that given the general loosening of extended family bonds in contemporary society, sex between cousins does not "feel" like incest. Nonetheless, because it is a taboo of which almost everyone is aware in modern society, we will include it within our definition of incest.

Step-relations, too, are sometimes included, and sometimes not, under the laws concerning incest. But regardless of legalities, many step-parents and step-siblings live together in relationships that are virtually indistinguishable from those maintained by natural parents and siblings. At issue here is whether the taboo applies primarily to a biological bond or to a social one. Those who tend to see the importance of the taboo in its prevention of inbreeding and the alleged genetic consequences thereof are less concerned with incest between step-relations. Those who see the taboo more as a protection of family relations tend to see incest with step-relations as equivalent to other kinds of incest. Our bias is in this latter direction.

The great frequency of this kind of incest, however (see below), does suggest that the taboo, or the mechanism that enforces it, is weaker in regard to step-relations. Nevertheless, incest with step-parents and step-siblings violates a taboo that does exist—especially in those families in which step-relations have taken on the trappings of normal family—and when violated, the consequences are similar to those in cases with natural family members. For this reason, we will consider sexual acts with step-relations as being incestuous.

Prevalence of Incest

Incest is often called "the ultimate taboo" or the "universal taboo" or something similar to classify it as the gravest violation of the rules of human society. It is usually described with terms like "horror," "revulsion," or some other strong adjective ("My husband," 1977). In fact, however, incest is regarded ambivalently. On the one hand, it is treated as a serious threat to the social order, which in this day and age means being associated with psychological abnormality and social degeneracy. On the other hand, unlike sexual abuse, which is almost never joked about, incest is often the subject of ribald humor, innuendo, and the like.

> A young man with passions quite gingery
> Tore a hole in his sister's best lingerie
> He slapped her behind
> And made up his mind
> To add incest to insult and injury.
>
> [Legman, 1964, p. 62]

There are also such jokes as: Jack has just been seduced by sister Jill. "Golly, Jack," says Jill, "you're much better than Paw." "Yeah," he replies, "that's what Maw always says" (Randolph, 1976).

As in the case of wife-batterings such an undercurrent of humor about a supposed taboo can be an indicator of a counterculture, a covert belief among people—often held simultaneously with the taboo—that "it's really not so bad" or that "under some circumstances" at least, it would be OK. The humor reflects a kind of challenge to the taboo, a message that it is not so serious that even joking about it would be in poor taste. In contrast, truly serious taboos like parricide or fratricide are not the subject of any humor to speak of.

More evidence of this counterculture is available at any drugstore. In the last five years, the pornography trade has begun to cater heavily to fantasies of incest. Titles like "Family Affair" and "Mother Love" are interspersed among more mundane themes in the shelves of erotic literature. Sexually oriented magazines often carry stories, ostensibly from readers, about experiences of incest described in graphic detail (Readers discuss, 1977).

This indulgence in fantasy about incest is not entirely restricted to males, as might be thought. The "true romance" magazines with their entirely female readership have also begun to capitalize on this theme. Recent story headings from a selection of such magazines include "Whenever Dad's on the road, Mom begs me for Love," "I love my brother . . . the wrong way," and "Sis and I fight over Daddy's bed; We take turns being his wife." Although the stories rarely approve of incest, as the male-oriented literature does, the convention of the genre clearly is intended to allow readers to participate in fantasies without having to feel guilty about them. There appear to be strong and growing fascination and covert approval of incest in the popular fantasy life.

Thus, although it does come as a surprise to discover that people engage in a substantial amount of incest, perhaps it should not. More people report a sexual experience with a family member (26 percent) in our survey than a childhood sexual experience with an older person (16 percent). The comparison is possibly unfair. Childhood sex experiences can only occur in childhood, whereas incest can occur at any age. However, this comparison is based almost wholly on experiences occurring before age eighteen. At any age period during childhood, there are more incestuous experiences than experiences with older persons—which suggests that the more serious taboo involves cross-generational sexual acts, no matter how the parties are related.

An inventory of incestuous partners appears in Table 6-1. In addition to the large number of reported incestuous contacts, note the range of partners. In this sample of slightly fewer than eight hundred individuals, a sexual experience was reported with every kind of blood relative recognized by our kinship system except for grandmothers. Mothers, aunts, and grandfathers made only one isolated appearance in the inventory, but nonetheless it indicates that such incestuous relationships are not com-

T A B L E 6 - 1.   Sexual Experiences with Relatives or Near-Relatives

PARTNER	NUMBER OF EXPERIENCES REPORTED BY:	
	Boys	*Girls*
Father	—	5
Stepfather	—	2
Mother	—	1
Brother*	15	72
Sister*	16	18
Uncle	1	16
Aunt	1	—
Grandfather	—	1
Cousin, male	9	48
Cousin, female	33	16
Brother-in-law	—	5
Parents' Friend	2	10
Total persons reporting incest†	60	151
Percent of sample	23%	28%

* Includes step-siblings.

† Does not include parents' friend. Column does not sum because some persons had multiple experiences.

pletely extraordinary. Even if we limit ourselves to incest in the nuclear family, the rates are high. Fourteen percent of the girls and 8 percent of the boys had had sexual contact with a mother, father, brother, or sister. For a crime of allegedly universal revulsion, sex within the family seems to be remarkably widespread.

The largest amount of incest occurs between partners of the same generation—brothers, sisters, and cousins. Only twenty-six of the reported cases, a slim 10 percent, involved cross-generation liaisons, the kind conventionally regarded as the most serious. This finding gives additional support to our earlier claim that although incest itself is touted as the ultimate taboo, what is really most taboo is cross-generational sexual contact, particularly within the family.*

Almost all the cross-generational incest involves girls. The boys reported one experience with an aunt and one with an uncle, and the rest of the twenty-six instances of cross-generational sexual acts were reported by girls. This ratio (corrected for sample size) of about four to one is much more lopsided than for sexual incidents with older persons outside the

---

* This statement presumes, of course, that prevalence itself is some sort of barometer of the strength of the taboo. Such is probably true, but it needs to be established by comparing prevalence rates with attitudes, an analysis we will undertake elsewhere.

family, where boys report experiences at least half as often as girls. Members of the older generation are much more likely to sexually approach girls in the family than boys. For girls, then, the family would appear to be a more sexually dangerous arena.

Father–Daughter Incest

Of all kinds of incest, the one receiving the most attention at the current moment is that between a father and a daughter. Mental health workers once thought it to be extremely rare and confined to exceptionally degenerate families, but more recently they have revised their outlook. Based on experiences with clientele of both ordinary psychotherapy and special centers organized to treat victims of sexual abuse and incestuous families, many clinicians and social workers have concluded that father-daughter incest is rampant and of epidemic proportions.

Our own data give some support to this concern. Five girls reported sexual experiences with fathers, and two with stepfathers. In a sample of 530 women, this figure is over 1 percent, which is in keeping with the only other surveys on the subject (Gagnon, 1965; Hunt, 1974).

Although such small numbers are not a reliable basis on which to calculate prevalence accurately, with the support of the previous surveys, they do show that the problem is significant. One percent may seem to be a small figure, but if it is an accurate estimate, it means that approximately three-quarters of a million women eighteen and over in the general population have had such an experience, and that another 16,000 cases are added each year from among the group of girls aged five to seventeen. It puts father-daughter incest clearly in the same category as other clinical phenomena of great interest to the mental health profession, such as schizophrenia, which also has an estimated prevalence of 1 percent.

Two of the seven cases (29 percent) were with stepfathers. Once again the small numbers require caution, but this figure does confirm the widespread impression that incest with stepfathers is a particularly common form of father-daughter incest. When one considers that only 5 percent of the sample reported having a stepfather, one can see to what extent stepfathers contributed disproportionately to the rate.

Any one of several explanations are available to account for the vulnerability of stepdaughters. First, the taboo on incest between two such partners—who do not have a true blood relationship—may be less severe. Second, stepfathers, who may not have known their stepdaughters as young children, may therefore have acquired less of the paternal, protective, tender, or whatever impulse that acts as a shield or deterrent in natural fathers to incest. That is, they may be more likely than natural fathers to have unalloyed sexual feelings. Third, families with stepfathers may just be more disorganized. The familes have obviously been through the loss of one parent. If, as we suspect, father-daughter incest is more likely in disorganized families, and disorganized families are more likely to have stepfathers, this fact alone may account for the high rate. Of course several of these explanations may be at work simultaneously (for more discussion, see Chapter 9).

These factors suggest that stepfather incest may have dynamics that distinquish it from ordinary father-daughter incest. It probably should be studied as a matter in its own right. Within this study, unfortunately, the number of cases is too small to allow us to contemplate such a separate analysis. So for almost all our purposes we will group cases of father and stepfather incest together, and call them father-daughter.

Sibling Incest

Of the various kinds of incest, that between father and daughter is the kind reported most frequently to hospitals, clinics, and police (De Francis, 1969; Burgess *et al.,* 1978; Queen's Bench, 1976; Weinberg, 1955; Weiss *et al.,* 1955). However, many in the field have doubted whether it was really the most common form. It has often been speculated that in fact brother-sister incest was the most common, but that it rarely came to public attention—in part because it was less taboo, in part because it involved minors, but perhaps most importantly, because it did not set up a similarly explosive family conflict. Although it violates norms against sexual acts within the family, brother-sister incest does not create an intense rivalry which threatens to upset all family roles, in the same way as does father-daughter incest. This aspect would explain both why the latter would occur less often—family members, especially mothers, have a special stake in preventing it—and why it would be reported more often—an aggrieved family member would be more likely to take some public action. Brother-sister incest, in contrast, may be less offensive, both to the partners involved and to other family members. Thus it would be less often discovered, and when discovered, more easily dealt with within the family.

All these explanations are speculative, but the facts on which they are based are well confirmed by our survey. Brother-sister incest is far more common than father-daughter. Thirty-nine percent of the incest reported by girls and 21 percent reported by boys was of the brother-sister sort, while only 4 percent of the girls' experiences involved fathers. Even if we only consider brother-sister experiences that occurred to girls as adolescents, the number still exceeds that of their father-daughter experiences.

More surprising, however, is the large amount of homosexual incest between siblings. Brothers were sexually involved with other brothers almost as often as they were with sisters, and sisters also reported a fair number of homosexual experiences, one-fifth of all their sibling contacts. When homosexual experiences are lumped together with heterosexual ones, it is clear that sexual acts among siblings are impressively common. Fifteen percent of the girls and 10 percent of the boys had such a sexual experience, which accounted for about half of all the incest and 94 percent of all incest within the nuclear family.

Much of the incestuous activity of our respondents with brothers and sisters took place at a fairly early age. Ninety percent of the girls and 80 percent of the boys were twelve or under at the time. A particularly large portion of it occurred around the ages of nine or ten.

However, it is mistaken to conclude from this statistic that most of the sibling incest amounted to "playing doctor" and preadolescent sex experimentation. If we look at the partners to these experiences we can see why. For the girls, almost half the partners were *not* preadolescents but were adolescents and adults. Twenty-three percent of the partners were in fact more than five years older than our respondents at the time, putting them into the category of older partners. Although sexual acts between siblings occur among members of the same generation, these partners are not necessarily peers. Many are substantially older.

For example, we mentioned earlier the interviewee who reported that when she was eight, she had several sexual experiences with her brother and some of his friends, who were thirteen. The brother had bribed and manipulated her and her sister into letting them attempt intercourse on several afternoons when the parents were away. The woman remembers feeling ashamed and degraded by the experience for a long time afterward.

SIBLING INCEST AS AGGRESSION

Many of the experiences involved similar kinds of coercion, particularly for the girls, who reported that about 30 percent of the sibling incest took place under force or threat of force. When Walters (1975) writes, "It is rare for an older brother to force a younger sister into sexual relations" (p. 128), we believe he is being misled by the scarcity of such instances coming to public attention. In fact, these experiences are alarmingly common, and their scarcity among reported cases is merely another indication that they are unlikely to be revealed, either by victims or their families.

The use of force was not limited to partners who were adolescents nor to partners who were much older. Some of the experiences that took place between siblings fairly close in age also involved force and coercion. For example, another of our interviewees told of being gang-raped at four by his brother and his brother's friends, who were only two years older.

> **R:** [My brother] was an extremely angry person. He was extremely angry to me all the time. He's always claimed it was sibling rivalry, but the things he did to me I don't consider sibling rivalry at all. Like whipping. He was sort of into whips and tools of torture he had developed. He used to whip me and my friends. He strung one of my friends up by his toes upside down. He used to throw me down the stairs all the time. He tried to stuff a dead bird in my mouth once. These are just examples of the kinds of stuff he used to do.
>
> My parents couldn't deal with him. They turned deaf ears. Whenever I said, "Carl's doing this, Carl's doing that," after a while they didn't listen. They didn't want to hear it. They would either say, "You're lying," or they'd say, "Go deal with it yourself." That started the whole process that they never really trusted me. I really felt like he had permission to do it.
>
> At the time [age four] we were living in a house that had a full basement. Across the hall from the playroom was my father's storeroom. He had a liquor closet and a gunroom. I was walking out of the playroom to go upstairs and I heard some noise in the storeroom so I went in. There was my brother and one of the kids from across the street. And maybe a couple of others. There were four or five people in there. They had their pants down. I remember kind of looking eye to eye at these two people, I don't remember who, having anal intercourse right there. They'd gone into my father's liquor cabinet and the place was reeking. I tried to run, I tried to run away immediately. That's where my memory stops until later, I remember being in that room alone, covered with whiskey and this whiskey smell and then being discovered by my parents and getting punished for getting into the whiskey. And not being able to say what I had experienced.
>
> I'm pretty sure they made me go along with whatever was happening. My guess is that people were kind of taking turns on one another. And that I was put up on that table and used by some of the other children there. I don't see how it could be any other way. It was something I was immediately terrified of. I think they manhandled me.

Thus sibling incest should not be romanticized as it sometimes is in literature and in men's magazines (Pomeroy, 1978). The stereotype of innocent childhood sexual games has only limited applicability. A substantial portion of sibling incest involves much older partners and some coercion. The same is true for the experiences of incest reported with other partners of the same generation: cousins and brothers-in-law. For example, two of the interviewees reported sexual assaults by older cousins. In one instance, the older boy tackled his fourteen-year-old cousin and ripped her shirt in an attempt to have sexual relations with her. She finally fended him off, but she was shocked and upset and was never able to talk with him subsequently nor reveal the incident to her mother or any other relative.

AN INCEST–AVOIDANCE INSTINCT?

The large amount of sibling incest reported here does pose some paradox to at least one common theory about the nature of avoidance. Westermarck's (1894) old idea that "familiarity breeds contempt" or at least "avoidance" has been resurrected in recent years by certain anthropologists (Fox, 1962) to help explain incest-avoidance behavior. According to this view, when children are raised in close proximity to one another, a kind of bond develops that "innoculates" each of the children against sexual involvement with the other. They fail to find one another sexually and romantically attractive.

Some ingenious empirical support for this idea has been gathered by Shepher (1971). Among 2,769 marriages of Israelis raised in the communal nurseries of the Kibbutz, he could not find a single sexual relationship or marriage between two former nursery mates, even though no overt taboo exists against it. Shepher believes that this aversion develops among siblings and nursery mates between birth and age six by a process similar to what ethologists call imprinting.

Such data would suggest that sexual avoidance between siblings would be quite routine, as long as they were brought up in fairly close proximity. Our finding of a large number of incestuous involvements, however, would suggest that such a mechanism was weak, easily by-passed, or nonexistent.

Of course, two considerations could reconcile these two sets of findings. For one thing, perhaps a large amount of the incest reported in our survey occurred among siblings who were not raised in close proximity, or who had not been inoculated in childhood because of large age differences or other circumstances in their upbringing. However, a more detailed examination of the sibling incest experiences in this sample shows this to be of limited validity.

A second consideration is also possible. Shepher's data refer to marriages and (to a lesser extent) to adolescent sexual experiences. His theory argues that the imprinting takes place between birth and age six, which is earlier than most of the sibling incest reported to us. One might suppose that the avoidance mechanism takes effect as soon as the imprinting has occurred, but perhaps this is not so. Shepher himself says that the kibbutz children he studied have many childhood sexual experiences with their nursery mates up through preadolescence. Thus children may be innoculated against pair-bonding as adults with early age-mates and siblings but not against childhood sexual activity with these same people. Such a delayed reaction kind of mechanism needs further explanation to be plausible. If the imprinting notion of incest-avoidance is going to stand, in any case, it will have to take account of the fairly large quantity of reported experiences of sibling incest in childhood.

Mothers and Other Relatives

Since recent experience has brought about a revision in people's thinking about the incidence of father-daughter incest, one wonders if conventional wisdom has been wrong about other kinds of incest as well. Traditionally, for example, mother-son incest has been looked upon as exceedingly rare, occurring only in the context of psychosis or extreme family disorganization. Few cases are ever reported or prosecuted (Weinberg, 1955). Nonetheless, devotees of men's magazines are often treated, more and more in recent years, to allegedly true accounts by readers of mother-son sexual encounters ("Readers discuss," 1977). Conceivably, the low rates of reported cases could be attributable to reporting bias and to the reluctance of police and social agencies to recognize its existence, thus misrepresenting true prevalence.* Zaphiris (1978), who takes this point of view, has studied twenty-eight cases of mother-son incest, of which eleven occurred in military families.

However, our data support the conventional wisdom. No respondent reported a case of mother-son incest. One girl, however, did report being sexually approached by her mother, although the experience did not go beyond genital exhibition and occurred only once. On the whole when it comes to overt sexual activity with children, mothers appear to be fairly benign—which follows the general finding of this survey that adult women rarely make sexual advances toward children (see Chapter 4). Mothers may nonetheless have enormous, perhaps even overpowering, influence on their children's—both male and female—sexual development, and sometimes, if one trusts psychoanalytic theory, this influence takes very insidious forms. One form it does not take, however, is direct sexual involvement with children, as is more often the case with fathers.

A variety of other adult relatives make sexual approaches to children and adolescents. Our survey documents instances of incestuous contact with uncles and aunts, a grandfather, and several brothers-in-law.

Aside from knowing that these are adult relatives, it is hard to formulate a picture of these kinds of relationships, without much more detailed information on the family constellation. Ties with extended kin vary so much in our current society—from ethnic group to ethnic group, from social class to social class, and from family to family—that to know that someone is an uncle says very little about the exact nature of the relationship. An uncle may be a man whom a child has known all her life, with whom she may have lived for various periods, and in whom she has a great

---

* Similar speculation has taken place on the subject of father-son incest. It too, seems to be rare and the dynamics very different from father-daughter incest (Langsley *et al.*, 1968).

deal of trust; or he may be a virtual stranger, who suddenly appears for a visit and then departs. Some uncles, in other words, have hardly more relationship to a child than some of the strangers reported on in earlier sections. Other uncles may in fact be quasi-parents or parent surrogates.

By the same token, there are even some partners who are not relatives at all, but whose relationship to the family may be that of a virtual relative. The most striking instances of this sort are the not uncommon cases in which the boyfriend of a mother becomes sexually involved with her children. Another such situation occurs when a close personal friend of the father makes a sexual advance toward his friend's daughter. Although we do not know them for a fact to be of these two sorts, we do note in Table 6–1 that twelve sexual experiences reported by our respondents were with friends of their parents.

One woman reported just such a situation. For five years she dated a man who spent a great deal of time with her and her young son but who never actually lived with them. The man was at times physically abusive to her and also to her son, but he had a good sexual relationship with her and seemed to show a lot of concern for her boy. He was always very hostile to homosexuals.

Several years after she had broken up with this man, and after her now teenage son had spent some time incarcerated for exhibitionism, the son came to her and told her that during those five years the boyfriend had made frequent sexual advances toward him. Those experiences, he said, had really "fucked him up." He had never told her about the incidents, she speculates, because he realized how badly she needed this boyfriend. Although the man was not formally a parent, the dynamics of the situation bear some similarity to a case of parent-child incest and illustrate well how kindship categories do not necessarily capture the true nature of the sexual victimization taking place.

Such relationships have many of the elements of incest. For one thing, there is the betrayal of trust on the part of someone who is a member or a quasi-member of the family unit. For another thing, such relationships set up a volatile triangle of conflict and rivalry that is or can be extremely damaging to family ties. However they develop, such encounters place in jeopardy the child's relationship to his or her most trusted adults, and in some cases may be functionally similar to incest in the nuclear family. In some instances parents themselves have complicity in the situation by their negligence in failing to protect the child (De Francis, 1969). In the case just noted, the boyfriend had once mentioned that he found the son sexually attractive, but the mother had dismissed this revelation.

The lesson from this discussion of the nature of sexual acts with so-called uncles and family friends is that labels may be deceiving.

Some Discrepancies

A reader with an agile mind for figures may have noticed some interesting possibilities in Table 6-1. Do brothers report as many sexual experiences with sisters as sisters do with brothers? Theoretically, in a representative sample of a population—which this unfortunately is not—reports by brothers and sisters, should be equal. If they were, it would provide a reassuring confirmation on the validity of the reports.

The rates are not identical, leaving us with some serious unanswered questions. Twelve percent of the girls report an experience with a brother, but only six percent of the boys report an experience with a sister. The difference is large enough so that there is a less than 5 percent probability that it occurred by chance.

Two things might account for this difference in rates. For one thing, some brothers may have several experiences with different sisters. Then, more sisters than brothers within the same population would report experiences of incest. Unfortunately within our survey, the exact opposite seems to hold: it is the sisters who have multiple experiences and not the brothers.

A second possibility is that girls are more candid than boys, give a more honest report, and thus have a higher rate. The boys, more often the older partners and aggressors in these situations, may feel more guilt about them and be less willing to admit to them.

This line of thinking is reinforced when we note differences in the kinds of experiences men and women tend to report. Women report a fairly large number of experiences with much older brothers, but men report fairly few experiences with much younger sisters. The average age difference reported by girls is three years, but by boys, less than one year. These older brother–younger sister cases are the ones the men in the sample are most likely to feel guilty about, and most likely not to report.

However, there is also some evidence against this theory. For example, incest between cousins can be subjected to the same comparison as that between brothers and sisters. Presumably, male cousins should report as many experiences as female cousins. In this case, the disparity reverses itself; more male cousins (11 percent) report an experience than female cousins (8 percent). It appears to undermine the claim that girls are more candid in their reports. It would require convoluted logic to explain why they are more honest about experiences with brothers but more reticent about ones with cousins. This is especially true since males are every bit as much the aggressors in cousin incest as in brother-sister incest.

Unfortunately, these figures pose a riddle for which we have no adequate explanation at the present moment. It strikes right at the heart of the very important but inadequately researched subject of the validity and reliability of sex surveys. We can assume with some confidence that many people fail to report or underreport their sexual experiences, but we know very little about what kinds of people underreport which kinds of experiences. We will have to set these questions aside for surveys better equipped methodologically to grapple with them.

Conclusion

Sexual experiences among family members are more frequent than many people would expect. Twenty-eight percent of the women and 23 percent of the men reported incestuous sex. Even limiting consideration to the nuclear family, one in seven women and one in twelve men had had such an experience. Most of these incidents are between children of the same generation, although not necessarily the same age. A remarkable number involved some coercion or force.

7

SOURCES
OF
TRAUMA

RESPONDENTS REACTED to their childhood sexual experiences in different ways. Most reported them negatively, but some said that the experiences had been rather positive. Sixty-six percent of the girls' experiences with much older partners were negative, but boys' experiences and peer incest for both sexes were less so. Why the differences?

On a subject so loaded with moral implications, it is hard not to allow strong moral prejudices to affect our thinking about it. When we hear that a child's genitals were fondled by her uncle on a regular basis over a six-year period, starting when she was six, we immediately form a judgment about the seriousness of the experience. Most people are apt to see such an event as much more traumatic than one in which a six-year-old girl was invited by her eight-year-old brother to undress in front of him.

They will not have a hard time explaining why. The uncle is an adult, after all, and the brother only another child; and cetainly the actual genital contact by the uncle is more serious because of its intrusiveness compared to merely being seen naked. Finally, the first experience continued over quite an extended period of time, whereas the other happened only once. Surely its duration must have contributed to its negative impact.

At least two authors have tried to formalize these assumptions by listing factors that increase the trauma of sexual victimization for a child. Groth (1978) sees trauma as a function of four factors: (1) The closer the relationship between the child and the older partner, the greater the potential trauma. (2) The longer the experience goes on, the greater the harm. (3) More trauma results from more elaborate kinds of sexual activity, actual penetration being the most, and simple exhibition without physical contact being the least, traumatic. (4) Experiences involving aggression are likely to be the most negative.

To this list, McFarlane (1978) adds three other factors, ones on which other authors are not so generally agreed: (1) If the child participates in and enjoys the experience, he or she will be burdened with more guilt and negative feelings about it. (2) If the parents react severely and emotionally to the event, the child will be more harmed. (3) Finally, the older or more mature the children, the *more* traumatic the experience, because of their better comprehension of its meaning.

These principles, with the possible exception of the last one, correspond to common sense, based on what we know about adult sexuality. However, we should be reminded that we are dealing with children's sexual experiences, not adults', and that we may need a different framework. Contemporary sex research has pointed out more and more that sex for humans is as much in the head as in the body (Gagnon and Simon, 1973). Because what is in a child's head about sex cannot be assumed to be the same as what is in an adult's, we need to look critically at our assumptions about the trauma of children's sexual experiences.

Measuring Trauma

Each respondent in our survey rated the experience on a scale from positive to negative, which we can take as a measure of how traumatic they thought it was. Then, using this level of trauma as a dependent variable, we can determine what kinds of experiences were associated with greater trauma, and we can assess what aspects of the experience contributed most to the negative feeling about it.

A caution is in order about this procedure. For one thing, there is some ambiguity in the meaning of our measure. Our question asked, "In retrospect, would you say this experience was positive? mostly positive? neutral? mostly negative? or negative?" Although "in retrospect" usually means "looking back on things past from the perspective of the present," not all respondents may have understood it in that way. Some may have interpreted it to mean, "How did you feel about the experience *at the time it happened*?"

In either case, the scale is a highly subjective measure of trauma, and it may be affected by guilt or denial. Some people who may have been tremendously affected by it may refuse to admit as much, and others who were barely affected may distort the experience out of proportion.

Nonetheless, the scale is a measure of *some kind* of evaluation of the experience, and thus worthy of consideration. As we will discover later on, we can explain much of the kind of reaction a child had with reference to features of the experience itself. This finding lends credibility to the assumption we are operating on here: that what we are measuring is a reaction to something about the experience itself and not other extraneous developments in a person's history and outlook that occurred later.

Age Differences

Perhaps the first assumption we should hasten to test is the one on which much of the study so far has been based, that a large age difference between a child and his or her partner creates a victimizing experience. For much of the discussion about sexual abuse, we have analyzed a group of experiences in which the partners were at least five years older than the respondents (ten years in the case of adolescents). Is there some justification in assuming that such an age difference creates more potential for trauma?

Table 7-1 gives strong support to this assumption. Especially for girls, the larger the age difference, the greater the trauma. If a child's partner is five or more years older, the experience is much more negative than if the partner is relatively the same age. If the partner is ten or more years older, the experience is more negative still. Thus the study's underlying assumption is confirmed.

Consistent with this result, we also find that the older the partner, the more traumatic the experience. When the child's partner is another child, even an older child, it is not so traumatic an event as when the partner is an adult. This finding is quite expected, and in fact, would be surprising if it were otherwise.

However, there is something else not expected. Since a larger age difference creates more trauma, it would also be anticipated that a younger child would be more vulnerable. Many people have argued that very early childhood sexual experiences are veritable time bombs set to explode as the

TABLE 7-1. Trauma by Age Difference between Child and Partner

	MEAN TRAUMA SCORE FOR:	
AGE DIFFERENCE	*Girls* (N = 245)	*Boys* (N = 84)
Respondent older	2.9	3.0
Partner 0–4 yrs. older	2.8	2.3
Partner 5–10 yrs. older	3.8	3.0
Partner 10+ yrs. older	4.2	3.5
	F = 26.07**	F = 3.64*

Scale: 1 = positive; 2 = mostly positive; 3 = neutral; 4 = mostly negative; 5 = negative.
Analysis of Variance: *$p < .05$; **$p < .01$.

child matures. Certainly in the moral perception of sexual relations, the younger the child, the more outrageous the act.

However, experiences at earlier ages do not produce more trauma. If anything, they produce less. Respondents whose experiences occurred at ages four to nine remember them as just as negative or less so than those whose experiences occurred at later ages (Table 7-2). For girls it is especially remarkable that the most negative experiences occurred between ages sixteen and eighteen.*

Why aren't experiences at a younger age more traumatic? Several factors undoubtedly contribute to this result. For one thing, the findings here present some evidence for the phenomenon mentioned earlier: a child's understanding of the situation deeply colors his or her reaction to it. The full meaning of sexual activities is acquired fairly late by most children, just prior to or in the early stages of adolescence. Some children who entered into sexual relations at an early age report that at first they were unaware that they were violating a taboo. They did not realize that others regarded the activity as wrong until they were eight or nine, when their sexual and moral awareness more fully crystalized. Such naivete may exert a protection against trauma. It may be that activities undertaken under the cloak of innocence do not cause so much pain (McFarlane, 1978; Sloane and Karpinsky, 1942).

In contrast, older children, especially adolescents, are much more aware of what is happening. They no doubt experience much more guilt in regard to their activities, and this guilt may increase the negativity they report (Summit and Kryso, 1978).

Even more importantly, older children, because of their greater awareness of taboos and even their greater physical strength, are less apt

T A B L E 7- 2.   Trauma by Age of Child

	MEAN TRAUMA SCORE FOR:	
AGE OF CHILD	Girls (N = 245)	Boys (N = 84)
4–6	3.1	3.1
7–9	3.3	2.5
10–12	3.7	3.0
13–15	3.2	2.8
16–18	3.9	3.1
	F = 2.79*	F = .86

Scale: 1 = positive; 2 = mostly positive; 3 = neutral; 4 = mostly negative; 5 = negative. Analysis of Variance: *p < .05.

* The age range for children extends beyond sixteen because some of the participants in incest were that old at the time of the experience.

than younger children to cooperate naively with the sexual advances of adults and family members. They are more likely to be wary and resist, which means that the adults need to use force more often, a fact confirmed by the survey. When force is involved, as we will see later, it dramatically increases the trauma of an experience. Thus the negative reactions of older children result more than anything else from the greater degree of force used against them—a point confirmed later by our regression analysis.

In summary, there is certainly no evidence that a younger child will be more traumatized by a sexual experience than an older child. Older children tend to react more negatively only because they more often encounter force and coercion. We are apt to be more protective of young children because of their innocence, and we are more likely to be outraged as a result when adults take sexual advantage of it. But the popular "time bomb" view, the idea that the earlier a trauma occurs the more pervasive are its effects, does not appear to be true.

Closeness and Trauma

Almost all researchers agree that experiences with close family members are potentially more traumatic than those with acquaintances or strangers. This belief seems to be based on a number of assumptions: (1) The closer the relationship the greater the violation of the child's trust and security. (2) The closer the relationship the more complicated the family dynamics triggered by the sexual relationship. (3) The closer the relationship the more serious the taboo violated, and hence, the greater possibility for guilt. In addition, family members, police, and agency personnel all seem to coalesce in support of a child who is victimized by a stranger, whereas when the partner is closer to home, the child always faces divided loyalties and suspicions.

The starkest contrast is between a child victimized by a parent and one victimized by a stranger. Our findings give full support to the belief that father-daughter incest is indeed the most traumatic kind of sexual experience that can occur (Table 7–3).

However, the findings are much more equivocal about this "closeness principle" in general. For example, it would lead us to expect that experiences with other adult relatives would be more traumatic than those with strangers. However, in our sample, respondents found the latter highly traumatic and rated them just as negatively as, for example, experiences with grandfathers and uncles.

A corollary to the closeness principle might be that sexual acts within the nuclear family, at least, were more traumatic than outside of it. This theory is supported by the finding that incest with fathers and stepfathers is more traumatic than with uncles or grandfathers.

T A B L E 7 - 3. Trauma by Partner's Relationship to Child

PARTNER'S RELATIONSHIP TO CHILD	MEAN TRAUMA SCORE FOR:	
	Girls (N = 239)	Boys (N = 84)
Father	4.8	—
Stepfather	4.5	—
Mother	3.0	—
Brother	3.2	2.4
Sister	2.9	3.1
Uncle	4.0	3.0
Grandfather	4.0	—
Cousin, male	3.1	3.0
Cousin, female	2.4	2.4
Brother-in-law	4.0	—
Friend or Acquaintance (a)	4.0	3.2
Stranger (a)	4.0	4.0
	F = 3.94**	F = 2.10*

Scale: 1 = positive; 2 = mostly positive; 3 = neutral; 4 = mostly negative; 5 = negative.
Analysis of variance: *$p < .05$; **$p < .01$.

(a) No peer experiences are included. All experiences in category "friend or acquaintance" and "stranger" were with partners at least 5 years older.

However, even here the verdict of the data is mixed. Let us look not only at cross-generational experiences but also at peer experiences. For example, for girls, experiences with brothers are more negative than those with male cousins, as would be expected, and experiences with sisters are more negative than those with female cousins. However, an experience with a male cousin is more negative than one with a sister. Similarly for boys, an experience with a male cousin is more negative than one with a brother. Thus the closeness principle does not produce consistent predictions, and closeness of kinship may not be related to the degree of trauma.

Homosexual Experiences

On first consideration, one might expect homosexual experiences to be more negative than heterosexual ones. In general, society views homosexuality as deviant, and such experiences might thus entail more shame and result in a more negative reaction.

However, the issue is blurred concerning homosexual incest. Incest is already a taboo. Is homosexual incest more taboo than heterosexual incest? Is sex between brothers more shameful than sex between a brother and sister? The same question can be asked about homosexual abuse. Since sexual abuse itself is taboo, is homosexual abuse any worse?

As it turns out from the survey results, homosexuality was not the issue. The issue was whether the child's partner was a male or a female. Experiences with males were consistently more negative than experiences with females, whatever the sex of the child.

What this finding means is that homosexual experiences were more negative for boys and less negative for girls. For example, girls' experiences with their sisters were more pleasant than those with their brothers, and their experiences with female cousins were more pleasant than those with male cousins. Boys' experiences with women were in general less traumatic than those with men.

Trauma and Particular Sexual Acts

People are often surprised, we explained earlier, that adult-child sexual contacts involve so little intercourse. However, even people who acknowledge that intercourse is not the primary kind of sexual activity between adults and children still use the standard of intercourse to judge the seriousness of a child's sexual experience. In other words, they presume that experiences involving intercourse are the most traumatic. It is a well-ingrained prejudice. After all, penetration is the standard used to judge virginity, and it is used in law to determine rape. In addition, most of us spend our adolescence being drilled in the difference between intercourse and other sexual activity.

A very clear hierarchy of sexual seriousness exists in our culture, from kissing through touching breasts to touching genitals to intercourse, and these stages have a surprisingly rigorous order to them and are surprisingly universal in America (Reiss, 1967). Most people assume such a hierarchy applies to childhood sexual experiences as well.

However, our data show the opposite; that is, the seriousness of sexual activity as it is usually understood does not seem related to greater trauma in children. Children who have been involved in intercourse do not seem more negative about the experiences than those who only have had their genitals touched. Intercourse certainly did not stand out as a particularly negative factor in an experience, and for both girls and boys, simple fondling was about as negative as any kind of actual physical contact.

This is a rather remarkable finding. It gives substantial support to our decision not to rule out any experience from consideration because the sexual activity seemed too minor. It suggests that the actual sexual activity involved is less important than its context.

This kind of finding should also alert people who work with victims of sexual abuse. It is possible that adults may discount certain kinds of ex-periences because they seem too innocuous, as for example, did Kinsey (1953, p. 121).

Two other characteristics of the experience—duration and repeti-tion—are also remarkably unrelated to the trauma. Just because the ex-perience runs on for some time and occurs with some frequency does not necessarily imply that it is going to have a more negative impact. This find-ing violates some other assumptions about sexual abuse. If anything, the shorter, one-time experiences were reported as more negative.

Actually there is a logic to this finding that is not apparent at first. What it probably means is that when a child is approached sexually and finds the experience highly negative, the child often takes quicker action to end the relationship than the child would if he or she were feeling am-bivalent. Thus the highly negative experiences occur once, and then they end. Children are apparently more assertive in terminating negative ex-periences and keeping them from reoccuring than many people would have thought. If children defend themselves in this way, it would certainly ex-plain why short-term, one-time experiences might be reported more negatively than long-term, repeated ones.

Trauma and Force

If the kind of sexual activity and the duration of the experience do not make it traumatic, then what does? We have shown that the age difference between partners is important, but isn't there anything in the nature of the occurrence between the partners themselves that affects the child's feel-ings?

Indeed, the most important factor in determining the trauma of the ex-perience is an obvious one: was force involved? When it was, respondents reacted to the experiences very negatively. When no force was involved they were much more likely to see the experience as neutral or even positive. Of all the factors we measured, the use of force by the partner ex-plained more of the negative reactions than anything else. For girls, it cor-related .53 with trauma.

It is not surprising that force should be such an important factor. Unlike force, sexual activity and duration both are ambiguous in their im-plications. A longer relationship and one involving intercourse indicate greater intensity. Intensity may be more harmful, but it could also be an in-dicator in some cases of a positive, or at the least, an ambivalent, bond. In contrast, the presence of force would almost always signal something negative about the relationship. It is a concise symptom of a whole negative context—the reluctance of the child, the pressure exerted by the partner, the difference in power and control. The primary recollection of the child is of the coercion. That there was sex involved is perhaps less important than the fact that there was aggression.

If coercion, not the elaborateness of the sexual activity, is the main traumatic factor, it would appear to contradict one popular theory about the source of trauma in childhood sexual experiences. This theory holds that damage is caused primarily by guilt. The more a child imagines that he or she had complicity in the affair, the more guilty he or she will feel, and the harder it will be to get over the experience (McFarlane, 1978, p. 94).

In this theory a child whose experience was brutal and coerced would be less traumatized than one whose experience was more consensual. The consensual child would have to deal with the idea that he or she somehow caused the experience to happen, with all the attendant self-blame of such a realization. The coerced child, however, would know that the act had been against his or her will, and although perhaps more hurt at first, the child would be spared the long-term harm of guilt and self-doubt (Benward and Densen-Gerber, 1975, p. 11). As one victim put it:

> **R:** If it had been an isolated incident, especially if it had happened when I was so young, I would have understood I had no control. But it lasted so long, and it made me feel there was something in me that made him continue. It was my fault in the sense that this continued. [Armstrong, 1978, p. 175]

This theory predicts the exact opposite of the findings reported here. On the one hand, it predicts more trauma for those whose experiences last longer and were more sexually involved—both implying complicity. And it would predict less trauma for those who were threatened or coerced—relieving a child of complicity. Neither of these predictions holds. Instead, the conclusion seems to be that it is not complicity but coercion that causes trauma and determines how the experience is viewed retrospectively.

To Tell or Not to Tell

After the experience guilt can enter the picture from various angles. A victim may feel guilty for participating, as mentioned above. In addition, other people can reinterpret or label the experience, and thus create guilt in a victim where none had existed before. This theory—that other people make a child feel bad about an event—is one of a set emphasizing that the main impact of a childhood sexual experience is determined by subsequent events. In such theories, what happened at the time is less important than what happens later on (Summit and Kryso, 1978). Much of what happens later on is affected by the reactions of other people, and there is an interesting controversy surrounding what role third parties, like parents and confidants, play in the subsequent trauma.

A child may have an experience, for example, and not think much of it—many things can be strange to a child—until he reports it to his parents. When the parents become hysterical, interrogate the child, act as though a catastrophe has happened, and perhaps blame the child in the process, suddenly the event assumes traumatic proportions it did not previously have (McCaghy, 1971). In this way, minor events can balloon into major traumas.

If one follows the logic of this theory, the healthiest course for many children would be not to tell their parents. Of course, ideally the children should tell their parents, and parents should react in a supportive fashion. But given that most adults in current society are likely to be shocked, upset, and anxious, much as they might try to hide it, it can be safely assumed that most parents are more likely to frighten a child than comfort him or her. Assuming such a parental reaction, proponents of this theory would expect that on the whole children who tell their parents should be more traumatized than those who do not.

However, there is an alternative theory which hypothesizes that the most traumatic thing about such an experience is *not being able* to talk about it (Armstrong, 1978). According to this point of view, some people harbor the experience all their lives, unable to reveal it, and it leaves a permanent scar. Never able to be reassured about the experience, never able to find out what others think, they feel an ineradicable sense of differentness and stigma. Only by sharing the experience can the scar be healed. This theory predicts that children who *don't* talk about the experience should be more traumatized.

Our study supports neither of these theories. Only about one-third of our respondents told anyone about their experiences, but those who did, both boys and girls, fared no better or no worse than those who didn't.

One conclusion to draw is that it does not matter whether a child tells or not, that other factors are more important in creating trauma. This belief would certainly contradict the idea (implicit in the theories about guilt and reaction) that it is not what happens *during* the experience but what happens *after* that creates the trauma. Our data would indicate the opposite.

Multiple Regression Analysis

Various factors contributing to the negativity of an experience have been reviewed in this chapter: age, sex, and relationship to partner; sexual activity; the use of force; the duration; and whether anyone was told. In order to better understand just how they compare to one another, all these variables were entered into a multiple regression equation.

This equation allows us to see how closely associated two variables are, independent of the effect of other variables. For example, the data might show that whether a partner was drinking or not made a difference in how negatively the experience was perceived. However, drinking contributes to trauma not in and of itself, but rather because all the partners who drank in the sample were also adults and were much more likely to use force (because they were drunk)—two other factors that are crucial in producing a negative reaction. Thus the regression would show us which variables are really associated with the trauma and which are just reflecting the effect of other variables.

Table 7-4 shows the results of the regression equation for girls. (Unfortunately, there were too few cases to perform a meaningful regression analysis on the boys' experiences.) They are consistent with what we have gleaned from an analysis of the individual tables in this chapter. In the experiences reported by girls, the overwhelmingly most important factor was force, and then the partner's age.

The coefficients for other factors are so small as to be inconsequential in comparison to force and the age of the child's partner. The duration of the relationship made no contribution at all, and the seriousness of the sexual activity only added in a miniscule way to the trauma, confirming the surprising findings we mentioned earlier. Telling someone reduced the trauma very slightly. Also an older child was slightly less affected, and a more closely related relative actually decreased the negativity a tiny bit. But only two factors were statistically significant: 1) whether force was used to gain the child's participation and 2) how old the older partner was.

One other factor that seemed important earlier does not appear as important now by itself. We mentioned that experiences with male partners were consistently more negative than experiences with females. From the

T A B L E   7 - 4. **Regression of Trauma on Characteristics of Childhood Sexual Experiences**

	BETA
CHARACTERISTIC	*Girls*
Use of force	.416*
Partner's age	.313*
Told anyone	− .068
Child's age	− .064
Relatedness	− .024
Male partner	.018
Seriousness of sexual act	.013
Duration	——
Multiple R squared	.335

* $p < .001$.

very small coefficient here, however, it is clear that, when all things are considered, the fact of a partner being a male is not what causes the difference. If experiences with males are more negative, it must be because males are more likely to be older and are more prone to use force.

For girls, the regression equation explains 34 percent of the variation in negativity. A fairly high level of explanation for regression analysis of this sort, it suggests that we have most of the important explanatory variables included.

Conclusion

This chapter has cast doubt on some of the conventional assumptions about what causes a traumatic reaction to sexual victimization. In particular, there is little evidence from our respondents' reactions that the length of a relationship or the presence of intercourse or other serious sexual acts made the experience more traumatic. Experiences with relatives and more closely related kin were also not necessarily more negative than those with strangers and more distantly related kin, with the one exception of father-daughter incest. Nor is there any evidence that being able to confide in a parent or friend about the experience eases the ultimate pain.

Only two major factors stood out. Experiences were much more negative for the child if force was involved. In addition, the older the partner, the more unpleasant the experience.

8

SOCIAL BACKGROUNDS OF SEXUALLY VICTIMIZED CHILDREN

THE LITERATURE ON SEXUALLY ABUSED CHILDREN is rich in speculation on what is special in their backgrounds. But only once or twice in the whole history of this problem have the backgrounds of abused children been compared to those who have not been abused within the same population.

We will make this comparison in this and the following chapter. The family backgrounds of the 125 children in our sample who had experiences with older persons will be compared to those of the 671 children who did not. We will make a similar comparison for those who did and did not have incestuous experiences.

The kind of reasoning we will be applying is crucial for advancing both the theoretical and practical understanding of the problem of sexual victimization. From the practical point of view, it is essential to know how the victims' backgrounds differ so (1) we can more easily identify victims, especially since the circumstances of the problem so often defy identification; and (2) we can begin to conceive of measures to prevent sexual victimization in those environments where it is most likely. From a theoretical point of view, if we know how the victims' backgrounds differ, we will begin to have a catalog of items associated with sexual victimization that our theories should explain.

Social Isolation: Theory

As we pointed out in Chapter 3, one of the most prominent theories about the cause of incest is extreme social isolation.* Isolated families are

---

* In the following discussion, many of the theories and much of the previous research reported refer specifically to incest. However, the conclusions can easily be extended to apply to sexual victimization in general.

more insulated from public scrutiny and more ingrown, which is said to encourage family members to interact sexually.

However, from another perspective, isolation may not be the cause of incest so much as a symptom of other underlying causes more directly related. For example, one frequently encountered point of view is that certain subcultures are more tolerant of incest. Such cultures, by choice or by exclusion, may become peripheral to the social mainstream. Or isolation may be a symptom of poverty or family disorganization or social incompetence, since all these factors may cut a family off from full participation in community life. But whatever the cause of incest, a degree of isolation is usually believed to accompany it.

Researchers, however, have been able to marshall only limited evidence in support of the social isolation theory. Of course, one of the most common stereotypes about incest is that it occurs frequently among isolated backwoods families, such as in the hollows of Appalachia or the rural reaches of Maine. The movie *Deliverance* capitalized on this stereotype, implicitly suggesting that the backwoods Georgians it portrayed had a deviant kind of sexual culture.

Theorists, too, have capitalized on the stereotype to give the social isolation theory plausibility, but the idea does have some substance. Studies have been made of rural incest in Sweden (Riemer 1940), Japan (Bagley, 1969), Poland (Pilinow, 1970), and France (Scherrer, 1959), and the similarities in these diverse cultures are great enough to make Bagley identify them as a phenomenon in itself, which he calls "functional incest," in whose etiology rural isolation plays an important part.

However, it is possible that incest is only more *conspicuous* in rural areas and not more common. There have been no surveys comparing incidence rates in urban and rural populations, and the best evidence is highly inferential. Benward and Densen-Gerber (1975) found no tendency for drug-abusing incest victims to come from more rural regions of the country. On the other hand, the twenty incestuous families Tormes (n.d.) studied in New York City were more likely to be recent immigrants from the (presumably rural) South than were a comparison group. Landis (1955) noted that students from rural and urban backgrounds reported not so much different rates as different *kinds* of sexual abuse: urbanites encountered more exhibitionists, and rural residents more fondling, but the differences were not large.

Certainly there is no dearth of incest and sexual abuse in urban areas (De Francis, 1969; Szabo, 1958; Weinberg, 1955). The reporting rates for such areas as New York and San Francisco are quite high, and studies in urban areas have had no difficulty finding cases. In fact, Miller (1976) in a large random sample of Illinois teenagers found molestation most common in suburban and least common in rural areas. Thus the evidence that incest is typically associated with rural isolation is of poor quality and inconclusive.

Subculture: Theory

Isolation need not be geographical; it can also be social and cultural. One aspect of the social isolation hypothesis emphasizes that incestuous families belong to subcultures that are more approving of incestuous behavior. These subcultures are often geographically isolated; that is one of the ways in which they maintain their deviant values, but it is not the only way to do so. They may also be isolated in urban settings.

As with rural incest, there are a few case studies of such subcultural incest. The Mormons of Utah in their isolated subculture apparently practiced incest along with polygamy up until the turn of the century, when it was outlawed (Bagley, 1969). Weinberg (1955) in his study of incest in urban Chicago noted that there appeared to be an overrepresentation of Sicilians and Poles in his sample of court-drawn cases, suggesting that they came from subcultures more tolerant of incest. Higher rates of sexual victimization have also been noted among blacks (De Francis, 1969; Miller, 1976). The theory of subcultural incest (like the subculture of violence) does offer a simple explanation, but unfortunately the evidence is much too sketchy.

Social Class: Theory

The evidence connecting incest and sexual abuse to poverty, in contrast, is much stronger, relatively speaking, although not in any absolute sense. Up until recently, virtually every study made on the subject showed that most victims of incest and sexual abuse came from deprived backgrounds. The mean income, for example, of families of sexually abused victims was $5,100 (De Francis, 1969, p. 54) in the New York study of reported cases. Benward and Densen-Gerber (1975) found victims of incest over three times more likely to come from families with incomes under $7,000 than were members of a comparison group. The major reviews in the literature (Devroye, 1973; Maisch, 1972) find extremely few cases of incest reported from the wealthier social classes.

This social distribution of incest and sexual abuse is certainly consistent with the hypothesis of social isolation. Poverty can in itself be isolating; and it also tends to accompany other isolating circumstances, such as rural residence and unemployment. However, the connection may have little to do with isolation. Rather poverty may be an indication of crowding, family disorganization, and social incompetence, all factors that have been connected to incest.

Recently, however, there has been an outcry against this conventional association in popular thinking between sexual abuse and poverty. The new position is that sexual abuse is indeed common in middle- and upper-middle-class families, but it has merely been better concealed. On the whole, wealthier familes are better organized, have more social resources at their disposal, and thus have been able to keep their secrets from becoming public.

The statistical association in other studies between sexual abuse and low income, it is now argued, is a result of the way in which these samples were recruited. It is natural for low-income backgrounds to predominate in reports based on police records, court cases, and child protection investigations, since it is low-income families who are the main clients of these institutions (Rhinehart, 1961). As the taboo on discussing sexual abuse has lifted and as "respectable" mental health programs for treating the problem have been established, a massive amount of middle-class sexual abuse has come to light. The clinicians in these programs report no class bias among their clientele at all (Anderson, 1977; "My husband," 1977). In fact a study with a scientifically selected, unbiased sample did show that a large percentage of upper-middle-class girls had been molested (Miller, 1976).

Findings

Our data cast some light on each of these questions. Tables 8-1 through 8-3 present the rates of children's sexual experiences with older partners and incest for various sociodemographic subgroups, and show a comparison of these rates to the rates for the sample as a whole. Not all the subgroups identified in the study are presented here, only those of some theoretical interest or those in which an important relationship seemed to be indicated.

At the top of each table appear the rates for incest and sexual victimization for the survey as a whole.* For the girls, 19 percent experienced sexual victimization, 28 percent incest, and 1.3 percent father-daughter incest. For the boys, 9 percent experienced sexual victimization, and 23 percent incest.

---

* The reader will recall sexual victimization refers to experiences of children under twelve with persons five or more years older (or children thirteen to sixteen with persons ten or more years older). Incest refers to sexual experiences with relatives, including aunts, uncles, cousins, grandparents, nuclear family members, and step-relatives.

There is overlap between the categories as they are not mutually exclusive. About 9 percent of the girls fell into both categories as we have defined them, and about 2 percent of the boys.

RURAL RESIDENCE

What conclusions can we draw about social isolation from our data?

Here we have survey evidence for the first time that incest and sexual victimization are higher in rural areas. The subgroup with the highest rates was the group of girls who spent their childhoods on farms (Table 8-1). Three-quarters of them had had an incestuous experience. Such children were over two-and-one-half times more likely than the rest of the sample to have had an incestuous experience and over twice as likely to have been sexually victimized by an older person. The rates were high for the boys, too, but given the smaller sample of boys, failed to reach statistical significance.

High as these rates are, they apply only to a small group within the sample; there were a mere sixteen such females from farm backgrounds. The smallness of the group does not vitiate the validity of the findings, however. The significance test takes account of the smallness, and if anything, because a small sample requires a much larger actual difference to produce a significant finding, its validity is greater (Bakan, 1970).

This finding is not generalized to all rural residents, just to those with farm backgrounds. Our sample, as we pointed out in Chapter 3, has an unusually large representation of students from nonurban backgrounds. Most of these come from small towns, of under 25,000 in size, a kind of residence that is sometimes thought of as rural. However, it is not these small-town residents that show particularly high rates, but only those from actual farms. The rates for those from very small towns (under 5,000) is somewhat elevated for boys but not for girls. Thus it is something special about farms, not just rural areas, that affects the rates. Since farms tend to

T A B L E 8 - 1. Girls' Experiences with Older Partners and Incest by Residence

Subgroup	Older Partner (%)	Incest (%)	Father–Daughter Incest (%)
Whole sample (N = 530)	19	28	1.3
Farm background (N = 16)	44*	75**	—

(a) Chi-square statistic compares rate for subgroup with rate for sample as a whole.
*$p < .05$; **$p < .001$.

be particularly isolated, this is strong support for the thesis of social isolation.

However, there is one anomaly. In spite of the overall high incest rate, none of the specific cases of father-daughter incest occurred on farms (Table 8-1). They still occurred primarily in rural areas, but in the small towns. Six out of seven of these cases came from towns of under 5,000. We have no ready explanation for this difference, since the thesis of social isolation would predict equally high rates of all kinds of incest in the most isolated settings. Unfortunately, with our small subgroup of both farm residents and father-daughter incest victims, we cannot pursue the analysis any further.

ETHNIC AND RELIGIOUS BACKGROUND

To test whether incest and sexual victimization were products of a particular subculture, we looked at the rates of incest for various ethnic and religious subgroups. These subgroups are, on the whole, too big to constitute real incestuous subcultures. But even if pockets of incest-tolerance existed within a larger ethnic group, they might show up in the form of slightly higher rates. Weinberg (1955) had noted higher rates for certain of his ethnic categories, and some social workers in Northern New England have led us to believe we might encounter high levels of incest among the French-Canadian population.

It was not these immigrant Catholic ethnic groups, however, who had high rates of incest in our survey. Rather it was the Yankee stock that showed consistently higher rates all across the board, although these differences are not statistically significant.

However, our figures do give one important piece of evidence for subcultural factors in sexual victimization. Boys from Irish-American backgrounds reported an unusually large number of experiences of sexual abuse (Table 8-2). They were almost three times as likely to have had a childhood experience with an older partner as other boys in the sample. This is a surprising and unanticipated finding.

Two facts should be noted about this peak among the Irish: (1) It applies only to boys. (2) It applies only to their experiences with older partners, not to incest. Since sexual experiences with older partners who are relatives appear in both categories, what accounts for the high Irish rate is a large number of homosexual experiences with older *unrelated* men.

This finding about the experiences of Irish-American boys has some plausibility. The Irish in America as a group are characterized by a high degree of sexual repression and segregation. There is much guilt transmitted in Irish families about sex. In a pattern of life that traces back to the old country, relations between the sexes are stilted and strained (Greeley, 1972).

TABLE 8-2. Boys' Experiences with Older Partners and Incest by Ethnic Background

SUBGROUP	OLDER PARTNER (%)	INCEST (%)
Whole sample (N = 266)	9	23
Irish (N = 40)	22*	28
Italian (N = 15)	7	13
French-Canadian (N = 52)	6	27
English (N = 74)	15	24

Chi-square statistic compares rate for subgroup with rate for sample as a whole.
*$p < .001$.

It would be wrong to conclude that the Irish have a subculture more tolerant of adult-child sex. But the repression and sexual segregation may foster an environment where this kind of deviance is more common. If Irish men are inhibited by training from relating sexually to Irish women, they may express their sexual impulses toward younger boys, who are less threatening and more accessible.

This explanation is speculative, but our evidence clearly suggests that some subcultural factors are at work. Why sexual victimization of boys is higher among the Irish-Americans is an intriguing question and worthy of more investigation.

SOCIAL CLASS

Table 8-3 also supports the idea that for girls, at least, these forms of sexual deviance are more common among lower social classes. Three separate indicators of class membership are presented—father's occupation, family income, and parents' educational attainment—and all three show significantly higher levels of the kinds of sexual experiences we have been examining.

However, this finding is true only for girls. Only in the case of income and only in the case of incest (not experiences with older partners) did class tend to make boys more vulnerable. Consistent with many of the other findings in the survey, the data for boys show much less coherence than those for girls. Therefore, for the rest of this chapter we will be speaking, except where noted, of girls' experiences alone.

OCCUPATION

The relationship between class and sexual experiences is weakest in the case of the father's occupation, but then, over half the fathers in the sam-

TABLE 8-3. **Girls' Experiences with Older Partners and Incest by Indicators of Social Class**

SUBGROUP	OLDER PARTNER (%)	INCEST (%)	FATHER–DAUGHTER INCEST[a] (%)
Whole sample (N = 530)	19	28	1.3
Blue-collar father (N = 326)	26*	34	1.2
Family income (N = 72) under 10,000	33*	46**	.8
Father not HS grad. (N = 91)	29	42*	1.1
Mother not HS grad. (N = 77)	38**	52**	5.2

[a] No significance test calculated.

Chi-square statistic compares rate for subgroup with rate for sample as a whole.

* $p < .05$; ** $p < .001$.

ple have blue-collar status. Two smaller occupational groups show higher rates. Predictably, families with farmers for fathers have high rates of incest and experiences with older partner, and incest also is more frequent in families where fathers have no occupation at all.

INCOME

Lower-income families also had markedly higher rates of incest for boys and girls, and rates of sexual abuse for girls alone. Lower-income girls were over 60 percent more vulnerable to both such experiences than the ordinary girl in the sample.

It must be borne in mind, moreover (as we pointed out in Chapter 3), that our sample underrepresents lower-income families, and the lower-income people it does represent are probably the healthiest and most upwardly mobile of that class. Thus, we suspect that in an even more accurate sampling of lower-income persons, the disproportion of incest and sexual victimization in that class would be even greater.

This is not to say that incest and sexual victimization are rare among the wealthier classes; quite the contrary. If anything, the fact that our largely middle-class sample shows a high incidence of incest and sexual victimization is evidence that indeed these things are common in this class. This seems to be the important point that many observers have been trying to make recently in arguing that incest and sexual abuse show no class bias. They are both right and wrong: it *is* much more common in the middle class than was previously thought, and it is not limited to impoverished environments: but it is still even more common among the poor.

EDUCATION

The figures for parents' education reinforce the findings from income and occupation. What appears to be interesting about these figures is that the mother's education makes so much more difference than the father's. Families of poorly educated mothers manifested almost all the father-daughter incest.

Since most spouses have similar education, different results for husband and wife are a bit unusual. They appear to indicate something special about the mother's connection with the problem—that it is the relationship between mother and father and not just social class that is influential. For this reason, we will delay further discussion of this finding until the next chapter when we take up internal family characteristics and their relationship to incest and sexual victimization.

Now that we know about the influence of social class, could it be that our earlier findings on rural incidence and the present findings on lower-class incidence are just different sides of the same phenomenon? Could incest be common on farms, for example, because people on farms might be poorer? This does not appear to be the case. Controlling for high or low income, rates on farms still appear to be higher than in the sample as a whole. Moreover, controlling for urban-rural residence, low income still appears to contribute to incest and sexual victimization.

In conclusion, there appears to be substantial support for the hypothesis of social isolation. We found incest and sexual abuse to be more common in rural areas. We also found at least one ethnic group with a peculiarly high incidence rate, suggesting that subcultural patterns play a role. Finally, we can give some substantiation to the belief that this kind of sexual victimization is more common among lower-class groups.

9

FAMILY BACKGROUNDS OF SEXUALLY VICTIMIZED CHILDREN

THE FAMILY HAS BECOME a more and more important factor in attempts to explain sexual victimization, as we pointed out in Chapter 2. Whereas once investigators looked only at what was wrong with the offender or what was wrong with the victim, today researchers ask questions like, who are the family members? How do they interact? and What are the family values about sex? In Chapter 2 we outlined several rudimentary theories about how families contribute to sexual victimization. In this chapter we will see if we can cast any light on these theories by contrasting the family backgrounds of those who have been sexually victimized and those who have not.

Marital Conflict and Disruption: Theory

There is hardly a social problem that has not been attributed to marital conflict and family disruption, and sexual victimization is certainly no exception. The literature is full of suggestions that children are more sexually vulnerable when parents fight or parents leave.

A stereotype that quickly comes to many people's minds, although not usually by name, is that of the "Oedipal triangle." In this model, incest occurs because a husband and wife become estranged and the father turns to his daughter for sexual outlet. However, marital conflict is extremely common, but father-daughter incest is not. Therefore, much more than just marital conflict is necessary for incest to develop. Moreover, father-daughter incest constitutes but a small fraction of the total amount of sexual victimization we have been discussing (see Chapter 3). If marital conflict is connected to sexual victimization, there must be other mechanisms besides the Oedipal triangle at work.

Other authors have proposed explicitly or implicitly three such mechanisms:

1. When children grow up in families marked by parental conflict, they receive contradictory messages, especially about sex. Such contradictions leave them confused, unclear about appropriate sexual values, and less capable of handling themselves in potential situations of abuse. They may be particularly vulnerable to older persons who entice them into sexual situations with offers of advice and instruction and assurances about the appropriateness of the behavior (Weiss *et al.,* 1955).

2. Similarly, in families with much conflict or ones that have been disrupted, children are less well supervised and thus more vulnerable to sexual victimization (De Francis, 1969).

3. If the family has been disrupted by the conflict or if separation has been threatened, the children may be anxious about losing loved ones. This feeling may produce a kind of desperation in a child, or "abandonment anxiety," and lead to a sexualization of ties to family members and other adults in an attempt to stave off loss (Lustig *et al.,* 1966).

No specific research has ever tried to investigate one or another of these mechanisms, but a number of studies confirm the general connection between marital conflict or marital disruption and sexual victimization. For example, De Francis' study of 250 cases of sexual abuse found that in 60 percent of the families, the children's natural father was not in the home. In 31 percent the mother was the sole parent, and of the families where two parents were present, 39 percent were marked by moderate to violent marital conflict (1969, pp. 76–77). Similarly, in one of the few nonclinical studies that actually had a control population, Landis (1956, p. 17) showed that "collaborative" victims at least were more likely to report that their parents' marriages were unhappy. In another survey, Miller (1978, p. 87) found that molested girls were more likely to come from homes in which the biological father was missing.

The Importance of Mothers: Theory

A number of theories focus on how a mother contributes in various direct and indirect ways to the sexual victimization of her daughter. Such theories usually implicate the mother specifically in incest, not sexual victimization in general. In one theory, she contributes because she abdicates her maternal responsibilities (Browning and Boatman, 1977). In another, she tries to exchange roles with the daughter (Machotka *et al.,* 1966). In still a third, she is seen as weak and unable to protect her daughters from their father (Tormes, n.d.). In a final theory, she is responsible because she knows about the incest but refrains from doing anything about it (Poznanski and Blos 1975).

It has also been suggested that mothers contribute to their daughters' resistance or vulnerability to sexual victimization in general, not just to incest. When mothers do not model self-protective behavior, do not provide daughters with information, or do not adequately supervise them, the likelihood of sexual victimization is increased.

A number of studies have offered empirical evidence to support these ideas. In the case of incest, Tormes (n.d.) reported that the mothers in her sample had married younger, had less education, were more intimidated by their husbands and had less power than mothers of a comparison group. Gligor (1967) described the mothers in her sample as being more rejecting than those in the control group. For sexual abuse, Landis (1955) showed that the victims in his sample had poorer relationships with their mothers, who were less educated and gave their daughters less sex information.

Miller's (1976) study dissents somewhat from the consensus of these earlier findings. She, too, finds that girls with poor affective relationships with their mothers are more likely to be victims. But in her study, mothers are no more important than fathers. With either parent, if closeness is missing and supervision poor, molestation is more frequent.

In summary, two themes stand out in theories about the family contribution to sexual victimization: (1) marital conflict and (2) unprotective mothers make children vulnerable. Both have received some empirical support. Can we add anything from our survey?

In Tables 9–1 through 9–4, we have assembled data allowing us to explore how family patterns may contribute to sexual victimization and incest. The tables show the rates for these two kinds of sexual experiences among respondents with various kinds of family backgrounds. These rates can be compared (and have been with statistical tests) with the rates for the sample as a whole. Column 1 shows childhood sexual experiences with older partners, what we are calling sexual victimization. Column 2 shows experiences with both older, same-age, and younger family members (nuclear family, cousins, step-relatives, in-laws), what we are calling incest. Column 3 shows experiences of father-daughter incest only. (For more detail, the reader can refer to Chapters 3 and 6.) As with the tables in Chapter 8, not all comparisons are listed but only those of some theoretical interest.

Marital Conflict and Disruption: Findings

The evidence in our study is very strong that marital conflict and family disruption are associated with sexual victimization of girls. Girls whose parents had unhappy marriages had higher rates of experiences with older persons. So did girls who had ever lived without their natural mother or natural father before the age of sixteen. If their parents' marriage was unhappy, they were about 25 percent more likely to experience sexual abuse. If missing a father, the increased vulnerability was 50 percent; if missing a mother, increased vulnerability was nearly 200 percent that of others in the sample. This finding supports all the theories mentioned earlier: sexual victimization is related both to family conflict and to family disruption. Moreover, missing a *mother* is the most damaging kind of disruption.

Note, however, that these findings apply more strongly to experiences with older partners than to incest. This fact is curious. It suggests that of the various proposed links between marital conflict and sexual victimization, the theory of abandonment anxiety (mentioned previously) is *not* a good explanation. If a child were worried about losing family members, we might expect that it would be the family ties that would be sexualized first. Instead, what increase most are sexual experiences with older persons who are not family members.

Either of the other two theories presented above, the absence of supervision or the presence of contradictory messages about sex, might account for this increase with nonfamily members only. Neither of them implies a necessary increase in incest but only a vulnerability to exploitation. These theories are adequate to explain the connection between marital disruption and sexual victimization.

However, if we look at some of the other figures in Table 9–1 we will

T A B L E 9 - 1. **Girls' Experiences with Older Partners and Incest for Indicators of Family Disruption**

Subgroup	Older Partner (%)	Incest (%)	Father-Daughter Incest [a] (%)
Whole sample (N = 530)	**19**	**28**	**1.3**
Parents had less happy marriage (N = 155)	25*	29	1.9
Lived without natural father (N = 86)	29*	35	3.5
Lived without natural mother (N = 19)	58**	53*	—
Had stepfather (N = 30)	47**	33	6.7
Had stepmother (N = 17)	35	35	—

[a] No significance test calculated.
Chi-square statistic compares rate for subgroup with rate for sample as a whole.
*$p < .05$; **$p < .001$.

see how the situation of children in disrupted households is much more complicated. If it were mostly a matter of inadequate supervision or conflicting messages that left a little girl more sexually vulnerable in a broken family, we might expect that a reconstituted family would provide her with increased surveillance and consistent messages and hence increased protection. Nothing could be further from the case. Rather the addition of a stepfather to a girl's family causes her vulnerability to skyrocket. Girls who are merely without fathers were about 50 percent more vulnerable than the average girl, but girls with stepfathers were almost 150 percent more vulnerable. The addition of a stepfather has been shown to increase dramatically victimization rates in another study, too (Miller, 1976). Why should having a stepfather so jeopardize a young girl?

INCEST WITH STEPFATHER

Clinicians have noted that in many cases of father-daughter incest the offender was really a stepfather. The situation is so stereotyped that even the romance magazines have a well-formulated opinion about how the dynamics work. A stepfather moves into a family with a sexually attractive girl who is a stranger to him. He does not feel himself to be really a father to this teenage or preteen girl he is suddenly living with. He has not had the parenting experiences with her as a young child, and so is more likely to respond to her sexually than paternally. Moreover, there is often a rivalry between daughter and mother at this stage, and the daughter is competing for the stepfather's attention and affection. In such a situation, sex is a possible outcome.

Indeed our data give support to this picture. The rate of father-daughter incest is much higher in the families with stepfathers than in any other subgroup in the whole survey—almost five times higher. The stereotype does indeed have some validity, and this is the first survey we know of to present evidence to this effect.

However, the numbers in our study are so small that the evidence must be accepted with a great deal of caution. There were only two cases of stepfather-daughter incest, and although this figure is large in comparison to the fairly small number of girls who had stepfathers (thirty), studies with larger base populations are needed to confirm the findings.

STEPFATHERS INCREASE GENERAL VULNERABILITY

Exactly because the number of cases is so small, it does not fully explain why girls should be so vulnerable in families with stepfathers. Other adults must be taking advantage of these girls.

This fact can be shown statistically. If families with stepfathers were like other families and did not make girls more vulnerable, six cases of sexually victimized girls from such families would have shown up in our sample just because of the ordinary rate. Instead there were fourteen such cases, eight more than expected. Some of this excess is accounted for by stepfather-daughter incest, *but only two* cases. The other six extra cases involved other adults. Thus girls in these families are more vulnerable to victimization, not just by their stepfathers, but by other men as well.

Part of the explanation might be that stepfathers are not the only step-relatives living in these families. Stepfathers sometimes have sons and daughters that accompany them into their new families. Even when the other step-relatives are not brought right into the same household, the child is likely to be exposed to a new group of relatives on visits and family outings.

Step-relatives may be more likely to sexually victimize a child than natural relatives. When no real blood tie exists, older males may feel less constrained by the incest taboo. Once again, not having seen the girl in her childhood, these other relatives, as in the case of stepfathers themselves, may view her less as a child to be protected and more as a sex object.

However, this explanation of the "stepfather effect" on sexual victimization is not really supported by our data. Most notably, having a stepfather is not associated with any increase in incest (beside father-daughter), just with an increase in sexual victimization by older persons. In our tabulations stepbrothers, stepsisters, stepcousins, and so forth are counted as relatives, and so sexual experiences with them would be counted as incest. If other step-relatives beside stepfathers were more likely to molest girls, we should see higher rates of incest too. But this is not the case. Rates of general incest (as distinct from rates of father-daughter incest) are not higher in families with stepfathers.

It is particularly noteworthy that incest with siblings is not at all higher in families with nonnatural brothers and sisters (this finding does not appear in the tables). However, the presence of nonnatural brothers (mostly stepbrothers) does, as in the case of stepfathers, increase the likelihood of sexual victimization. Once again, this is a case where step-relatives seem to increase vulnerability, not because they directly take advantage of relatives, but because other nonfamily members do.

Thus what needs to be explained is why in families with stepfathers and stepbrothers, girls have more sexual experiences with older persons who are not family members. Answers to this question are speculative, but there are three possibilities.

1. Stepfathers (and stepbrothers) may bring into the family a coterie of friends and acquaintances who are not so protective toward a stepdaughter (or stepsister) as they might be toward the real daughter (or sister) of a friend.

2. The problem may still be one of supervision. Instead of increased supervision, the entrance of a new father into a household may take up the mother's time and energy and actually mean less supervision of the child than previously.

3. Something in the Oedipal triangle may make the child more vulnerable. The daughter may feel betrayed by her mother, who has now married, or she may feel that her mother is paying less attention to her. She may be competing with her mother for the attention of the stepfather. Any or all of these factors may create a serious emotional conflict in the daughter, which since it involves sexual issues, may make her vulnerable to sexual victimization outside the family.

Moreover, what needs to be explained here is really a problem that goes beyond sexual victimization. Stepfathers apparently cause more difficulties for stepdaughters than just increasing their vulnerability to sexual abuse. Other research has shown that having a stepfather does not bode well for a young girl's future. For one thing, women who had stepfathers have higher rates of divorce—even comparing them to women whose parents separated but whose mothers did not remarry. (Pope and Mueller, 1976, Table 4). In addition, women who had stepfathers have higher rates of psychological disturbances later on in life (Langner, 1962), higher even than those who lost a father through death or divorce but did not have a stepfather.

Thus sexual victimization is but one part of a larger picture. It is even possible that a high level of sexual victimization is what lies behind the high level of divorce and psychological problems for these women. But more likely, all three have a common root in the family dynamics and psychological conflicts of a family with a stepfather. In any case, this research certainly contradicts the myth that fatherless children benefit from

TABLE 9-2. Girls' Experiences with Older Partners and Incest for Indicators of Maternal Disability

SUBGROUP	OLDER PARTNER (%)	INCEST (%)	FATHER-DAUGHTER INCEST [a] (%)
Whole sample (N = 530)	19	28	1.3
Mother often ill (N = 134)	35*	34	3.0
Mother often drunk (N = 23)	26	26	4.3
Mother not HS grad. (N = 77)	38**	52**	5.2

[a] No significance test calculated.
Chi-square statistic compares rate for subgroup with rate for sample as a whole.
*$p < .05$; **$p < .001$.

a replacement. For girls at least, finding a new father to replace the old hardly seems like a favor.

The Importance of Mothers: Findings

Our data also give strong confirmation to the idea that mothers are important in preventing sexual abuse. These findings are very consistent with those reported in the literature and mentioned previously. A group of girls in the sample highly vulnerable to sexual victimization were nineteen girls who at some time before the age of sixteen had lived without their mothers (Table 9-1). Fifty-eight percent of those girls had been sexually victimized, three times the rate for the sample as a whole.* Such girls were also more vulnerable to incest, although surprisingly, not father-daughter incest.

Unlike the case with stepfathers, when motherless girls then acquired a stepmother, their likelihood of victimization dropped. They were still much more likely than usual to have a victimizing experience, but the presence of a stepmother reduced the vulnerability somewhat, suggesting that the presence of a mother, even a stepmother, acts as protection.

Not just maternal absence, but also inability to protect can contribute to sexual victimization. Two findings are relevant here. In Table 9-2, we see that having a mother who was often ill is correlated with more sexual experiences with older partners. Moreover daughters of poorly educated mothers have about twice as many such experiences as is normal. Ill mothers, we presume, cannot supervise daughters and cannot be good role models. Poorly educated mothers may likewise be less capable of protecting because, in line with Landis' (1956) findings, they may not be able to give their daughters good sex information.

To further test the theory of maternal protection, we constructed an index of "role weakness," which included questions about whether the respondent's mother was energetic, was ambitious, took charge of things, had problems with relatives, was nervous, was ill, drank heavily, or complained about finances. The index as a whole was not predictive of sexual victimization or incest, however, even though individual items were—the main one being illness.

Of factors indicating maternal disability, poor education and alcoholism were particularly associated with father-daughter incest. This

---

* Miller (1976) presents some findings quite at odds with this, showing in fact motherless girls to have *lower* rates of child molestation. She argues that this finding makes sense because these girls live in families that have been disrupted primarily by the mother's death, not by divorce, with all its accompanying conflicts and rivalries. However, her question on family composition ("With whom are you living now?") is significantly different from the one asked in this survey ("Was there any time before age sixteen when you did not live with your mother?"), which may account for her divergent findings.

finding is quite consistent with the clinical picture of such incest. In the case literature, mothers are often described as weak, dominated by the fathers, unable to act in their own interest and on behalf of their daughters. The story of one of our interviewees illustrates well how mothers who are themselves victims have a hard time protecting their daughters:

R: My father was an educated man, and he was extremely critical of my mother because she had only a sixth-grade education. He always corrected her grammar. That was the one big thing I remember. Every word he corrected the grammar of it.

She was very, very passive, very accepting, and indicative of this was the fact that she stayed with him through all those years, through all his running around, through all the abuse of the children and her. I mean she was physically beaten many times. And through the conditions she had to live with: no water, no food, being cold. I don't think she ever would have left him, ever. I think she would have stayed until he killed her. She was very passive.

I was embarrassed of her many times. I was embarrassed by the fact that she wore hair curlers to the market, for instance. And I didn't respect her. I didn't think she had much wits about her. Of course, that was very much supported by my father because I was the smarter one and he made me feel that way.

She was the first person who told me that there was anything wrong about what was going on. She called me in from the apple orchard once when she noticed that my father had asked me to take my underpants off. So I came in and she scolded me and said that was wrong. After that I started being aware that these things were wrong, so I started telling her what my father was making me do. I remember threatening my father, saying, "I'm going to tell mother if you don't stop." He probably chuckled too because he knew it would do no good to tell my mother.

I did tell her a couple of times and she didn't really respond. It was like anything, no matter what you told her, she never really responded about anything. I would say, "Gee, he did it again last night." And she would say, "This man, I don't know what I'm going to do about him."

I always thought that one of the reasons she never really made a big deal of his advances to us was because it relieved her of the sexual burden. I think she was also very concerned in a distorted manner for the welfare of the children. She figured if anything happened to him, she wouldn't have the almighty dollar. She had to weigh that. I think she was almost willing to sell her children for that financial support.

These findings, all together, strongly suggest that the oppression of wives is connected to the sexual victimization of their daughters. When mothers themselves are victims, when they are not equal parents, they apparently cannot transmit effective coping and self-protective skills to their daughters. Such girls are more likely to be victimized both within the family, particularly by their fathers, and outside the family. In addition mothers play an important supervisory and guardian function. Girls who are without mothers or whose mothers are ill or extremely oppressed, miss the protection a mother provides. They are particularly likely to be taken advantage of sexually.

Large Families and Overcrowding

THEORY

A favorite theme in the early literature on incest was that it took place in conditions of overcrowding. When many people were crowded into few rooms, it was hypothesized, privacy broke down, family members were much more sexually accessible to one another, and incest occurred (Weinberg, 1955).

Weinberg criticized this oversimplified notion and showed that the ratio of rooms per person for his sample of over two-hundred incestuous families in Chicago was no worse than the average for the city.

Although the emphasis on overcrowding has abated, the idea that incestuous families and sexually abusive families are quite large has persisted. Tormes (n.d.) found that the former had an average of 4.7 children compared to 3.9 for nonincestuous families. In De Francis' (1969) study of sexually abused victims, 55 percent of their families had six or more members compared to the 14 percent of such families that would be expected by census estimate. Thus the evidence about large families is stronger than the evidence about overcrowding.

There has been little theorizing about why size per se (independent from crowding) might increase incest or sexual abuse. In large families, increased sexual abuse may be connected to the larger age span between youngest and oldest siblings. Younger children are more vulnerable when older siblings and their friends are beginning to experiment sexually and may not have learned to control their sexual impulses. The difference in age, as with stepsiblings, might mean that some of the usual deterrents to incest are not operating.

FINDINGS

We looked at several measures of family size and crowding to see what light they might shed on this discussion. In our sample, crowding in families does not promote sexual victimization or incest, at least for girls. Boys from crowded families (ones that had more than two people per bedroom) have slightly higher rates of experiences with older partners and incest but not enough to be statistically significant.

The situation is similar in the case of nonnuclear family members living in the household. We hypothesized that the chance for incest and sexual victimization to occur might increase if there were extraneous people living in the household—grandparents, cousins, boarders. These people would not only make conditions more crowded and effectively increase family size but also they are people, who because of their transience or more distant connection to the family, might be less inhibited from taking sexual liberties with children in the household. Once again, this situation had a small effect on the likelihood of incest for the boys, but it made no difference to the girls in the sample.

By contrast absolute family size did significantly effect at least one kind of sexual victimization. The largest families were not riskier environments for the girls in our sample, but they were for the boys. The boys from families of more than six people reported twice as many experiences with older persons than was normal for the other boys in our sample (Table 9-3). Surprisingly, they did not report an unusually large amount of incest, only of sexual victimization outside the family. This result is paradoxical, because our theories about family size would lead us to expect that it would increase sexual incidents within the family, not outside. It is also unusual that the size should affect the boys' experiences and not the girls'.

A further analysis shows, however, that this initial impression is misleading. Girls are in fact at risk in large families too, but only a particular kind of large family—those with many brothers. When a girl has four or more brothers, she is twice as vulnerable to sexual victimization and about 50 percent more vulnerable to incest (Table 9-4). She has to contend not only with her brothers but also obviously with many of their friends and playmates, which exposes her to increased possibility of sexual victimization both from within and outside the family.

Hence, our conclusion is that an oversized family does contribute to sexual victimization, but not through the mechanism of crowding, as has sometimes been thought in the past. Some other factor—the age span be-

TABLE 9-3. Boys' Experiences with Older Partners and Incest by Family Size

SUBGROUP	OLDER PARTNER (%)	INCEST (%)
Whole sample (N = 266)	9	23
Large family (6 +) (N = 46)	17*	26

Chi-square statistic compares rate for subgroup with rate for sample as a whole.
*p < .05.

TABLE 9 - 4. **Girls' Experiences with Older Partners and Incest by Family Size**

SUBGROUP	OLDER PARTNER (%)	INCEST (%)	FATHER– DAUGHTER INCEST[a] (%)
Whole sample (N = 530)	**19**	**28**	**1.3**
Large family (6 +) (N = 121)	21	30	—
4 or more brothers (N = 38)	42**	40	2.6

[a] No significance test calculated. Chi-square statistic compares rate for subgroup with rate for sample as a whole.

**p < .001.

tween the oldest and youngest or the decrease in individual adult supervision—must explain the phenomenon.

Ordinal Position of Siblings

The literature on incest pays a lot of attention to the ordinal position of siblings. It has been found that victims of father-daughter incest are almost always the oldest daughters (Tormes, n.d.). This fact illustrates well that such incest is not just a special alliance that occurs between a father and a particular daughter he may be close to. Rather, it is a family role configuration inherent in a particular kind of marital relationship. As the oldest daughter matures, she is being prepared for a certain role in such a family. Sometimes other daughters become victims too, but it is usually after the oldest daughter has rejected the father or left home.

No one to our knowledge has investigated whether ordinal position has any bearing on a child's likelihood of being sexually victimized in general. Within our sample it was possible to do so.

Ordinal position is not related to a child's chance of being sexually victimized or engaging in incest. Although oldest daughters are the most likely choice of fathers, they are not necessarily the most likely choice of other male relatives. If any position holds a slight vulnerability, it is the youngest who are most likely to be sexually victimized and the middle girls who are most likely to have incestuous experiences. However, neither of these differences is statistically significant.

The pattern is similar for boys. It is the youngest and middle children who if anything are more vulnerable, but once again the differences are small. The only conclusion to draw is that ordinal position does not make any difference.

Conclusion

Our investigation into the family backgrounds of children who are sexual victims and participants in incest has yielded some valuable and provocative results. On the whole, they are consistent with other research findings to this point, rudimentary as these have been, but they have helped to make the conclusions more specific.

Marital conflict and family disruption are environments that contribute to the risk of sexual victimization. Being the child of an unhappy marriage, missing a father, or particularly missing a mother leave a girl especially vulnerable to sexual abuse. In addition, a stepfather or stepbrothers, when they are present in the family, are associated with sexual victimization, not just because they themselves take advantage of a girl, but because they increase the likelihood of a nonfamily member also doing so.

Another conclusion that this research has reconfirmed is the importance of a mother in protecting a girl from sexual abuse. Girls without mothers are at very high risk, and so are girls whose mothers are inadequate or incapacitated because of illness, alcoholism, or poor education.

On the question of crowding, the findings are more equivocal. Crowding itself does not seem to increase sexual victimization and incest, but large families do. All large families make boys more vulnerable to sexual victimization, but only families with a large number of brothers do so for girls.

10

COMPARISON OF THE FINDINGS WITH OTHER STUDIES

IN THIS CHAPTER we turn our attention to two commonly asked questions about the sexual victimization of children: (1) Is it increasing? (2) Is there any difference between the kinds of cases that are reported and those that are not? To help answer these questions we will compare the findings of our own study, first, with studies that have been made at earlier times, and second, with studies that have only looked at *reported* cases of sexual abuse.

Given the inadequacy of almost all work that has ever been done on this subject, including our own, we need to recognize that these comparisons do not amount to hard science but are rather partially grounded speculations. We have some fragments of evidence that yield some plausible conclusions, but they are of almost entirely unsubstantiated validity. Nonetheless, trying to answer these questions even with flimsy evidence may be good intellectual preparation in anticipation of a time when we have something better to go on.

Is Sexual Victimization Increasing?

Reports of sexual victimization have been increasing dramatically in the last few years. Child protection workers all over the country report that they are overwhelmed by the influx of new cases of sexual abuse. Whereas ten years ago there was hardly a case anywhere, today the reporting rate is increasing exponentially and shows little sign of abating (Giaretto, 1976). The situation has been called an epidemic.

Despite the enormous increase, few observers have been willing to argue

131

that the true incidence of sexual abuse has actually risen. Most believe what we are witnessing is a revolution in consciousness, a situation where, because of changed mores, professionals are more sensitive to identifying instances of sexual abuse and victims and their families are more willing than before to seek help.

THE RECENT PAST

The curious history of interest in this problem does allow us to make some comparisons. Unlike physical abuse, which has only recently worried the public seriously enough to prompt emprical investigation, child molestation triggered a wave of interest in the 1940s and early 1950s, which produced, among other research, two sets of survey data of fairly high quality and comparable to that reported in the present study.

One of the studies was by Kinsey, who in the last wave of his interviewing, between 1947 and 1952, posed questions to 1,200 women about childhood sexual experiences with adults. Although not analyzed in his 1953 book, these data were later analyzed by John Gagnon in an article in 1965. In the other study, Judson Landis conducted a survey of 1,800 University of California at Berkeley students in 1952 on a similar topic. Although Kinsey and Landis gathered their data around the same time, Kinsey's effectively gives information on an earlier time period since his respondents were generally older. The overall incidence rates for only the

T A B L E 10 – 1. Prevalence of Childhood Sexual Victimization of Women as Reported in Three Studies (Percent)

Study	(1) As Originally Reported	(2) Under 13 Only	Col. (1) Excluding Exhibitionists	N
Kinsey-Gagnon (1947–53)	28(a)	28	14	(1,200)
Landis (1951–53)	35(b)	19	16	(d)
Finkelhor (1978)	19(c)	16	15	(530)

Sources: Gagnon (1965): Table 3
         Landis (1956): Tables 1, 2
(a) Children before puberty with person five years older.
(b) Children up to 21 with "adult sexual deviate."
(c) Children under 12 with person five years older and children 13–16 with adult ten years older.
(d) No N available for females. Males + Females = 1,800.

women in these two studies and the present one are shown in Table 10–1. They show a marked *decrease* between then and now.

A DECREASE IN SEXUAL ABUSE?

Could this decrease be due to methodological factors? The methodologies, although not exactly the same, are fairly comparable. Respondents in all three studies were college-educated women, reporting retrospectively on childhood experiences. Landis used a questionnaire, as in this study; Kinsey, as almost everyone knows, used personal interviews. The experiences counted were virtually identical, ranging from sexual approach, exhibitionism, fondling and touching genitals, attempted coitus, and coitus. However, the studies show some differences in their definitions of child and adult. For Kinsey (as analyzed by Gagnon) childhood sexual experiences with adults meant only those experiences prior to puberty with a person at least five years older. Landis, however, had a broader definition which included adolescent experiences with adults, although he did not state a precise definition of adult. (He said he excluded instances that appeared to be consensual but did not say what that meant.) The figures from the three studies can be recalculated to refer to as comparable an age group as possible: the experiences of victims twelve and under (see Table 10–1, column 2). They still show a substantial decline.

A DECLINE IN EXHIBITIONISM

One important part of the decrease can be pinpointed more exactly. Both Landis and Kinsey-Gagnon show much higher rates of experiences with exhibitionists than in the current study: Kinsey-Gagnon, 50 percent of the experiences; Landis, 55 percent; this study, 20 percent. The rates for nonexhibition experiences only are shown in column 3. (It was not possible from the published statistics to correct these for age as in column 2; but since Landis reports that the experiences with exhibitionists were much more common for the older girls, eliminating these experiences makes the Landis study more comparable in its age distribution to the other two.) After eliminating experiences with exhibitionists, the findings of the three studies are remarkably similar. Thus one would conclude that the major item that has declined over the last thirty years has been the incidence of exhibitionism.

However, the large difference in the amount of exhibitionism between the earlier studies and this one may be due to factors other than an historical decline. Exhibitionism is an offense thought to be more often committed in urban areas, where the kind of anonymous public conditions conducive to the offense are more prevalent (Landis, 1956; MacDonald, 1973). The present study may be artificially low in its reports of exhibitionism because it has a large representation of rural and small-town respondents.

A comparison in this study of urban and rural students, however, shows no difference in rates of experiences with exhibitionists. The decline observed earlier would still hold if we compared Landis' and Kinsey-Gagnon's findings to only our urban group and excluded the large rural contingent. Thus we think on the whole that the drop is better attributed to historical change than to urban-rural differences between the samples.

In fact a historical decline in exhibitionism has been noticed elsewhere (Kutchinsky, 1973) and is usually related to increasing social acceptance of sexuality. Studies have shown that many exhibitionists are motivated by the desire to shock and humiliate their victims by exposing their genitals (Mohr et al., 1964). As people become more and more blasé about sexual matters, exhibitionists can no longer count on success. Hence, its frequency declines.

Therefore, the answer to our original question—is sexual victimization increasing or declining?—is as follows: In the last thirty years the incidence of adults actually physically molesting girls has probably stayed about the same. The incidence of exhibitionism toward girls has probably declined.

However, two cautions pertain to this speculation: (1) it applies only to girls; we have no comparative data on boys; (2) it does not apply to the experiences of children within the last five years or so, since it has been at least five years since even our most recent interviewees were children.

THE DISTANT PAST

If we extend our historical comparison further back into history, not a mere generation or two, but a whole century or two, we are almost certainly on solid ground in asserting that sexual victimization of children has decreased. Historians of children report that molestation was probably the rule rather than the exception for children of the sixteenth, seventeenth, and eighteenth centuries in Europe (Aries, 1962; De Mause, 1974). For example, the detailed diary kept about the childhood of no less a personage than Louis XIII of France by his personal physician reveals a child who was subject to the sexual whims of almost every adult in his environment—relatives and courtiers, not to mention servants and nurses (De Mause, 1974). Stone (1977) remarks that no one, including the child's parents, found this activity unusual. He doubts that this was a deviant upbringing in this respect and thinks it likely that such sexual behavior toward children was a common practice of the period.

SOCIAL CHANGE

Taking now another speculative approach to the problem, how would we expect the incidence of sexual victimization to change, given what we know about contemporary historical developments? Would the most recent changes in the nature of family and society be likely to ameliorate or to aggravate the problem.

Take, for example, the increasing rate of divorce. The new willingness of parents (particularly women) to terminate unsatisfying marriages probably means that fewer children than before are trapped in brutal situations. To the extent that incest and child molesting are connected with parental authoritarianism, sexual problems, and marital discord, this development would seem to bode well.

However, our findings and others indicate that loss of a parent or acquisition of a step-parent increases vulnerability to sexual victimization. There is some dispute about whether the current high rate of marital dissolution deprives more children of parents than did the high mortality rates in earlier times (Bane, 1976). Remarriage rates have undisputedly increased (Carter and Glick, 1976), so children today have more step-parents than before. This and the fact that they may possibly live more often in single parent families are both factors conducive to sexual victimization. Thus the impact of the new family patterns accompanying divorce might either increase or decrease rates of sexual victimization.

Another phenomenon whose effect is ambiguous is the decline of extended family relations and the fact that children today grow up knowing fewer people of older and younger generations. In such circumstances, children probably have contact with fewer adults (for example, extended relatives living with the family) who would be in a position to take sexual advantage of a child's trust. But by the same token, there are fewer adults in the child's environment to supervise him or her and thus deter such situations from arising. Thus the change cuts both ways.

Finally, as we indicated in Chapter 1, it has been argued that increased sexual freedom makes children both more and less vulnerable to molestation. On the one hand, under liberalized conditions, children learn more about sex and are better prepared to handle themselves. Fear and shame about revealing that something has happened should be reduced, and the consciousness of parents and other caretakers will increase. Even potential child abusers may benefit by having alternative and now less guilt-ridden sexual outlets.

On the other hand, sexual freedom appears to bring with it, at least in the short run, a greater sexualization of everybody, including children, as we have seen in advertising and in the recent blossoming of kiddie porn. Moral inhibitions about all kinds of sexual activity are loosened, which may weaken the taboo against sexual activity with children also, especially among certain people with already weak controls. Therefore sexual liberalization too may promote sexual victimization of children, or it may lessen it, or it may do both simultaneously. This open question is one, unlike many others, that we may all live long enough to find out the answer to.

SEXUAL LIBERALIZATION AND SEXUAL ABUSE IN DENMARK

At least one study on another country shows that social progress and sexual liberalization result in a decline, not an increase, in sexual abuse. Kutchinsky (1973) has meticulously analyzed police reports on child molestation in Denmark during the period 1959 to 1971. This period saw dramatic increases in sexual freedom, combined with dramatic decreases in the number of reported sexual offenses. Kutchinsky tried to see if the marked decline there could be attributed to changed practices in reporting by the public or police rather than an actual decline. However, after eliminating such other possible explanatory factors, he concluded that some of the decrease in child molesting had been real, reflecting the fact that in a more sexually liberal society potential child molesters have other sources of sexual gratification.

It is curious, however, that sexual liberalization occurred simultaneously with a *decrease* in reported cases of sexual abuse in Denmark, whereas it appears to be occurring simultaneously with an *increase* in this country. If sexual liberalization in effect makes it easier to talk about such matters, and this development accounts, as many have argued, for the particular epidemic in reporting that we currently have, then why did not a similar increase in reports occur in Denmark. This difference suggests that the social dynamics in the two countries relating to the two phenomena are not the same. It will be interesting to know whether rates will continue to fall in Denmark or whether they will have the same kind of rise as in this country under the impact of increased international awareness of the problem.

Reported and Unreported Cases

If the current epidemic of sexual abuse is really (or at least in part) an epidemic of reporting and not an actual increase in incidence, the question of why some cases are reported and others not becomes very interesting. All researchers believe that there is a vast number of unreported cases for every reported one, but what is not known is whether these unreported cases are similar or quite different.

This is an important issue for both researchers and practitioners. Since most research has been based on reported cases, it is crucial to know whether there are special characteristics about them that would prevent us from generalizing research findings on their basis. For example, some people think that the reported cases are biased because they exclude a large number of "positive" adult-child sexual experiences, which naturally never come to the attention of therapists, child protection workers, and police (Nobile, 1978). Others think that what characterizes reported cases is the presence not of sexual deviance but of intense family conflict, which is what results in the reporting. If either of these things were true, what many researchers are analyzing as the sexual abuse syndrome would only apply to the limited number of cases that come to public attention, not to the apparently large majority of cases "out there."

For practitioners, the question is of interest in the process of case finding. If unreported cases are different, then using profiles based on known cases to identify other unknown cases will not bring great success.

On this question there has been much speculation but little evidence. Some think that more serious cases are less likely to be reported than superficial ones. A family, in this view, will be less likely to report an uncle than a stranger, whom they have no desire to protect (Green, 1977).

Others argue the opposite, however: that more serious cases are more likely to be reported. Families only involve outsiders when a truly difficult situation arises. Unless it involves great force, a case of exhibitionism or fondling by a stranger or a neighbor will be handled by the family on its own (Rosenfeld, 1977). Only under conditions of serious threat and prolonged family conflict do outside authorities become involved.

Answers to most of these kinds of questions will have to await much more sophisticated analyses than we can make here, analyses involving detailed descriptions and comparisons of cases that were and were not reported. However, it is possible to make some global comparisons, using this study and studies made on the basis of reported cases. Differences about such things as sex, age, and relationship to the victim may provide some clues about the differences between reported and unreported cases.

There is one serious bit of presumptuousness to this procedure. We do not know for sure how many of the cases in our sample actually were reported to police or social agencies. No such explicit question was asked of respondents. Our presumption that the sample is made up mostly of unreported cases is based on two pieces of evidence. (1) In previous surveys of this sort, only a small portion of cases had been reported to the police; Kinsey-Gagnon (Gagnon, 1965) found only 6 percent, and Landis (1956) only 10 percent. (2) Two-thirds of our respondents said they did not talk about their experiences to anybody, parents or siblings, let alone police or social workers. Since a virtual precondition of reporting to police or social agencies is telling parents or some other adult, we can be confident that the experiences of at least two-thirds, and probably quite a bit more of the sample, never reached public attention.

FEWER BOYS AMONG REPORTED CASES

In our study and in one other survey (Landis, 1956), boys revealed substantial numbers of childhood sexual experiences with adults, 9 percent, or about half the frequency reported by women. Yet, most studies of reported cases display an overwhelming preponderance of girls. A ratio of ten girls to one boy, coming from the De Francis (1969) study, is the figure most commonly quoted in the literature. A great many studies fail to report on the experiences of boys at all, so small is the number of cases they receive. (For two recent notable exceptions see Queen's Bench, 1976, and Swift, 1977).

There are many possible reasons why the sexual victimization of boys does not come to public attention so readily. Processes are probably at work at various stages along the route that screen it out; for example:

1. Boys appear less likely to report the experience to anyone (see Chapter 4 and also Landis, 1956, p. 99), perhaps because they feel greater shame or because they have been indoctrinated into an ethic of greater self-reliance. In either case, if no one is told, the case is never reported.
2. Boys are older when they have their experiences (see Chapter 4 and Table A-1) and thus less likely to report them to adults.
3. Boys seem to be less frightened by their experiences (Chapter 4 and Landis, 1956, Table 5), and thus perhaps manifest fewer symptoms by which others might recognize their experiences.
4. Professionals in the field may be less prepared for the possibility of sexual victimization of boys and thus less likely to identify it.
5. Sexual victimization of girls may arouse a more protective response and thus be promoted to case status by various public and family authorities.

In short, there is a "victim" role for women in the society, into which they are cast both by themselves and others (Chapman and Gates, 1978). This bias may facilitate the discovery and establishment of cases against girls more readily than against boys.

YOUNGER CHILDREN MORE OFTEN REPORTED

What else can we learn from comparing reported and unreported cases? Almost all studies report the average age of the victims. In Appendix A-1 we assembled all the studies according to whether they were general surveys of the incidence of sexual victimization (like the present one) or based on victims who had brought reports to public agencies or on the court records of convicted offenders.

This comparison shows the average age of girls in reported cases (9.1) to be younger than in general survey cases (10.2). These figures indicate that the experiences of younger children are more often reaching agencies, than those of the older children.

This is not an anticipated finding. Most observers have felt that younger children are less likely to come to public attention because they are less able to act autonomously, and parents and other caretakers would try to protect them from the trauma of police or agency investigation.

However, it would seem from these data that it is the older children who are less likely to report, possibly because they are more conscious of embarrassment and less willing to tell. Another possibility is that cases involving teenagers are more morally and legally ambiguous, and both families and victims fear that blame for the sexual experience will be placed on the victim. Perhaps older victims have more control over whether, once discovered, a report is made, and they act to discourage reporting. All these are mere speculations about why older victims would report less. Much more study of this issue is warranted.

PARENTS AND KNOWN OFFENDERS MORE OFTEN REPORTED

As mentioned earlier, some people have thought relatives would be less likely to be reported when discovered; others have thought the opposite. Fortunately, quite a few studies have published figures on the nature of the relationship between offender and victim. Although they have not always used equivalent categories, we have assembled them in Appendix A-2 in as comparable a form as possible.

Two generalizations hold: (1) Cases involving parents are more likely to appear among reported cases than their proportion in the general population would indicate. (2) Offenders who are known to victims are more likely to be reported. Experiences with strangers are underreported.

Parents (mostly fathers and stepfathers) make up a large proportion of reported cases for several reasons. For one thing, they are conspicuous, create concern, and are thus likely to be pursued by those who know about them until they become official statistics. For another thing, although many families try to contain knowledge about parent-child incest, the dynamics are so volatile and the potential for conflict so great that they must be much harder to hush up permanently than other kinds of children's sexual abuse. Thus even though the motivation for silence may be greater, the actual ability to contain it is less.

The underreporting of strangers is really an underreporting of exhibitionists. For example, Landis' and Gagnon's figures show a higher number of strangers compared to the studies of reported cases, but the present study shows a much smaller number. The Landis and Gagnon studies, as mentioned earlier, are characterized by a large number of exhibitionists compared to the present one. This study's figures, by contrast, are quite in line with those from reported cases.

Exhibition may not be reported because children and parents do not take it seriously enough to bother. Moreover, once reported, the victims of exhibitionists are much less likely to be referred from the police to a social agency.

This fact is illustrated by the variation of the rates in different studies according to the kind of agency involved. The Queen's Bench study, which was an actual police blotter count, shows a fairly high proportion of strangers. Burgess' (1977) and Peters' (1976), however, are hospital-based studies, which probably see few victims of exhibitionists. Similarly, De Francis' (1969) study was based on a child protection agency and thus was also less likely to be referred such cases. As the strangers are harder to locate, fewer of them are found and convicted; thus it is not surprising that fewer of them appear in the Mohr (1964) study of convicted offenders.

In summary, although it would appear that there are motivations for both reporting and not reporting cases of sexual victimization involving kin and acquaintances, on the whole the balance tips slightly toward reporting; in cases involving strangers, the balance is against reporting. No doubt, however, the vast majority of both kinds of cases are never reported.

YOUNGER OFFENDERS NOT REPORTED

Several different kinds of studies also supply information on the age of offenders. We have assembled in Appendix A-3 the statistics from one general survey, two studies of reported victims, and two studies of convicted offenders. The comparison shows that the age of offenders is lowest in the general survey and highest in the studies of offenders—which means that experiences involving younger offenders tend not to reach public attention, whereas those involving older offenders are the most reported and prosecuted.

As a caveat, it must be pointed out that the ages are exact only in the studies of offenders. In those based on victims' reports, the victims have mostly estimated the ages of their partners, often in situations, as with strangers, where they have had little time and peace of mind in which to make their observations. For some reason such estimates might be systematically low and thus explain the difference in reported ages. However, another feature allows a more compelling explanation: although many acts of sexual abuse are committed by juveniles, such offenders are not likely to be in prison; instead they are disposed of by the juvenile justice system.

It is only a little harder to explain why offenses by younger persons, in addition to not reaching the courts and prisons, also are not so frequently reported to police and social agencies. It is likely that potential reporters—adults, friends, and parents—are somewhat more reluctant to report a juvenile. They feel less threatened by the situation (realistically so), better able to handle it without recourse to outside intervention, and perhaps even more compassion for the offender.

REPORTED CASES NOT MORE COERCIVE

This study has emphasized the importance of force and coercion in affecting the impact of the experience on a child. On this basis and on the basis of other analysis (Gagnon, 1965, p. 182), we might expect reported cases to involve more force and violence. In cases of force the victim is more obviously a victim, and other people would be less likely to suspect collaboration. That should be exactly the kind of situation victims and parents would feel most comfortable about reporting to police.

A comparison of this study with studies of reported cases, however, does not support this conclusion (for details see Appendix A-4). A little over 50 percent of the victims in this survey reported that force was used against them, yet three studies of reported cases find an average use of force that was about equivalent. The expected greater degree of force in reported cases does not appear. In a study made of offenders, the use of force in these reported cases was even found to be much lower. (However, this finding should probably be discounted, since offenders probably minimize the extent to which they coerced their victims.)

If we consider this finding concerning force more critically, it is hard to know whether equivalent evaluations of force are used in the various studies. The present study, for example, relied on respondents' own perception of whether force or threats of force were used. The other studies do not indicate how they arrived at their determination, but it is likely that they used different criteria. Thus our figure may be inflated in comparison.

Reported Cases: Conclusion

We have assembled here some fragmentary evidence of the ways in which reported cases differ as a group from the cases of children's sexual victimization that are not reported. Female victims are more often reported to police and social agencies, as are younger victims and cases in which the offender is known, is an older person, or is a parent. We also saw that reported cases are not necessarily more violent. Interesting as this evidence is, it does not answer concerns about whether reported cases are so special as to undercut any attempt to extrapolate from discovered to undiscovered instances of sexual victimization.

Unfortunately, we are still a long way from knowing why some cases are reported and others are not—our original question. What is missing from this analysis is an appreciation of the process that determines whether a case comes to public attention. Like the branching of tracks in a railroad yard, some cases must take a route past a set of crucial junctures leading to reports whereas others become permanently side-tracked at one or another point.

Some of these crucial junctures might be (1) the degree of discomfort the child feels about the situation; (2) the confidence the child feels in being able to get help by telling versus the fear of perhaps being hurt or blamed; (3) the family dynamics surrounding the sexual victimization; situations of intense family conflict may work either to stifle reporting or to promote it, depending on power relations within the family; (4) family members' and even the local subculture's attitudes to bringing in outside authorities; this factor may depend in part on whether such agencies are connected to or remote from the family's operating network.

Finding out about some of these things is a high priority. As they become known, they will certainly help to explain some of the conclusions we have uncovered here.

11

CONCLUSION

THE LAST TEN CHAPTERS have touched on many issues. We shall review some of the salient findings of the study and then try to draw them together in a commentary on some of the questions posed at the outset.

Findings Reviewed

This study should leave no doubt that a large number of children are sexually victimized. Nearly one in five girls and one in eleven boys say they have had a sexual experience as a child with a much older person. The experiences cut across social class and ethnic lines and involve children of all ages. Boys as well as girls are frequent victims.

Boys' experiences are somewhat different from girls'. They are primarily homosexual, and they less often involve family members. However, boys do seem to be the victims of force and coercion just as often as girls. Both girls and boys report that in over half the incidents some form of coercion was used.

Preadolescent children are the most vulnerable. The youthfulness of the children most often victimized suggests to us that it is not the onset of physiological puberty that makes children prone to sexual victimization. Rather, we theorize that it is the independence of preadolescents and their inexperience with newly learned sex-role gestures that account for the vulnerability of this age group.

Many of the experiences are perceived negatively, especially by girls. Very few children of either sex say anything about their experiences to anybody. Most are afraid that parents will be angry or will blame them for what happened.

The victimizers are mostly men, and a very small number of women. They are more often young than old. Contrary to the image of the child molester, a large number are friends and relatives of the children they victimize. About 75 percent of the female victims know their older partners. Almost half are family members.

Parents and siblings are all too often the culprits. If this sample is any estimate of the population as a whole, about 1 ½ percent of all women have had incestuous sex with a father. As many as 5 percent have been victimized by a much older person within the nuclear family. Even in cases of incest between siblings and cousins, we find that often there is a great disparity in age between partners, and in many cases force is used.

Very few women are reported as older partners to the children in the sample—not, we argue, because women play a physiologically passive role in the sexual act, but because they have a different orientation toward sex and toward children. In the case of the few female offenders in the sample, however, the children's experiences with them were not very different from those with men. Yet the experiences with women are somewhat less traumatic, and for some of the boys, they are pleasurable initiation rites.

The study found that the sources of trauma in the experiences are not quite so obvious an many others have thought. Based on respondents' ratings of the experiences, neither the duration of the relationship, the seriousness of the sexual activity, nor the degree of the partner's family closeness directly relates to the negative perception of girls. (However, father-daughter incest is by far the most traumatic type of relationship.) The factor that produces the most trauma is the use of force, and next to force is the age of the partner. The experiences get worse as the partners get older. From these findings, we conclude that it is not true that children feel worse about experiences they have somehow cooperated in. Rather they feel worse about experiences that are intrinsically unpleasant.

The study confirms various long-standing impressions about the kinds of backgrounds most commonly associated with sexual abuse. Social isolation is connected to victimization, as demonstrated by the large number of victims among those who grew up on farms. People from low-income families are more often affected. At least one ethnic group—the Irish—displays particularly high rates of victimization for boys, indicating that some subcultural factors may contribute to a child's vulnerability.

A child's parents play a crucial role in affecting a girl's vulnerability to sexual victimization. Girls whose mothers are absent, sick, or poorly educated run a particularly high risk. Similarly, having a stepfather increases a girl's chances of being sexually abused, not just by the stepfather, but by other persons outside the family. When the parents' marriage is unhappy, rates are also high.

Comparing this study to some earlier ones, we are able to marshall evidence that sexual victimization of children has not increased in the last thirty years. Offenses involving actual physical contact have stayed at about the same level over this period, while the number of experiences with exhibitionists has probably declined. The fact that sexual victimization of children has not increased, despite the decline in sexual restrictions over the last generation, is a good sign; but we do not know whether it holds true for the last five years or whether it will continue to hold true in the future. Certain recent changes in family life, like increases in the number of compound families, may have the potential to increase the amount of sexual victimization.

Based on a comparison of this study with agency-based studies, some interesting differences were found between reported and unreported cases of sexual victimization. Reported cases involve fewer boys, younger children, and offenders who are both older and more likely to be relatives.

Future Directions

PREVALENCE

We have devoted a great deal of attention in this study to descriptive data about children's sexual victimization, and we have shown how widespread it is. However, the sample leaves something to be desired, casting some doubt on whether the results can be generalized. One obvious priority for future research is to use more refined sampling techniques. Miller's (1976) work and also Gagnon's (1977) suggest that randomly chosen respondents, adolescents or college students, be interviewed. A sample like one of theirs, combined with a questionnaire as detailed as this one, might produce some excellent results.

The frequency with which boys are victimized is another important finding of the study, as its extent would appear to be widely underestimated. More work is needed on this subject; a good start would be a survey with a much larger sample of males. The experiences of boys should be compared to those of girls, particularly to decide whether boys' experiences are as victimizing. If indeed, as we tend to believe, boys' experiences are similar to girls' in this respect, then public energies must be mobilized to find and intervene in the large number of male cases.

Despite its usefulness in uncovering findings such as this one, the descriptive and statistical approach of this study should be counterbalanced by a study of how such experiences are perceived by the victims themselves. There is much to be learned about childhood and the nature of sexual development. In the testimony of victims themselves, there are also certain to be new insights about the causes of the problem. The second phase of this study, the analysis of interviews with victims, should begin to fill this need.

TRAUMA

This research has challenged some assumptions about what is traumatic about sexual victimization. Chapter 7 offered substantial evidence that certain classic features of these experiences, such as how long they lasted or whether they involved intercourse, did not predict the degree of trauma.

In the future, this whole matter needs to be approached in a much more complicated, multidimensional way. First, we need to assess trauma with more objective indicators, ones based on life experiences and life adjustment as well as on the kind of subjective measures we have used here.

Second, a complex causal analysis should be made to distinguish the traumatic factors in the general environment—poverty, family disruption, social and emotional isolation—from those of the sexual experience itself. We also need to distinguish the trauma induced by the experience itself from that induced by the reactions of friends, family, and institutions. The problem is certain to involve conditional relations and interaction effects that must be disentangled.

Our understanding of trauma could best be enhanced by a longitudinal study, perhaps as part of a study on the whole family, which managed to observe children before and after sexual victimization. Such studies are expensive, invasive, and rare. In their absence, statistical regression techniques on survey information can be used to good advantage to disentangle some of the complexities alluded to.

HISTORICAL TRENDS

We have suggested that important theoretical implications can be derived from knowing whether sexual victimization is increasing or decreasing over time. The findings of this study, compared to those made a generation ago, suggest that rates have stayed the same, or in the case of exhibitionism, have dropped. However, other of our findings suggest that changes in contemporary family life—for example, increasing numbers of compound families and increasing social isolation—could mean a rise in the amount of sexual abuse. Unfortunately, it is hard to obtain statistics for a past that is out of reach. However, we can certainly compare the experiences of cohorts of people of different ages who are still alive today. We can also begin to compile statistics that will be of use in answering this question in the future.

REPORTING CASES

We have illustrated one way to discover whether reported cases of sexual victimization are consistently different from unreported ones. The findings of this study, most of whose cases are unreported, were compared to findings from studies of reported cases. The latter appear to differ in that they involve fewer boys, younger children, and offenders who are older and more likely to be relatives.

This whole topic of inquiry needs to be extended, but by methods that yield more trustworthy results. For example, if a large enough sample can be taken of a national population, an analysis could contrast the reported and unreported cases within that same sample. The problem here would be getting a large enough group of reported cases.

Moreover, as we suggested in Chapter 10, reporting should be examined as a process, not just as an outcome. An experience of sexual victimization may be reported at various junctures, and various forces influence whether it is more or less likely to happen. We need to study the factors and conditions that determine who tells whom about the experience and how these decisions culminate in a reported case.

A THEORY OF SEXUAL VICTIMIZATION

Ultimately we return to the question, why are children sexually victimized? Unfortunately, we do not believe it is going to be possible to find a simple one- or two-factor explanation for this problem. We need to recognize, as some are beginning to do (Summit and Kryso, 1978), that there are many different kinds of sexual abuse, and that each kind may require a separate explanation. For sexual victimization in isolated rural areas, for example, we will need one kind of explanation that takes into account the effects of isolation or of an unusual subculture. For sexual victimization that is part of a psychotic episode, we would be better off with an explanation based on individual psychology, that is, how certain patterns of development lead to such behavior.

This study cannot distinguish well among the many different types of sexual victimization that are represented in its sample. In that respect, it does not have a good vantage point from which to theorize. As an exploratory study in an area of little research, its objective has been to describe some of the main features of a kind of experience about which all too little is known. Still, the findings can point the way for future theoretical developments. What follows are suggestions for directions to pursue in future attempts to explain sexual victimization.

We hope we have firmly established the idea that the family plays a crucial part in creating vulnerability to sexual victimization. In Chapter 2, we tried to show that it was increasingly the consensus in the literature that attempts to understand sexual abuse must focus on the family environment. In Chapters 8 and 9, we demonstrated that family factors are indeed empirically associated with higher rates of sexual abuse: family size, ethnicity, social class, and family composition. More efforts must be made to apply what we know about other aspects of the family—family interaction, socialization, the development of values specific to individual families, power relationships among family members, the strains of parenting, and so forth—to understand why some children are sexually victimized.

Mothers

Based on the findings here, we believe special attention ought to be paid to the relationship between mothers and daughters. Our data show that girls without natural mothers are particularly vulnerable to sexual victimization, as are the daughters of poorly educated, ill, and alcoholic mothers. Girls without mothers or with incapacitated mothers are probably not well protected or supervised. Their education about sexual matters may well be incomplete. They lack strong models from whom they can learn how to defend themselves. In fact, since their mothers may be victims of various sorts, their most available model may be that of women as victim.

It is a highly plausible inference from this finding that the oppression of women as wives and workers promotes the sexual victimization of their daughters. If girls are going to learn self-protective coping behavior, especially in sexual situations, they will have to do so from their mothers. When mothers themselves are demoralized and disorganized, and are victims themselves in their relationships with husbands and other men, they are in a poor position to transmit these skills. This is a good example of how the oppression of women can have repercussions that extend for generations, affecting not only the women themselves but also their children and conceivably their grandchildren.

More research is needed on the possible connection between the oppression of wives and the victimization of daughters. More substantial indicators of sexual inequality and incapacitation than the ones used here should be employed. For example, is sexual victimization more common in families where husbands beat their wives? Where large inequalities exist in matters of family decision making? Where wives have no income?

Moreover, more should be known about the way in which the mother-daughter relationship provides protection against sexual victimization. Is it the direct supervision and concern a mother maintains over her child? Is it the education and information she provides? Is it the modeling of coping behavior? The testimony of victims on their relationships with their mothers will be helpful in deciding among the alternatives, but actual observations of mother-child interactions could provide us with the richest source of information on this subject.

Stepfathers

Another intriguing family factor highlighted in this research is the role played by stepfathers. Girls with stepfathers suffer higher rates of sexual victimization, and although the stepfathers themselves account for some of it, that is not the whole story. Such girls are also more vulnerable to victimization by persons from outside the family.

One can imagine various connections. The key problem may be in the relationship itself, which may be an easily sexualized one. Once sexualized, it may lead to a girl's victimization at the hands of either the stepfather or other men as she tranfers styles of relating she has learned inside the family to the outside.

On the other hand, the difficulty may arise through the girl's mother. A girl who watches her mother go through courtship and remarriage learns things about sexual behavior other girls may not learn. Perhaps by imitating this behavior prematurely, she attracts potential sexual abusers. Or even more simply, perhaps a girl is angry with or jealous of a mother who remarries. Vulnerability to sexual victimization may develop from the emotional conflict.

Perhaps the environment of remarriage is somewhat precarious as far as sexual victimization is concerned. A child may be poorly supervised or exposed to more strangers and more relatives.

In any case, our findings here fit into the pattern of previous knowledge about the relationship between stepfathers and stepdaughters, which shows that girls with stepfathers often have difficulties in later life with mental and marital instability. The fact of sexual victimization is another piece of a puzzle which needs to be explained.

Social Isolation

Social isolation is an important ingredient in some kinds of sexual victimization. We have pointed out how research on different aspects of the problem has converged on social isolation as a possible cause. Our finding in Chapter 8 that girls from farm backgrounds are more commonly victims supports this analysis.

We think the concept of social isolation should be understood in a broad sense. It should include not just geographic isolation but isolation caused by poverty, family constellation, shyness, or unusual value systems. Such isolation may foster sexual victimization because family members take advantage of one another for sexual gratification, because the families develop deviant values which encourage victimization, or because the families are not exposed to community supervision. These different possibilites must be disentangled.

It also seems a strong possibility that social isolation, although associated with sexual victimization, may not be a causal factor in it at all. It may be a spurious association. In other words, other problems—poverty, unusual values, or family disorganization—may be responsible for both the sexual victimization and the isolation. Even if it is not a causal factor, however, knowledge about the connection between social isolation and sexual victimization will be useful to the process of prevention and case identification.

Research should establish more clearly the aspects of social isolation that are connected with sexual victimization. What are the best indicators of this pathological type of social isolation? Weak ties with extended family? Children who have few friends and outside contacts? Or a family with few organizational and community involvements?

If, in fact, there are communities, for example, in rural areas, where incest and sexual abuse are more common, it might be extremely fruitful to conduct in-depth studies of them. Hard as it might be to penetrate these communities, such a study would be likely to provide a clearer picture of the sources of at least one particular type of sexual abuse.

Policy on Family Sexuality

In Chapter 1, we pointed out that there may develop in the near future a controversy about the wisdom of increasing sexual openness and interaction among family members. Specifically the issue pits certain reformers, who are eager to free society from the burden of sexual repression, against those concerned with the large amount of sexual trauma sustained by children at the hands of family members.

We suggested several questions that had bearing on this debate, among them the following: (1) Is sexual abuse the consequence of too much sexual repression in the family or not enough? (2) Is there evidence that increased family sexuality promotes benefits in family life and in subsequent personal developments? (3) Is sexual contact among family members harmful to children, and if so, does it stem from something intrinsic to the experience or only to the prejudices of our culture about such experiences? (4) Are the benefits and dangers of sexual openness in the family of equal magnitude for men and women?

Although nothing from this study gives a conclusive answer to any of these questions, it is interesting to look at the findings in their light. Do the findings tend toward one point of view or another? Do they suggest other avenues of research?

The strongest argument in favor of liberalizing family sexuality is the evidence that sexual victimization has not increased in the last thirty years. Society as a whole, and families in particular, have undergone dramatic liberalization in that period. Sexually oriented media have become much more available, sex is now more freely discussed, and attitudes toward childhood sexual play and masturbation have relaxed. If these changes have not increased, and have in fact possibly decreased, the number of children who are sexually abused, then further liberalizations may also take place without harm.

Of course, these changes of the last three decades have not sexualized the family quite so directly, as would some of the more zealous proposals now being made. There may be little correspondence between the effects produced by an increased toleration of masturbation and those produced by overt displays of parental sexuality in front of children—the kind of family sexualization now being proposed in some cases.

In favor of those concerned with protecting against sexual abuse, on the other hand, one must cite the sheer quantity of sexual victimization. This burden does not fall equally on all children; girls sustain the disproportionate share. The data here suggest one girl in five is a victim during childhood. On top of that, studies have shown that over half of all college women report being victims of sexual aggression during college (Kanin and Parcell, 1977), and the U.S. Justice Department estimates that twenty women per hundred thousand are raped every year. The chances that any given women will encounter sexual victimization in her lifetime are quite high, which would certainly argue in favor of a policy that gives priority to reducing harm before experimenting with new freedoms.

Of course, some have argued that increased sexual openness in the family is the way to reduce victimization as well. In this view, sexual abuse is the result of too much repression. More controls, in an effort to promote the protection of women, will only aggravate the problem.

One finding from the study supports the idea that more repression does lead to more victimization. We know from this study that there is more sexual abuse in lower-class families. We also know that they are much more sexually repressive (Newson and Newson, 1968; Sears *et al.,* 1957). It is possible that the repressive atmosphere in such families leads to the abuse.

On the other hand, much other evidence from this study points to the conclusion that weak rather than tight controls are associated with sexual victimization. For example, victimization is more common when mothers are weak, absent, or sick, possibly because they cannot enforce norms and protect their daughters. It also occurs more often in families with stepfathers, possibly because they and their affiliated kin feel less strongly the sanction of the incest taboo. When sexual abuse occurs in rural areas, where it is apparently more frequent, it may be because the family is isolated from community supervision; or when it occurs in a large family, it may be caused by a similar lack of supervision.

We know well by now that responsible behavior is not produced merely by rigid rules of correct conduct. But we also know that in many contexts, especially where people are not otherwise well integrated into family and community, weakening of norms or social supervision can result in an increase of antisocial behavior. There is some reason to be concerned, on the basis of the findings indicated here, that a weakening of taboos on sexual interaction between adults and children would have that effect in some family environments.

What about the idea that the harm of an adult-child sexual experience is mostly in the societal reaction, that the experience becomes traumatic only because people react to it as being so? This is a point of view that favors de-emphasizing the dangers of sexual relations between family members and encouraging a freer, less self-conscious family atmosphere. What we can contribute, on the basis of the present study, is the assurance that within our own culture these experiences are predominantly negative. In the majority of cases, they are foisted on the children, involve force and coercion at least of a psychological sort, and are reacted to negatively, especially by the girls. In our statistical profiles there is little room for romanticizing these experiences. There is clear evidence that they are noxious and traumatic.

The discomfort may be aggravated by the reaction the child receives from others about the experience. However, our study finds that there is much that is discomforting in the experiences themselves, independent of the reaction of others. In short, the general impression that adult-child sexual experiences are in fact abusive is not just an anachronistic prejudice. It accurately describes the majority of the incidents.

Our conclusion is that priority should be given to the problem of sexual victimization. We must say in all honesty that this was a conclusion we held at the outset of the study and that drew us to the topic in the first place. However, we feel it is a conclusion warranted and advanced by the findings here.

This is not to argue that sexual liberalization of the family is an evil. Rather, if there are culprits to the problem of children's sexual victimization, we suspect they are things like family disorganization, the commercial exploitation of sexuality, sexual inequality, and values that encourage the sexual exploitation of others.

To give priority to the issue of sexual victimization means acting on it directly, teaching children who may be potential victims how to avoid it, and re-emphasizing for the benefit of potential abusers that such behavior is damaging and wrong. It means doing more than merely creating a sexually more open environment and hoping that in the fall-out, children will understand more about sex, and adults will find healthier modes of sexual expression.

There is always the fear that in emphasizing the dangers of sexuality we will reinforce the old puritanical attitudes. This is an unrealistic fear, based on the idea that there are only two postures one can take toward sexuality—permissive or repressive. There is no reason why we cannot raise children who can recognize both the dangers and delights of sexuality, who can be realistic about the possibility of being victimized, yet at the same time have a positive and exploratory outlook.

Appendix A:

COMPARISON OF STUDIES

TABLE A-1. **Mean Age of Victim in Selected Research Reports of Children's Sexual Victimization**

STUDY	GIRLS	BOYS	BOTH
General Surveys			
Finkelhor (1979)	10.2 (122)	11.2 (22)	10.6 (144)
Landis (1956)	10.4 (531)	15.4 (215)	
Gagnon (1965)	9.9 (400)		
Benward [a] (1975)	10.3 (60)		
M =	10.2	15.0	10.6
Studies based on Victims'			
Reports to Public Agencies			
Burgess *et al.* (1977)	8.8 (44)		
Queen's Bench (1976)	8.7 (89)	8.5 (42)	8.6 (131)
Peters (1976)			7.9 (64)
Weiss (1955)	9.9 (73)		
De Francis (1969)			11.6 (250)
M =	9.1	8.5	10.2
Studies Based on Incarcerated			
Offenders			
McCaghy (1967)			9.0 (158)
Gebhard *et al.* (1965)	11.3 (643)	12.8 (291)	
Mohr (1964)	9.4 (33)	12.2 (25)	10.0 (68)
Frisbie (1959)	8.8 (594)	12.4 (271)	
M =	10.1	12.6	9.3

[a] Only sexual experiences with family members.
Source and type of population:
   Landis: Table 2. College students
   Gagnon: Table 4. Adult women
   Benward: Table 10. Female drug abusers
   Burgess *et al.*: p. 237. Visitors to hospital clinic
   Queen's Bench: Table 1. Cases reported to police
   Peters: p. 414. Visitors to pediatric emergency room
   Weiss: Table 4. Psychiatric referrals from prosecutor
   De Francis: p. 56. Cases in files of protection agency
   McCaghy: p. 79. Convicted sex offenders against children
   Mohr: Table I. Court-referred offenders to psychiatrist
   Gebhard: Tables 132, 133, 124. Convicted sex offenders
   Frisbie: cited in Mohr, Table II. Convicted sex offenders.

TABLE A–2. Relationship of Female Victim to Offender in Selected Research Reports of Children's Sexual Victimization

Study	Parent	Other Relative	Friend	Total Known	Total Stranger	N
General Surveys						
Finkelhor	6	37	33	76	24	(120)
Landis	(a)	(a)	(a)	34	65	(531)
Gagnon	2	13	26	42	58	(400)
Benward	31	42	27	(b)	(b)	(60)
Studies Based on Victims' Reports to Public Agencies						
Burgess et al.	56	44	(b)	(b)	(b)	(44)
Queen's Bench [c]	14	9	33	65	45	(89)
Peters [c]	14	18	59	78	22	(64)
De Francis [d]	17	11	37	75	25	(250)
Weiss	33	7	45	85	15	(72)
Studies Based on Offenders						
Mohr	15	6	43	85	15	(33)

Header spanning Parent through Total Stranger: OFFENDERS KNOWN TO CHILD %

(a) Total only known. Not broken down by category.
(b) Incest and near incest cases. No strangers considered.
(c) Columns do not add properly because of cases with multiple offenders.
(d) Males and Females.

Source:
Landis: p. 97
Gagnon: Table 5
Benward: Table 9
Burgess: p. 238
Queen's Bench: Table IV
Peters: p. 416
Weiss: Table 3
De Francis: Table 27
Mohr: Table V.

TABLE A-3. Age of Offender in Selected Research Reports of Children's Sexual Victimization

STUDY	MEDIAN AGE
General Survey	
Finkelhor *(N = 119)*	27.9
Agency Reports	
De Francis *(N = 250)*	31.3
Queen's Bench *(N = 123)*	32.8
Offender Studies	
Mohr *(N = 53)*	35.3
McCaghy *(N = 158)*	37.3

Source:
  De Francis: Table 23
  Queen's Bench: Table VI
  Mohr: Figure 2
  McCaghy: p. 79.

TABLE A-4. Use of Force or Threat of Force in Selected Research Reports of Children's Sexual Victimization

STUDY	FORCE OR THREAT (% OF CASES)
General Survey	
Finkelhor *(N = 119)*	55
Agency Reports	
Queen's Bench (*N = 131*)	44
Peters *(N = 64)*	31
De Francis *(N = 250)*	60
Offender Studies	
McCaghy *(N = 158)*	24

Source:
  Queen's Bench: Table VI
  Peters: p. 48
  De Francis: Table 11
  McCaghy: p. 80.

Appendix B
QUESTIONNAIRE

Dear Student:

We would like to ask you to participate in this study of the family and sexual behavior by filling out this questionnaire.

Some of the questions here are very personal. Because they are personal, social scientists have been reluctant to investigate them in the past. But as you are certainly aware, family life has been undergoing profound changes in recent years, as have people's attitudes toward sex. If social scientists are to help families become healthier environments for living and growing up, if we are to help answer questions about important social issues like teen-age pregnancy, sex education, child abuse and so forth, we need to know more about these personal things.

We hope with this in mind, and the knowledge that *everything you answer here is completely anonymous,* that you will decide to participate.

To help you decide, we want to say a little more about the questionnaire. The highly personal questions here include questions about sexual attitudes and sexual experiences, as well as questions about your family. Some of the information you will be providing here is probably not information you would want others to know about. For one thing, it may be personally embarrassing or painful. For another thing, it may involve people beside yourself, who would not want information divulged. Finally, believe it or not, some of the things you may be reporting in the questionnaire may be against the law. This gives you some idea of how sensitive an area this is. So consider carefully whether you really want to participate.

157

However, we do not want you to take risks that might endanger yourself or others in any way. As a matter of fact, we feel that you are perfectly safe in participating in the study, and we want to tell you the steps we are taking to safeguard your privacy.

First of all, you are under no obligation to participate. It is *not* a course requirement. Much as we would like your co-operation, you should feel free not to fill out a questionnaire. In fact, if at any point while filling out the questionnaire you decide you no longer wish to participate, you may stop wherever you are and fill out no more. Moreover, if there are any particular questions which you want to skip, you may do so.

If you decide not to participate you may do so very discreetly. All questionnaires have a blank cover sheet. If you decide not to fill out any part, just turn in your questionnaire at the end of the period along with everyone else, and no one will be aware that your questionnaire is incomplete.

Secondly, all questionnaires are completely anonymous. Nowhere on the questionnaire do we ask for your name, and we have carefully avoided asking questions that might identify you indirectly. Your questionnaire will be one of over 800 that we will be collecting, so the possibility of anyone identifying your questionnaire is virtually nil. All questionnaires will be guarded by us with the utmost care. No one but the researchers will have access to them.

Thirdly, because of the sensitive nature of the research, it is important that we have your fully informed consent to use your questionnaire. If you choose to participate, make a check in the box below indicating your consent.

Unfortunately, if there are some of you here who are not *at least 18*, and thus still legally minors, we will not be able to use your questionnaire. According to law, minors need to obtain parental consent in order to participate in scientific research of this sort. If you are under 18, we are sorry to exclude you from the research, but unfortunately we have no other choice. So please just turn in a blank questionnaire.

Thank you for your cooperation.

I have read the above and I agree to participate [   ]
I have read the above and decided not to participate [   ]

PART A

1. Your sex (circle one answer number):
   1. Male
   2. Female
2. Your age at last birthday _____
3. Marital status (circle one answer number):
   1. Single
   2. Married
   3. Separated or divorced
   4. Widowed

4. In what religion were you raised?
   1. Roman Catholic
   2. Eastern Orthodox
   3. Episcopalian
   4. Congregationalist
   5. Methodist
   6. Presbyterian
   7. Other Protestant _____
      (please indicate)
   8. Jewish
   9. No religion
   10. Other _____
       (please indicate)

5. What is your predominant ethnic background (circle no more than 2):
   1. Irish
   2. Italian
   3. German
   4. French-Canadian
   5. Polish
   6. Other Eastern European
   7. Black
   8, Spanish
   9. English
   10. Scotch
   11. Other _____
       (please indicate)

6. In the first 12 years of your life, did you live mostly in (pick the one you lived in longest):
   1. a farm
   2. a town of under 5,000

3. a town of between 5,000 and 25,000
4. a town of between 25,000 and 100,000
5. a town of between 100,000 and 500,000
6. a town larger than 500,000

We would like to gather some information about MEMBERS OF YOUR FAMILY.

7. First, about your FATHER
   a. Is he:
      1. Living with your mother
      2. Divorced or separated from her
      3. Widowed
      4. Living apart for some other reason
      5. Deceased
   b. What is (was) his year of birth? (If unsure, put current age or approximate age.) _____
   c. Was there any time before you were 16 when you did not live with him?
      1. Yes   2. No
      If *Yes*, give your age, e.g., 6 to 10
      Age _____ to _____
   i. When you last lived with him, how close did you feel to him?
      1. Very close
      2. Close
      3. Somewhat close
      4. Not close
      5. Distant

8. Did you also have a STEPFATHER?
   1. Yes   2. No (If no, go to no. 9)
   a. Is your stepfather:
      1. Living with your mother
      2. Divorced or separated from her
      3. Widowed from her

4. Living apart for some other reason

5. Deceased

b. What is (was) his year of birth? (If unsure, put current age or approximate age.) _____

c. Was there any time before you were 16 when you did not live with him?

1. Yes   2. No

If Yes, give your age

Age _____ to _____

d. When you last lived with him, how close did you feel to him?

1. Very close

2. Close

3. Somewhat close

4. Not close

5. Distant

9. Now, about your MOTHER

a. Is she:

1. Living with your father

2. Divorced or separated from him

3. Widowed

4. Living apart for some other reason

5. Deceased

b. What is (was) her year of birth? (If unsure, put current age or approximate age.) _____

c. Was there any time before you were 16 when you did not live with her?

1. Yes   2. No

If Yes, give your age, e.g., 6 to 10

Age _____ to _____

d. When you last lived with her, how close did you feel to her?

1. Very close

2. Close

3. Somewhat close

4. Not close

5. Distant

10. Did you also have a STEPMOTHER?

1. Yes   2. No   If no, go to (no. 11)

a. Is your stepmother:

1. Living with your father

2. Divorced or separated from him

3. Widowed from him

4. Living apart for some other reason

5. Deceased

b. What is (was) her year of birth? (If unsure, put current age or approximate age.) _____

c. Was there any time before you were 16 when you did not live with her?

1. Yes   2. No

If Yes, give your age

Age _____ to _____

d. When you last lived with her, how close did you feel to her?

1. Very close

2. Close

3. Somewhat close

4. Not close

5. Distant

Now, about your BROTHERS (If none, go to no. 15)

Start with Oldest Brother, and work down to Youngest.

11. a. Oldest brother, is he:

1. A natural brother

2. A stepbrother (no parents in common)

3. A half-brother (one parent in common)

4. An adopted brother

b. What is his year of birth? ____

c. Was there any time before you were 16 when you did not live with him?

1. Yes   2. No

If *Yes,* give your age, e.g., 6 to 10

Age _____ to _____

d. When you last lived with him how close did you feel toward him?
   1. Very close
   2. Close
   3. Somewhat close
   4. Not close
   5. Distant

12. Next BROTHER (If none, go to no. 15)
   a. Is he:
      1. A natural brother
      2. A step brother
      3. A half-brother
      4. An adopted brother
   b. What is his year of birth? ____
   c. Was there any time before you were 16 when you did not live with him?
      1. Yes   2. No

   If *Yes,* give your age

   Age _____ to _____

   d. When you last lived with him how close did you feel toward him?
      1. Very close
      2. Close
      3. Somewhat close
      4. Not close
      5. Distant

13. Next BROTHER (If none, go to no. 15)
   a. Is he:
      1. A natural brother
      2. A stepbrother
      3. A half-brother
      4. An adopted brother
   b. What is his year of birth? ____
   c. Was there any time before you were 16 when you did not live with him?
      1. Yes   2. No

If *Yes,* give your age

Age _____ to _____

d. When you last lived with him, how close did you feel toward him?
   1. Very close
   2. Close
   3. Somewhat close
   4. Not close
   5. Distant

14. Next BROTHER (If none, go to no. 15)
   a. Is he:
      1. A natural brother
      2. A stepbrother
      3. A half-brother
      4. An adopted brother
   b. What is his year of birth? ____
   c. Was there any time before you were 16 when you did not live with him?

   If *Yes,* give your age

   Age _____ to _____

   d. When you last lived with him, how close did you feel toward him?
      1. Very close
      2. Close
      3. Somewhat close
      4. Not close
      5. Distant

Now about your SISTERS (If none, go to no. 19)

Start with Oldest Sister, and work down to the Youngest.

15. a. Oldest sister, is she:
      1. A natural sister
      2. A stepsister (no parents in common)
      3. A half-sister (one parent in common)
      4. An adopted sister
   b. What is her year of birth? ____

c. Was there any time before you were 16 when did you not live with her?

1. Yes   2. No

If *Yes*, give your age, e.g., 6 to 10

Age _____ to _____

d. When you last lived with her, how close did you feel toward her?
1. Very close
2. Close
3. Somewhat close
4. Not close
5. Distant

16. Next SISTER (If none, go to no. 19)
a. Is she:
1. A natural sister
2. A stepsister
3. A half-sister
4. An adopted sister
b. What is her year of birth? ____
c. Was there any time before you were 16 when you did not live with her?
1. Yes   2. No

If *Yes*, give your age.

Age _____ to _____

d. When you last lived with her, how close did you feel toward her?
1. Very close
2. Close
3. Somewhat close
4. Not close
5. Distant

17. Next SISTER (If none, go to no. 19)
a. Is she:
1. A natural sister
2. A stepsister
3. A half-sister
4. An adopted sister
b. What is her year of birth? ____

c. Was there any time before you were 16 when you did not live with her?

1. Yes   2. No

If *Yes*, give your age.

Age _____ to _____

d. When you last lived with her, how close did you feel toward her?
1. Very close
2. Close
3. Somewhat close
4. Not close
5. Distant

18. Next SISTER (If none, go to no. 19)
a. Is she:
1. A natural sister
2. A stepsister
3. A half-sister
4. An adopted sister
b. What is her year of birth? ____
c. Was there any time before you were 16 when you did not live with her?
1. Yes   2. No

If *Yes*, give your age.

Age _____ to _____

d. When you last lived with her, how close did you feel toward her?
1. Very close
2. Close
3. Somewhat close
4. Not close
5. Distant

19. Which of these family members were you living with at age 12?

a. Father	g. 3rd brother
b. Stepfather	h. 4th brother
c. Mother	i. 1st sister
d. Stepmother	j. 2nd sister
e. 1st brother	k. 3rd sister
f. 2nd brother	l. 4th sister

PART B

The rest of the questionnaire applies to your family when you were *age* 12. All questions should be answered with reference to the members of your family when you were *age 12* (unless otherwise indicated). That means when a question asks about your "father," it means the father you lived with when you were 12.

If you did not live with one or both parents when you were 12, answer for that parent at some earlier age when you *were* living with him or her.

20. What were your parents' occupations when you were 12?

Father	Mother	
1	1	Semiskilled or unskilled worker (factory worker, hospital aide, truck driver, etc.)
2	2	Skilled worker or foreman (machinist, carpenter, cook)
3	3	Farmer (owner-operator or renter)
4	4	Clerical or sales (but not manager)
5	5	Proprietor, except farm (owner of a business)
6	6	Professional (architect, teacher, nurse) or managerial position (department head, store manager)
0	0	No occupation outside home
X	X	Don't know

21. When you were 12, which of the following came closest to your parents *annual income before taxes?*

Father	Mother	
0	0	Not employed
1	1	Less than $4,000
2	2	$4,000 to $5,999
3	3	$6,000 to $7,999
4	4	$8,000 to $9,999
5	5	$10,000 to $11,999
6	6	$12,000 to $14,999
7	7	$15,000 to $19,999
8	8	$20,000 to $29,999
9	9	$30,000 and over
X	X	Don't know

22. What was the highest level of education attained by your parents?

Father	Mother	
1	1	Some grade school
2	2	Completed grade school
3	3	Some high school
4	4	Completed high school
5	5	High school and some other training but not college
6	6	Some college
7	7	Completed college
8	8	Some graduate work
9	9	Graduate degree (M.D., M.A.)

23. How many of your grandparents were born in the United States?
    1. 1
    2. 2
    3. 3
    4. 4
    0. None

24. Did either of your grandparents grow up on a farm?
    1. mother
    2. father
    3. both
    4. neither

25. How many bedrooms were there in the house your family lived in when you were 12?

    _____

26. How many people were living in the house at the time?

    _____

27. At age 12, did you share a bedroom with:
    1. No one, had own bedroom
    2. One brother
    3. More than one brother
    4. One sister
    5. More than one sister
    6. One or more brothers and sisters
    7. One or both parents
    8. Someone else
    9. Other combination _____
           (please indicate)

28. Did any other people live with you for *more than a year* while you were growing up, besides mother, father, sisters and brothers? (Circle as many as apply.)
    A. Grandfather
    B. Grandmother
    C. Uncle
    D. Aunt
    E. Other relative
    F. Other nonrelative (e.g., boarder, housekeeper, etc.)

29. When you were 12, did you have:
    1. Many good friends
    2. A few good friends
    3. One or two good friends
    4. No good friends

30. Answer the following questions about the set of parents you had *when you were 12*.

How true was this of your Mother and Father?

	Father					Mother				
	____ No father					____ No mother				
	Never	Rarely	Sometimes	Often	Very Often	Never	Rarely	Sometimes	Often	Very Often
A. Influenced other people or took charge of things	1	2	3	4	5	1	2	3	4	5
B. Was ambitious, worked hard	1	2	3	4	5	1	2	3	4	5
C. Lacked energy	1	2	3	4	5	1	2	3	4	5
D. Had problems with relatives	1	2	3	4	5	1	2	3	4	5
E. Was tense, nervous, worried	1	2	3	4	5	1	2	3	4	5
F. Was ill	1	2	3	4	5	1	2	3	4	5
G. Drank heavily	1	2	3	4	5	1	2	3	4	5
H. Complained about finances	1	2	3	4	5	1	2	3	4	5
I. Kissed you	1	2	3	4	5	1	2	3	4	5
J. Hugged you	1	2	3	4	5	1	2	3	4	5
K. Put you on his/her lap	1	2	3	4	5	1	2	3	4	5
L. Roughhoused or played tickling games with you	1	2	3	4	5	1	2	3	4	5

31. When you were 12 how happy would you say your parents' marriage was?
    1. Unhappy
    2. Not very happy
    3. Somewhat happy
    4. Happy
    5. Very happy
    X. Not applicable. Only one parent

32. How often do you remember your parents:

Kissing	Hugging	Holding Hands	
1	1	1	Never
2	2	2	Rarely
3	3	3	Sometimes
4	4	4	Often
5	5	5	Very often
X	X	X	Not applicable

33. Did you *ever* see or hear your parents in the act of sexual intercourse?
    1. Yes   2. No

34. If you had to make a guess, how often would you estimate that your parents had sexual intercourse when you were 12. (You are not expected to know; just make a guess.)

   0.   Never or less than 1 time per year
   1.   1 to 6 times per year
   2.   1 time per month
   3.   2 or 3 times per month
   4.   1 time per week
   5.   2 times per week
   6.   3 or 4 times per week
   7.   More than 4 times per week
   X.   NA. Only one parent

35. Would your Father and Mother have agreed or disagreed with the following statements? (Circle number from 1 to 4 to indicate degree of Agreement or Disagreement.)

	Father				Mother			
	Agree			Disagree	Agree			Disagree
(_____ No Father) (_____ No Mother)	—	—	—	—	—	—	—	—
A. Children should never be allowed to talk back to their parents or they will lose respect for them.	1	2	3	4	1	2	3	4
B. In making family decisions, parents ought to take children's opinions into account.	1	2	3	4	1	2	3	4
C. Women should not be placed in positions of authority over men.	1	2	3	4	1	2	3	4

36. Every family has different, sometimes unspoken, rules about personal contact among family members. Think about your family when you were twelve. Who would you do these things with?

Answer *yes* or *no* to each question in the case of (a) your mother, (b) your father, (c) the sister closest in age to you, and (d) the brother closest in age to you.

	Mother (__ None)		Father (__ None)		Sister closest in age (__ None)		Brother closest in age (__ None)	
	Yes	No	Yes	No	Yes	No	Yes	No
If you were going on a trip, who would you								
a. Hug goodbye	1	0	1	0	1	0	1	0
b. Kiss goodbye	1	0	1	0	1	0	1	0
c. Kiss on the lips goodbye	1	0	1	0	1	0	1	0

	Yes	No	Yes	No	Yes	No	Yes	No

In your house when you were getting up in the morning, who could

	Yes	No	Yes	No	Yes	No	Yes	No
d. See you in your underwear without embarrassing you —	1	0	1	0	1	0	1	0
e. See you naked without embarrassing you ————	1	0	1	0	1	0	1	0
f. Go into the bathroom if you are already there without embarrassing you ————	1	0	1	0	1	0	1	0
g. Who could you tell a dirty joke to ————	1	0	1	0	1	0	1	0
h. Who could you tell about a sexual experience you had————	1	0	1	0	1	0	1	0
i. If you were in your bedroom alone who could enter without knocking ————	1	0	1	0	1	0	1	0

37. The next series of question are about *how* and *when* you learned about sex. How old were you when you *first* learned about the following things? Where did you learn them from? If you can't remember exactly how old, make an approximate guess. In case of several sources of learning, *circle all that apply.*

Source: (Code for answers below)

1. Mother
2. Father
3. Brother
4. Sister
5. Friend (same sex)

6. Friend (opposite sex)
7. Sex-education course
8. Other adult
9. Book or magazine
10. Self-discovery
11. Other or don't know

	Age you first learned	Source you learned it from
a. That men and women have different sexual organs ————	_____	1 2 3 4 5 6 7 8 9 10 11
b. That babies result from sexual intercourse ————	_____	1 2 3 4 5 6 7 8 9 10 11
c. That your parents engaged in sexual intercourse ————	_____	1 2 3 4 5 6 7 8 9 10 11
d. How to obtain and use contraceptives ————	_____	1 2 3 4 5 6 7 8 9 10 11
e. How to cope with menstruation (for women) ————	_____	1 2 3 4 5 6 7 8 9 10 11
f. How to arouse a sexual partner ————	_____	1 2 3 4 5 6 7 8 9 10 11
g. How to arouse yourself ————	_____	1 2 3 4 5 6 7 8 9 10 11

38. In response to each of the following statements, please answer the question in each of the five columns:

	How do you feel about this?		Did your Mother ever tell you this?		How do you think she felt about this idea?		Did your Father ever tell you this?		How do you think he felt about this idea?	
	Agree	*Disagree*	*Yes*	*No*	*Agree*	*Disagree*	*Yes*	*No*	*Agree*	*Disagree*
a. Men often try to take advantage of women sexually —	1 2	3 4	1	0	1 2	3 4	1	0	1 2	3 4
b. Masturbation is unhealthy ————	1 2	3 4	1	0	1 2	3 4	1	0	1 2	3 4
c. Sexual relations between two persons of the same sex are abnormal ————	1 2	3 4	1	0	1 2	3 4	1	0	1 2	3 4
d. Sex games among small children are unhealthy ————	1 2	3 4	1	0	1 2	3 4	1	0	1 2	3 4
e. Sexual relations between brothers and sisters are unhealthy ————	1 2	3 4	1	0	1 2	3 4	1	0	1 2	3 4
f. Sexual relations between children and their parents are unhealthy ——	1 2	3 4	1	0	1 2	3 4	1	0	1 2	3 4

PART C

It is now generally realized that most people have sexual experiences as children and while they are still growing up. Some of these are with friends and playmates, and some with relatives and family members. Some are very upsetting and painful, and some are not. Some influence people's later lives and sexual experiences, and some are practically forgotten. Although these are often important events, very little is actually known about them.

We would like you to try to remember the sexual experiences you had while growing up. By "sexual," we mean a broad range of things, anything from playing "doctor" to sexual intercourse—in fact, anything that might have seemed "sexual" to you.

39. Did you have any of the following experiences *before the age of 12* (6th grade) (circle any that apply)?
    a. An invitation or request to do something sexual.
    b. Kissing and hugging in a sexual way.
    c. Another person showing his/her sex organs to you.
    d. You showing your sex organs to another person.
    e. Another person fondling you in a sexual way.
    f. You fondling another person in a sexual way.
    g. Another person touching your sex organs.
    h. You touching another person's sex organs.
    i. Intercourse, but without attempting penetration.
    j. Intercourse.
    k. Other:

    _____
    _____
    _____
    _____

Choose three sexual experiences—or however many up to three—that you had *before* the age of 12 *with other children*, including friends, strangers, brothers, sisters, and cousins. Pick the three most important and answer the following questions about them. Take one experience and answer all the questions on the 2 pages that pertain to it, and then return to answer the same questions about experience # 2 and # 3.

No such experience [   ] Go to page 172
With regard to the
first experience

	Experience #1	Experience #2	Experience #3
40. About how old were you at the time —	_____	_____	_____
41. Approximate age of the other person(s) ———	_____	_____	_____
42. Sex of the other person(s): 1. for male 2. for female	1 2	1 2	1 2

43. Relationship to other person(s)

	#1	#2	#3
Stranger	1	1	1
Person you knew, but not friend	2	2	2
Friend	3	3	3
Niece or nephew	4	4	4
Cousin	5	5	5
Brother	6	6	6
Sister	7	7	7

44. What happened? (Circle 1 for Yes or 0 for No
    for each line.)

	Yes No	Yes No	Yes No
a. An invitation or request to do something sexual--	1 0	1 0	1 0
b. Kissing and hugging in a sexual way -------------	1 0	1 0	1 0
c. Other person showing his/her sex organs to you---	1 0	1 0	1 0
d. You showing your sex organs to other person --	1 0	1 0	1 0
e. Other person fondling you in a sexual way	1 0	1 0	1 0
f. You fondling other person in a sexual way ---	1 0	1 0	1 0
g. Other person touching your sex organs --------	1 0	1 0	1 0
h. You touching other person's sex organs --------	1 0	1 0	1 0
i. Intercourse, but without attempting penetration ---	1 0	1 0	1 0
j. Intercourse --- ----	1 0	1 0	1 0

k. Other: please mention   #1 _____

                             #2 _____

                                #3 _____

	You Other	You Other	You Other
45. Who started this? (Circle 1 for you or 2 for Other Person.)	1 2	1 2	1 2
46. Did other person(s) threaten or force you? 1. Yes	1	1	1
2. A little	2	2	2
3. No	3	3	3
47. Did you threaten or force other person(s)? 1. Yes	1	1	1
2. A little	2	2	2
3. No	3	3	3
48. About how many times did you have a sexual experience with this person? ----------------------------------	_____	_____	_____
49. Over how long a time did this go on? (Give number of days, months, years.) ----------------------------	_____	_____	_____

50. Which of these would best
describe your reaction at the
time of the experience?
1. Fear 2. Shock 3. Surprise
4. Interest 5. Pleasure   1 2 3 4 5   1 2 3 4 5   1 2 3 4 5

51. Who did you tell about this experience, at the time?
   1. No one --- 1   1   1
     2. Mother -- 2   2   2
      3. Father -- 3   3   3
       4. Other adult ------------------------------------- 4   4   4
        5. Brother/Sister ------------------------------- 5   5   5
        6. Friend --- 6   6   6

52. If mother, how did she react? (IF YOU DID NOT TELL YOUR
MOTHER, HOW DO YOU THINK SHE WOULD HAVE REACTED?)
   a. Angry   1. Very 2. Mildly
                  3. A little 4. Not at all   1 2 3 4   1 2 3 4
   b. Supportive 1. Very 2. Mildly
                  3. A little 4. Not at all   1 2 3 4   1 2 3 4

53. If father, how did he react? (IF YOU DID NOT TELL YOUR
FATHER, HOW DO YOU THINK HE WOULD HAVE REACTED?)
   a. Angry   1. Very 2. Mildly
                  3. A little 4. Not at all   1 2 3 4   1 2 3 4
   b. Supportive 1. Very 2. Mildly
                  3. A little 4. Not at all   1 2 3 4   1 2 3 4

54. In retrospect, would you say this experience was:
   1. Positive --------------------------------------- 1   1   1
     2. Mostly positive --------------------------- 2   2   2
      3. Neutral --- 3   3   3
       4. Mostly negative --------------------------- 4   4   4
       5. Negative -- 5   5   5

Now go back to page 169
and answer the questions
about Experience #2

If no more experiences
go to next page

Now go back to page 169
and answer the questions
about experience #3

If no more experiences
go to next page

Now we want to ask you to think of three sexual experiences — or however many up to three — that you had *before* the age of 12 *with an adult* (a person over 16) including strangers, friends, or family members like cousins, aunts, uncles, brothers, sisters, mother, or father. Pick the three most important to you and answer the following questions.

No such experience [   ] Go to page 175

With regard to the first experience	*Experience #1*	*Experience #2*	*Experience #3*
55. About how old were you at the time?	_____	_____	_____
56. About how old was the other person?	_____	_____	_____
57. Was the other person: Circle 1 for male 2 for female	1 2	1 2	1 2
58. Was the other person:			
a stranger ------------------------------------	1	1	1
a person you knew, but not a friend	2	2	2
a friend of yours ---------------------------	3	3	3
a friend of your parents -----------------	4	4	4
a cousin -------------------------------------	5	5	5
an uncle or aunt ---------------------------	6	6	6
a grandparent ------------------------------	7	7	7
a brother ------------------------------------	8	8	8
a sister ---------------------------------------	9	9	9
a father --------------------------------------	10	10	10
a stepfather --------------------------------	11	11	11
a mother ------------------------------------	12	12	12
a stepmother -------------------------------	13	13	13
59. What happened? (Circle 1 for Yes or 0 for No.)	Yes No	Yes No	Yes No
a. An invitation or request to do something sexual ------	1 0	1 0	1 0
b. Kissing and hugging in a sexual way --------------------	1 0	1 0	1 0
c. Other person showing his/her sex organs to you -----	1 0	1 0	1 0
d. You showing your sex organs to other person	1 0	1 0	1 0
e. Other person fondling you in a sexual way -------------	1 0	1 0	1 0

f. You fondling other person
in a sexual way --------------   1   0   1   0   1   0

g. Other person touching
your sex organs --------------   1   0   1   0   1   0

h. You touching other
person's sex organs --------   1   0   1   0   1   0

i. Intercourse, but without
attempting penetration --   1   0   1   0   1   0

j. Intercourse ------------------------   1   0   1   0   1   0

k. Other: please mention   #1 _____

#2 _____

#3 _____

60. Who started this? 1. You
2. Other person   1   2   1   2   1   2

61. Did other person threaten
or force you?   1. Yes   2. A little
3. No   1 2 3   1 2 3   1 2 3

62. Did you threaten or force
other person?   1. Yes   2. A little
3. No   1 2 3   1 2 3   1 2 3

63a. Had other person been drinking?
1. Yes   0. No   1   0   1   0   1   0

63b. Had you been drinking?
1. Yes   0. No   1   0   1   0   1   0

64. About how many times did
you have a sexual experience
with this person? ------------------   _____ _____ _____

65. Over how long a time did
this go on? (Indicate number
of days, months, years.) --------   _____ _____ _____

66. Which of these would best describe
your reaction at the time of the
experience?
1. Fear   2. Shock   3. Surprise
4. Interest   5. Pleasure   1 2 3 4 5   1 2 3 4 5   1 2 3 4 5

67. Who did you tell about this
    experience, if anyone?
    1. No one --   1   1   1
    2. Mother -----------------------------------   2   2   2
    3. Father ------------------------------------   3   3   3
    4. Other adult ----------------------------   4   4   4
    5. Brother/sister ------------------------   5   5   5
    6. Friend --------------------------------------   6   6   6

68. If mother, how did she react? (IF YOU
    DID NOT TELL YOUR MOTHER, HOW DO YOU
    THINK SHE WOULD HAVE REACTED?)
    a. Angry   1. Very   2. Mildly
                     3. A little
                     4. Not at all   1 2 3 4   1 2 3 4   1 2 3 4
    b. Supportive   1. Very   2. Mildly
                     3. A little
                     4. Not at all   1 2 3 4   1 2 3 4   1 2 3 4

69. If father, how did he react? (IF YOU DID
    NOT TELL YOUR FATHER, HOW DO YOU THINK
    HE WOULD HAVE REACTED?)
    a. Angry   1. Very   2. Mildly
                     3. A little
                     4. Not at all   1 2 3 4   1 2 3 4   1 2 3 4
    b. Supportive   1. Very   2. Mildly
                     3. A little
                     4. Not at all   1 2 3 4   1 2 3 4   1 2 3 4

70. In retrospect, would you say this
    experience was
    1. Positive   2. Mostly positive
    3. Neutral   4. Mostly negative
    5. Negative   1 2 3 4 5   1 2 3 4 5   1 2 3 4 5

Now go back to page 172
and answer the questions
about Experience #2

If no more experiences
go to next page

Now go back to page 172
and answer the questions
about experience #3

If no more experiences
go to next page

Now we would like you to think of sexual experiences you had *after the age of twelve with a family member or relative*, including cousins, uncles, aunts, brothers, sisters, grandparents, mother or father, or a guardian or close friend of a parent. (If this relationship was described in a previous section, do not repeat it.) Pick the three most important to you and answer the following questions.

No such experience [   ] Go to page 177

With regard to the first experience	*Experience #1*	*Experience #2*	*Experience #3*
71. About how old were you at the time?			
72. About how old was the other person?			
73. Was the other person: Circle 1 for male or 2 for female	1 2	1 2	1 2

74. Was the other person:

	#1	#2	#3
a cousin --------------------------------- 1		1	1
an aunt or uncle ---------------------- 2		2	2
a grandparent --------------------------- 3		3	3
a brother or sister ---------------------- 4		4	4
a parent ----------------------------------- 5		5	5
a step-parent ----------------------------- 6		6	6
a guardian --------------------------------- 7		7	7
a close friend of a parent ---------------- 8		8	8

75. What happened? (Circle 1 for Yes or 0 for No for each.)

	Yes No	Yes No	Yes No
a. An invitation or request to do something sexual ------	1 0	1 0	1 0
b. Kissing and hugging in a sexual way ---------------------	1 0	1 0	1 0
c. Other person showing his/ her sex organs to you -----	1 0	1 0	1 0
d. You showing your sex organs to other person --	1 0	1 0	1 0
e. Other person fondling you in a sexual way --------------	1 0	1 0	1 0
f. You fondling other person in a sexual way --------------	1 0	1 0	1 0
g. Other person touching your sex organs --------------	1 0	1 0	1 0

	Yes	No	Yes	No	Yes	No
h. You touching other person's sex organs -------	1	0	1	0	1	0
i. Intercourse, but without attempting penetration	1	0	1	0	1	0
j. Intercourse -----------------------	1	0	1	0	1	0

k. Other: please mention #1 _____

#2 _____

#3 _____

76. Who started this?   1. You.
    2. Other person   1   2   1   2   1   2

77. Did other person threaten or force
    you?   1. Yes 2. A little 3. No   1   2   3   1   2   3   1   2   3

78. Did you threaten or force other
    person?   1. Yes 2. A little
    3. No   1   2   3   1   2   3   1   2   3

79a. Had other person been drinking?
    1. Yes   0. No   1   0   1   0   1   0

79b. Had you been drinking?
    1. Yes   0. No   1   0   1   0   1   0

80. About how many times did you
    have a sexual experience with
    this person? ----------------   _____   _____   _____

81. Over how long a time did this go
    on? (Indicate number of days,
    months, years.) -----------------   _____   _____   _____

82. Which of these would best describe
    your reaction at the time of the
    experience?
    1. Fear 2. Shock 3. Surprise
    4. Interest 5. Pleasure   1 2 3 4 5   1 2 3 4 5   1 2 3 4 5

83. Who did you tell about this experience,
    if anyone?

1. No one -----------------------------	1	1	1
2. Mother -----------------------------	2	2	2
3. Father ------------------------------	3	3	3
4. Other adult -----------------------	4	4	4
5. Brother/sister ---------------------	5	5	5
6. Friend -------------------------------	6	6	6

84. If mother, how did she react? (IF
    YOU DID NOT TELL YOUR MOTHER, HOW
    DO YOU THINK SHE WOULD HAVE REACTED?)

a. Angry	1. Very 2. Mildly 3. A little 4. Not at all	1 2 3 4	1 2 3 4	1 2 3 4
b. Supportive	1. Very 2. Mildly 3. A little 4. Not at all	1 2 3 4	1 2 3 4	1 2 3 4

85. If father, how did he react? (IF
    YOU DID NOT TELL YOUR FATHER, HOW
    DO YOU THINK HE WOULD HAVE REACTED?)

a. Angry	1. Very 2. Mildly 3. A little 4. Not at all	1 2 3 4	1 2 3 4	1 2 3 4
b. Supportive	1. Very 2. Mildly 3. A little 4. Not at all	1 2 3 4	1 2 3 4	1 2 3 4

86. In retrospect, would you say this
    experience was

1. Positive   2. Mostly positive
3. Neutral   4. Mostly negative
5. Negative   1 2 3 4 5   1 2 3 4 5   1 2 3 4 5

Now go back to page 175
and answer the questions
about Experience #2

If no more experiences
go to next page

Now go back to page 175
and answer the questions
about Experience #3

If no more experiences
go to next page

Finally, we would like you to think of any sexual experience that occurred to you *after the age of 12*, which you did not consent to. That is, a sexual experience which was forced on you, or done against your will, or which you didn't want to happen. (Once again, do not repeat describing a relationship you described earlier.) Pick the three most important and answer the following questions:

No such experience [　] Go to Page 180

With regard to the first experience	Experience #1	Experience #2	Experience #3
87. About how old were you at the time --	_____	_____	_____

88. About how old was the other
    person ----------------------------------   _____   _____   _____

89. Was the other Person:
    Circle 1 for male or
        2 for female   1   2   1   2   1   2

90. Was the other person:
    a stranger ------------------------------ 1   1   1
    a friend of yours ---------------------- 2   2   2
    a friend of your parents -------------- 3   3   3
    a cousin -------------------------------- 4   4   4
    an aunt or uncle ---------------------- 5   5   5
    a brother or sister -------------------- 6   6   6
    a parent -------------------------------- 7   7   7
    a step-parent -------------------------- 8   8   8
    a guardian ------------------------------ 9   9   9

91. What happened? (Circle 1 for Yes or 0 for No for each.)

	Yes	No	Yes	No	Yes	No
a. An invitation or request to do something sexual ------	1	0	1	0	1	0
b. Kissing and hugging in a sexual way ---------------------	1	0	1	0	1	0
c. Other person showing his/her sex organs to you -----	1	0	1	0	1	0
d. You showing your sex organs to other person ---	1	0	1	0	1	0
e. Other person fondling you in a sexual way -------------	1	0	1	0	1	0
f. You fondling other person in a sexual way -------------	1	0	1	0	1	0
g. Other person touching your sex organs -------------	1	0	1	0	1	0
h. You touching other person's sex organs ---------	1	0	1	0	1	0
i. Intercourse, but without attempting penetration --	1	0	1	0	1	0
j. Intercourse ------------------------	1	0	1	0	1	0
k. Other: please mention #1						

#2 _____

#3 _____

92. Who started this? 1. You
                       2. Other person   1   2   1   2   1   2

93. Did other person threaten or force
you? 1. Yes 2. A little 3. No   1 2 3   1 2 3   1 2 3

94. Did you threaten or force other
person? 1. Yes 2. A little 3. No   1 2 3   1 2 3   1 2 3

95a. Had other person been drinking?
1. Yes 0. No   1   0   1   0   1   0

95b. Had you been drinking?
1. Yes 2. No   1   0   1   0   1   0

96. About how many times did you
have a sexual experience with
this person? ------------------------   _____   _____   _____

97. Over how long a time did this go on?
(Indicate number of days, months,
years.) -------------------------------   _____   _____   _____

98. Which of these would best describe
your reaction at the time of the
experience? --------------------------
1. Fear   2. Shock   3. Surprise
4. Interest   5. Pleasure   1 2 3 4 5   1 2 3 4 5   1 2 3 4 5

99. Who did you tell about this experience,
if anyone?
1. No one --------------------------------   1   1   1
2. Mother --------------------------------   2   2   2
3. Father ---------------------------------   3   3   3
4. Other adult ---------------------------   4   4   4
5. Brother/Sister ------------------------   5   5   5
6. Friend ----------------------------------   6   6   6

100. If mother, how did she react?
(IF YOU DID NOT TELL YOUR MOTHER,
HOW DO YOU THINK SHE WOULD
HAVE REACTED?)
a. Angry   1. Very   2. Mildly
3. A little
4. Not at all   1 2 3 4   1 2 3 4   1 2 3 4
b. Supportive 1. Very   2. Mildly
3. A little
4. Not at all   1 2 3 4   1 2 3 4   1 2 3 4

101. If father, how did he react? (IF
YOU DID NOT TELL YOUR FATHER, HOW DO
YOU THINK HE WOULD HAVE REACTED?)

    a. Angry   1. Very 2. Mildly
                    3. A little
                    4. Not at all   1 2 3 4   1 2 3 4   1 2 3 4

    b. Supportive 1. Very 2. Mildly
                    3. A little
                    4. Not at all   1 2 3 4   1 2 3 4   1 2 3 4

102. In retrospect, would you say this experience was
    1. Positive 2. Mostly positive
    3. Neutral 4. Mostly negative
    5. Negative   1 2 3 4 5   1 2 3 4 5   1 2 3 4 5

Now go back to page 177
and answer the questions
about Experience #2

Now go back to page 177
and answer the questions
about Experience #3

If no more experiences
go to next page

If no more experiences
go to next page

PART D

103. Everyone gets into conflicts with other people and sometimes these lead to physical blows such as *hitting really hard, kicking, punching, stabbing, throwing someone down,* etc. The following questions ask about how often these things happened to you, and how often you saw them happen to others. Try to remember these events for a year *when you were around 12.*

    0 = Never
    1 = Once
    2 = Twice
    3 = 3-5 times
    4 = 6-10 times
    5 = 11-20 times

During that ONE YEAR: 6 = More than 20 times
    X = No such person in family

    a. One of my brothers or sisters did this to me   0 1 2 3 4 5 6 X
    b. A brother or sister did to another brother or sister   0 1 2 3 4 5 6 X
    c. I did to a brother or sister   0 1 2 3 4 5 6 X
    d. My father did to me   0 1 2 3 4 5 6 X
    e. My father did to a brother or sister   0 1 2 3 4 5 6 X
    f. My mother did to me   0 1 2 3 4 5 6 X
    g. My mother did to a brother or sister   0 1 2 3 4 5 6 X
    h. Father did to mother   0 1 2 3 4 5 6 X
    i. Mother did to father   0 1 2 3 4 5 6 X

104. When you were *12 years old,* how often would your Mother or Father spank you?

Mother	Father	
1	1	Never
2	2	Once or twice
3	3	A few times each year
4	4	Once a month
5	5	Every week
6	6	More often than once a week
X	X	No such parent

105. Were you ever punished, scolded, or warned about any of the following by your Mother or Father?

(Circle only highest number that applies.) 3 = punished
2 = scolded
1 = warned about
0 = none of the above

Mother	Father	
3 2 1 0	3 2 1 0	Touching your sex organs
3 2 1 0	3 2 1 0	Not having clothes on
3 2 1 0	3 2 1 0	Playing sex games with other children
3 2 1 0	3 2 1 0	Saying dirty words
3 2 1 0	3 2 1 0	Asking questions about sex
3 2 1 0	3 2 1 0	Doing something sexual on a date
3 2 1 0	3 2 1 0	Looking at sexual pictures or books
3 2 1 0	3 2 1 0	Masturbating
X	X	No such parent

106. How old were you when the following things first happened to you? If you can't remember exactly give approximate age. (Write age in space. If this never happened leave blank.)

Age
a. _____ started going out on dates.
b. _____ (Men) first ejaculated.
c. _____ (Women) first menstruated.
d. _____ first had sexual intercourse.
e. _____ first sexual experience with someone of the same sex after the age of 12.

107. Within the recent past, how often have you engaged in sexual intercourse with a person of the opposite sex?

0. Not at all in last year
1. Once or twice in last year, but not in last month
2. More than twice in last year, but not in last month
3. Once in last month
4. Twice in last month
5. 3 times in last month

6. 4 times in last month
7. 5 to 10 times in last month
8. 10 to twenty times in last month
9. More than 20 times in last month

108. The last time you had intercourse, did you or your partner use any kind of contraceptive device or method for avoiding pregnancy?
1. Yes   2. No   3. Don't know   4. NA

109. Within the last month, how often have you "made out" (b through h on page 11) with a person of the opposite sex?

0. Not at all
1. Once or twice
2. 3–4 times
3. 5–10 times
4. more than 10 times

110. In the *last year*, how many sexual experiences have you had with someone of your *own sex*? (For more detail on what is included as "sexual experiences," see page 169.)

0. None
1. 1–2
2. 3–5
3. 5–10
4. 11 or more

111. Below are some descriptions of attitudes about sex. Indicate on the right whether you agree or disagree with this attitude.

1 = Agree
2 = Agree somewhat
3 = Disagree somewhat
4 = Disagree

a. I find I spend too much time thinking about sex ————————— 1 2 3 4
b. I often find myself in awkard sexual situations ———————— 1 2 3 4
c. I really like my body ——————————————————————— 1 2 3 4
d. If I'm sexually interested in someone, I usually take the initiative to do something about it ——————————————— 1 2 3 4
e. After sexual experiences, I often feel dissatisfied ——————— 1 2 3 4
f. Someone my age should be having more sex than I am ———— 1 2 3 4

112. We would like to know how strongly you disapprove of the items listed below.

One item ("wife-beating") has arbitrarily been assigned a score of 100. Please rate each item according to its seriousness compared to wife-beating. If an item seems less serious than "wife-beating," give it a number less than 100. If it seems more serious than wife-beating, give it a number higher than 100. You may use any whole numbers greater than 0.

Do not give any 2 items the same rating. Even if you think they are about equally bad, give them slightly different ratings.

_____ Premeditated murder

_____ Sexual intercourse between a father and his teenage daughter

_____ Adultery

_____ Rape

_____ Sexual intercourse between a teenage brother and sister

_____ Premarital intercourse

_____ Sexual intercourse between a mother and her teenage son

__**100**__ Wife-beating

_____ Sexual intercourse between an uncle and his teenage niece

_____ Beating up someone

113. Tom and Janice Lawrence are a couple in their early twenties. How often would you guess that a couple like that have sexual intercourse?
    0. Never or less than 1 time per year
    1. 1 to 6 times per year
    2. 1 time per month
    3. 2 or 3 times per month
    4. 1 time per week
    5. 2 times per week
    6. 3 or 4 times per week
    7. More than 4 times per week

A PERSONAL INTERVIEW

We are grateful for your participation in this survey. If you have found any of it frustrating or unclear, then you probably realize how difficult it is to capture a person's real experience with a questionnaire. For this reason, we would like to ask you to volunteer for a *personal interview*.

Obviously we cannot interview everyone. So we will limit ourselves to those of you who have had *sexual experiences with relatives and members of your families*.

Such experiences may be hard to talk about. If you have had such an experience, however, we urge you to consider seriously giving an interview. Information of this kind is badly needed *to help other people with similar experiences*.

All the information from the interview will be strictly confidential. Your name, address and identifying information will not be attached to it anywhere. In fact, after your interview, we will destroy any record of your identity, so the information will actually become anonymous. In appreciation of your help you will also be paid $5.00.

If you would like to be interviewed, please indicate on the accompanying card how we can get in touch with you to schedule an interview. Please include a phone number and a good time to call. If there are only a few people living at your phone number, you can merely give us a first name or nickname by which to ask for you. This will insure even further anonymity since we will not know your last name.

Finally, if you wish even more anonymity than this, you can just call to make an appointment. All you have to do is phone the number listed below and ask for an interview appointment for the Family Survey. There is no need for you to give your name.

Interviews will be conducted by a male and a female number of our research team. If you have a strong preference, indicate this on the card. We will try to accommodate such preferences, as our schedules permit.

Remove the accompanying card. They are to be submitted independently of the questionnaire. They will not be used in any way to identify the questionnaire's respondent.

Appendix C

"I WAS DIFFERENT": THE PERSONAL ACCOUNT OF AN INCEST VICTIM WITH INTERPRETIVE COMMENTARY

BARBARA HENLEY (pseud.) lives in a New England mill town. She is twenty-nine, now in her second marriage, the mother of a 7-year-old girl and a pair of twins, less than a year old. She works as a nurse at the local hospital.

She heard about our research from a former employer, and volunteered to be interviewed. She had been sexually victimized by her father starting at age 3 and lasting well into her adolescence. She was eager to assist our research and to do whatever she could to help others who had had experiences similar to her own.

This is her story. It is taken from the transcript of two interviews with Barbara, edited only to give it chronological coherence and to remove any identifying information.

There is no such thing as a "typical" incest family, and this account does not purport to be such. However, it does illustrate many common features of father-daughter incest situations. Moreover, Barbara's articulateness about her experience is very helpful in understanding sexual victimization, as it is experienced by the victim.

The personal account is followed by a commentary which tries to draw attention to features of Barbara's experience which are shared by many sexual abuse and incest victims.

* * *

I was raised in the South. I'll call it the South. It's North Carolina. I was the oldest and there were five below me, three sisters and two brothers.

So far as I knew we were all one family, but very early in my childhood I learned that I was different from the others because I looked different. I was the only child with brown eyes, so I felt different. I thought that they were all prettier than I was because they had blue eyes and light hair. I had freckles, so I thought that I was not as attractive.

When I was eight years old, I learned in school that two blue-eyed parents could not produce a brown-eyed child. I raised my hand and I said, "But you're wrong, teacher, because I'm proof. I have brown eyes and my mother and father both have blue eyes." My teacher responded that one of them must not be my natural parent because it just wasn't possible. So I came home and I did a little digging on my own. My parents had a box with important papers in it that had dust all over it. They moved it everywhere they went. I dug through it and found records to prove my teacher was right. The records I found were my parents' marriage certificate. They were married in 1950 and I was born in 1947. So that gave me verification.

But at that point I still didn't know which parent I belonged to, although I knew that one of them wasn't my natural parent. So I started to quiz my parents about things like, how much did I weigh when I was born. My mother didn't know. She couldn't recall how much I weighed. She didn't know why I didn't have a birth certificate. All the other kids had theirs with little footprints on them. These things are very important to a child. I guess I was a little precocious as an eight-year-old, being able to put these things together.

Then I went and talked to my grandmother, my mother's mother, and she said, "Edna had been married twice." She told me I was my father's child. My grandmother told me the name of my stepmother's first husband. He was a fireman and his name was Montgomery. So I confronted my mother. I didn't say, "Is this true?" I just told her one day that a fireman had come to the door looking for her and his name was Montgomery, just to see what kind of reaction I could get.

One of the basic things that I felt as a child growing up was insecure. I felt a lot of dishonesty, and I felt my parents weren't being level with me. I knew that very early. There was a rocky atmosphere between my mother and father. I never knew what was going to happen. I didn't have enough foresight to envision what was going to happen, I just knew that something wasn't right.

My mother always worked. She usually worked in cigarette factories or clothing factories, and then later she went to waitressing. That was what she did for most of her life and is still doing now. It seemed to me like she was always pregnant too. I remember that. But she always went back to work like six weeks after the child was born, and so we were always left to the care of someone else. We usually had a black woman who'd come in and take care of us. Of course in the South this was very common. You would pay the black help fifteen dollars a week to take care of four or five children, do all the housecleaning and do the daycare work. Those black women we had were very good ones. I don't know how my parents were able to select such good ones. Probably we got better care and more love from the black mothers that we had than from our real mother. Often they would bake cookies and bring them to us. And one of the black mothers would give us lunch money many times because we didn't have it. She would take it out of her small wages and give it to us. This was up until the time I was eight or nine. It was shortly after that when I started becoming the baby-sitter.

My father was an educated man. He went to Princeton for two years but because of World War II, he was forced to leave school. He was always frustrated after that because he never got a chance to complete his education. He knew a lot and spoke quite well. He was from New England. He met my stepmother in Connecticut and they were married and went back to the South. He always hated the South. My mother was from the South, but he always hated the South. He had nothing good to say about it and was extremely critical of my mother because she had only a sixth-grade education. He always corrected her grammar. That was one big thing I remember. Every word, he corrected the grammar of it. He would always teach us children to speak differently. He didn't want us to have a Southern kind of language. He always tried to make us like he wanted. He always said we were going to leave someday, and we were going to go North, but we never did. We always had more kids and less money, and we never really moved.

My father worked most of the time. He had a very heavy drinking habit. Of course now you'd call it alcoholism, but back then I don't think we would have thought of it as alcoholism. He just drank a lot as far as I knew. He had a weekend drinking and a payday drinking kind of thing. He drank a lot at home, but he did go off at times. Sometimes he would go off for a weekend and we wouldn't see him. I remember there was a time in my life when I was ten, twelve, or thirteen when there was a possibility that he was going out with other women. I may have overheard arguments. I can't remember how I came by all that information, but they argued quite a lot. He'd come in quite late frequently, particularly on the weekends and paydays, drunk, and she would argue and there would be just a stormy atmosphere in the house.

He always appeared the family man. He was affectionate. He used to take us fishing. When he was being a father, I suppose he did as well as anyone. He was giving and fun and we enjoyed his company. But when he was drinking he was certainly very different. When he was making sexual advances to me, he was drunk about 99 percent of the time. I can't really say that there was a time when he came to my room when he wasn't drinking.

My father was the kind of person who always drifted from job to job.

He was gainfully employed most of the time, and he did support the family. He wasn't just a bum. But he had always thought he was too good for the job that he had. He would be very upset if there were some people who had worked their way through the ranks with less education than he had and who were telling him what to do, and using improper grammar while they were doing it. He would say that they were stupid or illiterate, or that they couldn't read a slide rule. This was one big thing he had about reading a slide rule. He used to make us learn to read a slide rule as children. He could care less that we didn't even know what a slide rule was. He was really into mathematics. We had to learn all of the tools in his tool box, and what was sixteenths and what was three-quarters and what did what. He would drill us. He was also a mechanic, an excellent mechanic. If I had to say what he was while I was growing up, I would probably say, half mechanic, half salesman, because he had white-collar jobs and he also had blue-collar jobs. We just moved around a lot. He seemed to be happiest when he was in his white-collar job, which was the salesman's job. He sold plumbing fixtures for a while. He sold fishing equipment. He did very well with fishing equipment.

He usually got into conflict with the boys at the job because he was not earning the salary he thought he deserved, or because he felt a supervisor was not competent. His skill was so good at the kind of job that he did, that most of his bosses tended to overlook the fact that he came to work with alcohol on his breath. He always boasted that they couldn't do without him.

He really was without a family. His mother died in childbirth and he was an only child. His father was an alcoholic, and he was raised by an aunt. But I don't think he was raised by her consistently. I don't think she was the one who was the sole provider for his care for all of his life. I got the impression from my father that he was thrown around a lot from family to family, that whoever could take care of him for a month or six months did. I have the feeling he wasn't treated much like a child. He was probably treated more like an adult and forced to grow up very rapidly. I know he used to tell us that he was served wine and beer at a very early age. And he used to tell us if he didn't eat his meal, he'd be served the same thing the next meal.

Apparently he and his father never got along, but his father would send us gifts occasionally. His father must have been pretty well-to-do, because at Christmas time he would send presents to the children and they were usually nice presents. My father always played it down because he didn't care for his father. Then when I was seven or eight, my father all of a sudden decided he was going to call up his Dad and make up. It was going to be forgiveness or something. So he called and he got his stepmother on the phone. His stepmother told him that his father had died three years prior to that. He hadn't known about it. That's how distant the family was: He was the only child. His father had died and no one had even bothered to call him and tell him his father was dead.

The aunt who raised him came to visit him once when I was fifteen. I can't remember her name. He used to mention her name frequently, but I can't recall. She came and he wasn't home and she said she was looking for him, and she said who she was. She was an instructor at Clark University. He always had a high regard for her because she had a good position and she was well educated. So she was okay. She never married, she was a single lady, and she came to visit him at the house where we lived. I told her he wasn't home but that he would be home later. I don't think she came back that night. But I remember telling my father that she had stopped by to visit. She had gone to Washington, D.C. for some reason and we were just on the way. She was going to some convention, so it was convenient for her to stop by. He was thrilled. It brought tears to his eyes, he was so excited that she stopped by to see him. But he never made any attempt to visit her or contact her. I don't think there was really anyone for him to contact.

He talked about having friends. That was most of his remembrances from the past, his friends. But when my stepmother would talk about the friends, usually they were people that my father liked right away but were later turned off to my father because of his drinking and his abruptness. Once he would get drinking he would get rowdy, abrupt, and abrasive to people—not physically abusive, just verbally abusive and not pleasant to be around. I remember when my father gave me leads on finding my natural mother. He gave the names of some friends to look up. But when I called them they didn't remember who he was. So I think he usually built them up to be closer to him then they actually were.

There was one person he was very close to. This man and his wife were very close to my stepmother and my father as a married couple. He did call my father once or twice throughout the years. And my father would call him too, but my father would always pick 2:00 or 3:00 A.M. in the morning. There was never any visiting, not much communication, only a phone call every five years or so. So he really had no one, just about no one.

He always talked about leaving the South and going back to the North. That seemed to be the thing he held in the highest regard because of the better education in the North: They were more advanced and they didn't have a Southern accent. North just made more sense. I know I had this vision of what the North was going to be like and then when I married in 1967 we went to Boston, I couldn't believe it. This is the North! My father should see it now. You know, the hippie style was big back in the sixties and in Boston it was even worse. If they were dirty in the South, they were even worse in the North. If he only could see it now he wouldn't praise it so much. I found it quite amusing after the picture he had painted. Actually the most clean-cut thing I saw was the Boston Red Sox. I guess he was a pretty lonely guy when I think about it.

I don't recall him ever making a lot of money. When I was in school, there would be occasions where we would have to put down how much he made. I was always nosey and I always knew what the real figures were. I knew it might be $7,500 or $8,000. He would put down $10,000. Probably if I had to categorize how much money they made jointly, between $8,000 and $12,000 was an accurate figure.

Financially though, I would say we were lower class. We always lived in middle-class areas, but we were always forced to move. We tried to keep up with what our class should be, or somehow thought it should be, but we never quite made it. We always lived far out in the country. Outside of school I really didn't have any friends that would come over and visit. We just always lived on farms miles away from the next neighbor, just very distant rural places.

We lived in one middle-class neighborhood once from the time I was a sophomore in high school through nursing school when the other kids were growing up. It was in a brick home, which to my mother and the Southern people is the ultimate no matter what it looks like. If it's made of brick, that's it. It was incomplete when they bought it. There was no plumbing, no water, no bathroom, and they made this deal. The house was $8,000. That's how much it cost for an acre of land and a brick house. To me it looked glamorous, because the house had new wallpaper inside and shiny hardwood floors. The other homes on the road were pretty decent. Some of them were stately.

But I remember that the most tragic part of our lives happened in that house, as far as the conditions we lived under. There was no plumbing. In most of the places we lived we had some kind of resource for cleanliness. There would be an outside well, there'd be an outhouse, and some way to properly handle cleanliness and sanitation. Whereas in this home, there wasn't any of those things. We resorted to getting water daily from the town. We lugged it in a five-gallon jar. For a family of seven kids and two adults, we had to live with five gallons of water. That was for bathing and cooking and drinking. For everything. You can see how tough it was. And my father sometimes wouldn't get the water, or he wouldn't be home to get the water. So we'd have to take a pot over to the neighbors and borrow a gallon of water, just to cook potatoes. I think that was the most horrible conditions we lived in.

Our bathroom was a pot like the kind you would have in real poor countries or Tobacco Row. It was as bad as you can think of. My father wouldn't dump this. We had no place to put it. We couldn't dump it on the lawn, so we would store it and when the pot got full, dump it into a big galvanized trash can. So there was a time when we'd have twenty-five gallons of literally shit and urine sitting in our house stagnant, growing bugs and bacteria and everything else. Consequently, the kids were sick many times. There was very little sanitation.

I don't know how I ever did it, but I never was very sick. I always managed to be clean in spite of it. That's one of the things I always prided myself on, whether it was doing it at school or whether it was visiting a neighbor, and sneaking in a shower or a bath. I used to baby-sit on Friday and Saturday nights and I used to sneak my brothers and sisters over there as well, so they could get a bath. And quite often I would take my laundry over there and clean it and iron it while I was there. Unbeknownst to the parents I was using all of their water and iron and stuff to help out the family.

When he wasn't drinking, my father was quite OK, although he was rather stern, very rigid, and had very specific guidelines for us to follow. I had to wear my hair a certain way. We had curfews to come in at a certain time. We had study hours. We had certain expectations that we had to perform in school. The ones that did well always were in his favor. The ones that didn't do well were shut in their rooms and forced to study.

We were always afraid of him. We knew that certain things had to be done. We always knew what we couldn't get away with too. I mean most kids do, but we always knew that there were certain things that had to be done, or else. The "or else" was usually physical. He would beat us. But I was exempt from much of it. It's like there were two families, because I was different. I was different in many ways, but I was definitely my father's pet. It was quite obvious. So in one respect I had it a little easier, but I paid in the long run because of the sexual abuse. But looking back on it from one point of view, I guess I had it made, because I was pretty special in that I wasn't beaten. I was a good kid. I mean, I did the things I was supposed to do. I made excellent grades. I always made the honor roll. I was always the one he made an example of. "Why can't you be like your sister?" or "Why can't you do as well as your sister?" I was always well liked. Since I was a good kid, I didn't really get beaten.

I had a bond with my father which may have been a source of strength even though he was my pursuer most of the time. But still I think that bond is important: to have someone that's looking out for you even if they're beating you at the same time. I think that as long as there is some bond and some way that a kid can get that protection and that love, it doesn't matter how it's dished out.

My parents had a very short courtship, I know that. They met in Hartford. My stepmother was visiting a girlfriend in Hartford. She was a Southern person from North Carolina. She just happened to be there for two weeks, and during that two weeks they met, courted, married, and came back. So it was a very quick courtship. My mother was very attractive. She still is attractive. Slim and attractive. She truly is a nice person and very giving, so I assume that during the courtship that "ain't" did not bother him much as all the other things she might have had going for her.

My stepmother was also a very passive, accepting person. Indicative of that is that she stayed with him all those years, through all the running around, through all the abuse of the children and of her. I mean, she was physically beaten many times. And through the conditions we had to live with: no water, no food, being cold.

She was always a very nice person. Everybody liked her. But I was embarrassed by her many times. I think part of it was my father's doing because he was always belittling her. I was embarrassed by the fact that she wore hair curlers to market, for instance. She put her makeup on in front of everybody. I always thought that was a private thing, that you shouldn't dress in front of people. She would go out with these bobby-socks on and she'd roll them down, and I used to be horrified because she had these rolled-up bobby-socks on. I didn't like it because she didn't shave under her arms. I could tell you a thousand things that I picked at her for.

I guess the important thing about her was that she always worked. We never went without food, and it was my mother who kept us with food and kept us with clothes, even though her priorities were warped sometimes, just because she didn't know how to cope. She thought she was doing the best for us. She would go out and buy new furniture for the house when the old stuff got ripped up rather than taking us to the dentist because she thought that's how it should be. That's what I mean by warped priorities. The dentist should have been more important than the furniture, but it wasn't. But anyway, she tried. I guess I really never gave her credit when I was growing up for the things that she did do. I was always picking her apart for the things I didn't like.

Quite often she worked evenings because most of her life she worked as a waitress. She was home in the morning to get us off to school and she'd fix our breakfast but in the evenings I would come home and the house was mine. I was left to do the cooking and the dinner and getting the children ready for bed and helping with the homework and reading them stories and getting the school clothes ready for the next day and so on. It was just something I did. I didn't enjoy it. I resented it. In fact, I used to beat up on them because I didn't like having that responsibility. I was very strict because I would rather be out with my friends. It took away from what social life I might have had if I had not had this responsibility. I wished somebody else would hurry up and get to that age so I could go out and enjoy something else. I couldn't go to basketball games or anything.

I remember my stepmother as always being loving to the other children, comforting and consoling and things like that. But she never was to me. I don't think that's my imagination. I think that's really accurate, although when she and my father married, to hear her tell it, she was quite happy to have me and really took care of me. She was very proud of me and would dress me and cuddle me and do my hair and things like that. But the only part I remember about my mother is me being the oldest and me being forced to clean and me being the Cinderella type. Getting no comfort from her, even when the horrible things began to happen to me. I could never go to my mother.

One example, and I think it's important: I was menstruating for two years before I even told her. I just didn't tell her because there was no closeness there. She probably would have been helpful. She probably would have bought me some pads, but I didn't go to her. I would sneak them out of the box or buy them with my own allowance. I didn't respect her. I didn't think that she had much wits about her. And of course, that was very much supported by my father, because I was the smarter one and he made me feel that way. He used me as the lover, as the wife, as the mother, whatever. In his mind, I was the superior female in the family, in every respect. I suppose, when you get down to it, I was a much sharper women than my mother anyway, and probably did hold the family together, a lot more than she did.

It's sort of a paradox because my father showed her a lot of affection around us. When the family was together, he would love her, he would kiss her, and they would appear to be happy couple. He would express good feelings about her. He would say, "Your mother is a good person." He didn't want us to say bad things about her. And I feel that she loved him, for whatever reason I don't know, but she did. I wonder if that was part of the reason that she didn't leave him, that she tolerated all these terrible situations.

But when he was drinking they would fight. I've seen him hit her and throw her up against the wall. Lots of times she'd be meek because it was the safest way to be. It made more sense. She wouldn't get hurt that way. That was definitely a side of him. He would throw things and there would be holes in the wall and you'd see fists punched through the walls and dishes broken. We'd just hear it. We'd be in bed and they'd just be going at it. Probably once a week, at least once a week.

My mother always needed to get the children involved too, particularly if the argument was in the daytime. She would say, "Isn't that right?" or "Didn't he do that?" She always tried to pull us in.

I think lots of times my father staged a fight to get out of the house. He would start picking at her for something or other: her language, the dinner, the steak wasn't done right, or something. It was an excuse for him to leave. He would go speeding out, slamming the door, and then he'd be gone for the weekend, or he'd be gone for the night, or he'd be gone for hours.

And then of course, when he would come home drinking, a lot of their arguments were sexually oriented, because I think my mother was very prudish. She didn't really teach prudishness to my sister or me, but she just didn't talk about sex much at all. I think my father was just much more uninhibited. I think he was much more interested in sex, and I think the fact that she didn't supply his need, was why he went out or went to the children. They always slept together. There was never that separation. I'm sure they did have relations. There were many kids. We could see the evidence. They were very sloppy. They would leave their condoms out, they would leave their foam, or whatever form of birth control they were using. They would leave it hanging around and the kids would see it. There was one time I remember an argument they had. It was very sexually oriented. My mother didn't like my father's advances when he was drinking. I don't think she liked them anyway, but she used that as an excuse, not to like them more.

He's had a long line of women, my God. He's been married so many times, or at least paired up. I'm sure of one before my natural mother, then my natural mother, then my stepmother and at least one after that. So he's had at least four or five wives. And probably numerous other women.

My father is a very nice looking man, very physically attractive and whenever I would go anywhere with him, like to his work, he was always well thought of by the women. I could see that he was a charmer. Everybody that knew him among my friends, for example, thought that he was the greatest man in the world. My girlfriends thought, "Oh you're so lucky. You have the nicest father," because he was always polite. He was always johnny-on-the-spot if somebody needed something or needed some help. He would fix up cars or he would take people places. But he didn't do much for his own family.

To my knowledge he was pretty much aware socially of what's accepted. I don't think he was involved with any children outside his family. He could break the taboo in his own setting because he was the "ground ruler." But outside the family, he would have been a little bit too smart. He would have realized that it would have gotten him into legal trouble.

He would have affairs though. We used to go to parties and they would take us along. They had friends who had children and we would always be shoved in a room to play with the kids. I guess I was precocious because I always knew what was going on. I wasn't that precocious, but you just notice things. I saw my father chumming around with a wife of a friend, just standing there having a drink. But it was a friendly drink. I always noticed that they were very close and very friendly, and later on I would notice that he would be gone or he wouldn't come home, or my mother would be upset.

There was one time that my mother and I were sitting on the front porch and we saw his car go by and she said, "That was your father. Was Peggy in the car with him?" I said, "I don't know." But there was someone in it, and it was a woman.

I also used to go my father's place of employment a lot. There were always women there and they were always attracted to him. He would take them out to lunch. He would talk about them coming home! "Mrs. So-and so and I went to lunch." And I would meet Mrs. So-and-so and she was always attractive. Then he worked at a gas station. He was the manager and you could just tell that things were going on there. Of course, I was much older then. This was when I was fifteen, sixteen, or seventeen, and it was very obvious. It was subtle, but it was just very obvious.

My mother knew about it. She must have. I think she'd cry and she'd be disappointed but she never confronted him with it.

She probably was relieved because she didn't have to have the sexual burden and so she tolerated him having these affairs for that reason. I think on the one hand she was relieved and on the other hand she was probably disappointed. I always thought that the reason she never really made a big deal of his advances towards us was that it relieved her of her sexual burden. But then again that was just my idea.

At times, I guess I did wonder why my father did these things—to me and to others. I thought of it in relation to my stepmother. She was very, very inhibited sexually. From what I can gather she didn't like sex. She didn't want his advances and she used the excuse that he was drinking most of the time to ward him off. But I think she would have felt the same way regardless. She was very ignorant of sex. Knew very little and couldn't explain to me about menstration when it was time.

I don't know whether it's fair of me to put her in here, or if it's really relevant, but it's hard for me to separate them. I think it was her or her ignorance or her lack of interest that led him to go elsewhere. That was reinforced by the fact that he had extramarital affairs quite often, and he was always entertaining women outside the house, as well as coming on to his daughters and later on to his sons.

The sexual stuff with my father goes back a long way. I can remember as young as three years old sitting in front of the TV watching TV on a little stool. My father was always comforting and warming to me, so I would skoot my chair back and he would put his arm around me. Then he would put his hand in my underwear and fondle me. At three years old! I can hardly believe it. I thought nothing of it except that he did it. So that kind of behavior went on from three until five or six or seven.

My father would always take me places with him too. We'd be riding in the car and he would do the same thing, or he would put his hand on my chest. There was nothing there but he did it anyway. That went on until I was six or seven.

I was always getting poison oak too. He used to come and doctor the poison oak, and he'd always check the places I didn't have it to make sure I didn't have it, which were the places which were covered. "Oh, we'll check here." Of course, there was never anything there, but he would always check.

It wasn't until I was eight or nine that things started changing as far as I was concerned. I guess that's when your superego really comes into play. We were living in a lovely home. One of the nicest homes we ever had out in the country. It had a beautiful apple orchard. I was out picking apples with my father and he was under the tree and he asked me to take my underpants off. My mother was looking out of the window and she called me in and she said, "Don't ever do that again. Don't take your underpants off because that is wrong."

That was the only instruction I ever had from her at all up until that time that anything he had done might have been wrong. After that I started wondering. If that's wrong, you know, then what had been happening before must be wrong too. So I was torn between what my mother told me was wrong and what my father was telling me was right.

We also had this woman, Mary, a black woman, who was very well educated. She was a very fine woman and she used to talk to me many times about the little things I would find. I would find condoms haphazardly left around, and she would say they were not to play with, they shouldn't have been left there, your parents should be more careful. I don't know how she explained it, but she was very good at explaining it. She didn't say, "Don't touch that, it's nasty." She'd give me an explanation of what it was.

At about the time when I was eight, and in that same home, my father encouraged my mother to go to night school. She was going back to take an English course for this grammar problem she had. He really had this thing about grammar. So she went to night school for about three weeks and finally dropped out. But during the time that she was at night school he was at home alone with the children. One night he went to my room, picked me up and brought me to his bed, and then he masturbated on my chest. I thought he had urinated all over me. I was horrified because I couldn't understand why he would urinate on me. To me it was the vilest and most horrible thing that could be done. He never tried to insert himself, but that was the nearest he ever came to that point. I don't think I told my mother about that even though it was terribly horrifying, terribly awful. I don't think I told her about that.

During that same period, I remember he would be in the bathroom and he'd call me in to wash him, and he would get an erection. I didn't know that was what it was at the time. I didn't know anything about anything. He would ask me to wash his penis, soap him up, essentially masturbate him, but I don't ever recall him coming to climax except that one time on my chest.

So then I started talking to my father about it because my mother had said that it was wrong. He said that it should be our secret. That I shouldn't let my mother know. That I should never tell her what we did. That's the way he responded to it. It was the only explanation he gave. This was just our secret. "Don't tell your mother."

By that time, the TV thing had stopped. His advances were a little bit more subtle. He would invite me to go somewhere with him but I would decline the invitation because I knew what was coming and I didn't feel comfortable with it. But the thing that was hardest for me to decline were his advances at night, when he would come into my bedroom. That was the turning point, from about eight years of age. After that, nothing more happened during the day. Anything that I would participate in actively or that I would willingly consent to ceased. It changed to passive acceptance on my part. He would come into the room at night and I would pretend that I was asleep. Why I did it I'm not sure. I think partly because there was still that need for affection, partly because it felt good. Many times he would manually stimulate me. He didn't do any more of the masturbating on my chest. Mostly it was just putting his hands inside my pants and stimulating me at night in bed.

Whether he did anything to himself I don't know. I just wasn't that aware. I pretended I was asleep most of the time and tried not to participate in it. I'm not sure in my own mind what was going on except that I didn't want to admit to it. Maybe it was just a guilt thing. I just know I didn't want to be awake for it. I also knew that if I resisted or fought, I always got held back and I always got hurt. He would either hold his hands above my head or he would put his hand over my mouth, or he would hold me down. He was a very big man, like 6'1" and weighed 200 pounds. It didn't take much for him to restrain me. So I knew that if I resisted, I was going to get restrained anyway. So I usually would just lie there and accept his advances, and feel bad about it.

I can remember lying in bed at night awake just waiting for him to come home, afraid to go to sleep, petrified. There was a time when I put on four or five pairs of underwear under my pajamas hoping he would get discouraged. But then he set down ground rules that we couldn't wear underwear to bed, just pajamas. All of us children, we were not to wear underwear to bed, just pajamas. That was the house rule. One night I locked the door. He broke the lock off the door and told me never, never to lock the door again.

So it wouldn't be every night. Maybe only two or three times a week, but it was so bad that every night I would lie awake wondering if this was going to be the night. Lots of times he'd be out very late in the morning and I would fall asleep and wouldn't hear him come in. Then I would wake up and he'd be there, and I would be horrified. He wouldn't get into bed with me. We had bunk beds and I was always on the top bed. There was another child one deck below me. And whether she knew what was going on, whether she heard anything, whether he bothered her, whether he went to her first, I don't know. There were so many things that I just don't know.

I remember several times my mother would walk down the hall and would tell him to come to bed. She would see him standing there. She would get upset and she would say, "What are you doing? Come to bed."

And he did on several occasions. So there might have been one or two feeble attempts on her part to distract him from the children.

I remember threatening my father once, saying, "I'm going to tell my mother if you don't stop." He probably chuckled too, because it would do no good to tell my mother.

My mother knew what was going on with the daughters. Very, very definitely knew. And when my brother was here, he said that he knew that she knew what my father was doing, and she didn't stop him. He said that she stood there one night and watched my father make advances to my brother and she did nothing to prevent it. I think probably because I had seen her come and because she would call him away I thought that she would help me, so I started confiding in her more. I said that my father was in my room again last night. She would say, "Gee, I don't know what I'm going to do about this guy. I don't know how I'm going to help." And then realizing after four or five times, that she wasn't going to do anything about it, I just stopped.

My brother and I both felt the same way. We blame my mother much, much more for what happened to us than my father. It was easy to say he was sick and write it off. It's easy to be hostile to him and hate him and write him out of your life, but it's not so easy to write her off. And it's not so easy to rationalize why she did nothing to help us, when we couldn't help ourselves.

Nonetheless, I think she was very concerned in a distorted manner for the welfare of the children. But she felt if she did anything to him she wouldn't have the almighty dollar which was very important for taking care of the children. She had to weigh that. So she was willing in a sense to sell her children for that financial support. That's what she did later, once they were separated, and she was getting actual child-support payments. She would allow her children to go with their father knowing full well what would happen.

So things went on like that for just a long, long time. It was even worse when I started developing, you know, around twelve, thirteen, or fourteen. He was always very interested in when my periods were going to start. Whenever I was sick he would automatically assume that I was going to start my period. There was a time when he went out and bought me the Kotex and the belt. He just threw them on the bed and said, "Here, you'll need these." I didn't know what they were. That certainly wasn't what the problem was, so I didn't know what was going on. He seemed to think I needed them.

I remember that as I got older I got more resistant. The more secure I felt, the more I knew I had the strength to fight him off, whereas when I was younger I didn't try. So many times I would wake up and say get out of my room, or I would yell and scream so that he would be forced to leave.

Sometimes he would call me up to his room. He would read in his bed, and he would call me up and say, "Bring me an ashtray, bring me some cigarettes, bring me my magazine, bring me something to drink, bring me a beer, bring me anything," just to get me into the room. He would always be naked on the bed. He was always exposing himself, and he would try to force me to lie down beside him or comfort him or stroke him. I said forget it. I used to fight him all the time, and he used to scream, "Barbara, get up here." And I had to go. It got to the point where my brothers and sisters would look at me like, "You'll get killed if you don't," and I knew I had to go. I would usually wait or I'd try to go outside, or I'd send one of the other ones up, hoping that it would do. but it never really did. I'd say, "Jimmy, go take this to your father." But it just didn't work. I'd end up having to go myself.

One time I went up there and realized that it was one of his tricks, that he wanted some attention, and wanted me to give it to him. So I ran. I ran out the front door and into the woods and hid. It was about 9:30 then, and I knew he had to pick up my mother around 10:00. He would have to go pick her up because there was only one car. I was going to hide out until he left and then I would go back into the house. Shortly after, I saw him drive away. I felt a sigh of relief and I went back into the house. I was upstairs and was cleaning up when a few minutes later he appeared. He had driven the car down the road, parked it and walked back. I was horrified. I'll never forget the shock, because I thought I had beat him in this little game, and it turned out that he had snuck back. He said, "You thought you were smart, didn't you?"

So there was always a feeling that I couldn't get away from him. He was the supreme person. I was always trapped or caught, no matter what I did. I just couldn't escape this man. I even tried running away from home a couple of times. He always came and brought me back. Of course, I had nowhere to go except to my grandmother's. I always ran there and he always knew just where I was going to go. I just wasn't going to run away to New York. I didn't have it in me to run away to nowhere. I wasn't that courageous. So he always found me and brought me back.

One very significant thing happened when I was twelve or thirteen. We were very poor when I was in high school. We didn't have money for gym shoes, so I stole a pair of gym shoes out of someone's locker, because I was mortified that I didn't have gym shoes. I stole some gym shoes and later was caught. The gym shoes were marked and I didn't know they were marked. It turned out they belonged to one of my really good friends. That made it even more horrifying for me, because I didn't mean to steal from a good friend. Such morals! I should steal from my enemies! [laughter.]

So anyway, I was confronted by my gym teacher and best friend. I cried and cried. They took me to the office and my friend understood. She was very nice. She said don't worry about it. I was suspended from school for three days for the act of stealing. It was terrible. I had to take home this letter, this typed letter, and I knew I had to give it to my parents. I couldn't go to school for three days. What was I going to do? So I decided to give it to my father. I don't know why, I just did.

My father loved this. He blackmailed me. He said, "I won't tell your mother about this." He knew I was mortified. He said, "I'll get you back in school. Don't worry." The next day he called up the principal and I was back in school the next day, but he said, "I won't tell your mother about this if you're nice to me." So he blackmailed me. And I was nice to him, which meant I didn't fight his advances when he would come to my room.

I was nice to him for two or three months until it got to the point where I said, "Look, I don't care who you tell, just forget it. It doesn't mean anything to me any more." Of course, he didn't tell anybody and I was blackmailed all the time.

I had one friend who I really loved. Her name was Michelle. She came over once, and he made an advance to her while she was in my room. I couldn't believe it. So I confided in her. This was probably when I was about thirteen or fourteen. I confided in her and told her this horrible thing I was going through. She knew it, because she witnessed it firsthand. But I never told anyone else. I just didn't think they'd believe it or understand it, or else I didn't think I wanted to confide in anyone else. But I did tell Michelle. So for a couple of years she never came back to my house. I would go to her place, but she never came back to my house.

During this period, I tried to rationalize most of what was going on and put it out of my mind, and not only really think about it too much. I tried to live a normal life in spite of it. Normal, meaning going to school. That's why I put so much into my school life. School was the most important thing to me because it was my only escape from home. I got involved in a lot of extracurricular things and tried to stay late. Of course, I could get away with it when the kids were older. I couldn't get away with it when I was younger because I had to be home to take care of the younger children. I would spend nights with friends, and it was getting to the point anyway, where he couldn't control me as he had before. My voice was more powerful than his hand at that point. I wasn't going to have it, and that's where the real turning point was.

The years before nine I didn't even know that anything was wrong. The most tormenting time was between nine and thirteen. Between nine and thirteen I was certainly aware that it was wrong and that it was no good, but I had no idea of the effect it was going to have on me later. Nor did I know the effect it was having on me at the time. It wasn't until fourteen that I told my girlfriend. At that point I felt stronger and felt I could fight it off. It seemed like the belief came partly from confiding in someone, and partly from feeling stronger. I didn't have to put up with this thing. It was shortly after the blackmailing incident that I put it out. I said, "This is ridiculous, and I'm not going to continue to do this."

I remember confronting my father with the whole situation once when I was about fifteen. He used to wake me up at night to talk sometimes, just to talk. This time I said, "Why do you do these things? Why do you talk about my mother like this?" He was the most genuine I had ever seen him. He said, "Well, I guess it's because I'm sick." He actually said that he thought he was sick. I said, "You should get some help." And he said, "You're right, but I've never been able to do that." I never mentioned it afterwards and that was the end of that.

I guess when I think about it, I had it a lot less traumatic than a lot of kids, but at the same time, it was so very real. Even as an adult I would lay awake at night fearing he was still going to come and get me. Finally I realized that he can't bother me any more. First of all he is physically not here, and secondly, if he was physically here, it's a better match. I could protect myself. I don't feel threatened any more, but at the time I definitely felt that if I didn't comply I would be hurt. He had hit me and knocked me around. I wasn't totally free of what was going on with the other kids. I got less than the others, probably because I was a good kid. I guess I always did what he told me, and I was always the favorite child.

He was very protective of me. I wasn't allowed to go out. I wasn't allowed to date. I wasn't allowed to go out with friends. I was pretty much sheltered at home. God, when I got to be dating age, forget it! He wouldn't let me go anywhere. Absolutely forbade me to date, absolutely. He would say the guys weren't nice. No matter who I liked, no matter who I had crush on, he didn't approve.

Finally when I was a senior in high school, I had my first date. He told me he had heard all these terrible things about the guy I wanted to go out with, about how bad he was. But he was a nice guy. I just couldn't believe it. I said, "No, it couldn't be the same guy. You must have mixed him up with somebody else." So finally he did consent to let me go to this Christmas dance with this guy when I was a senior in high school. I had to be home at a certain time and that was it. The curfew was very strict. If the dance was over at 11:00, I had to be home at 11:15 or something like that. In fact, I think I did get home at 11:15. That's how rigid it was. After that I went to more parties, and he realized that he had to be a little more lenient. I said, "Look I'm not going to marry the guy; I'm just going to go out with him." Things did settle down a bit, and he did allow me a little more freedom.

Then when it was pretty evident that I was going to date, he introduced me to this guy that he had picked for me. It was an older guy. It was the guy I married, as it turned out. He was a nice guy, but my father picked him. I think that was part of the reason it didn't work out in the long run, because he was picked for me. No matter how great a guy he was, and he really was a nice guy, I just don't think it was destined to make it because he was picked for me. He was a college student, well educated, an older-looking type. Bob would have been about twenty-two and I would have been eighteen. That's not really that much older, but when you're a junior or senior in high school and he's a junior or senior in college, it's quite a big difference. So we dated and went steady for two years and got married. I was married when I was nineteen.

But I think the experience with my father affected me greatly in my relationship to men. Partly because I felt I was very ugly, and partly because I set up a dynamic where I was really "hands off" to anyone who made an advance. The ways guys make advances in high school are very strange, but I was very quick to cut it off. I was very sharp-tongued and would say, "Don't touch me," or "Stand back." So I really brought a lot of it on myself. I felt unattractive because I wasn't made advances to, but if they ever looked twice at me I was very quick to cut it off. I don't think I would have been so sharp to suspect evil or harm or being violated if it hadn't been set up by my father.

And then when I was married I was still very shy. I remember we waited a long time before there was any sexual thing at all. The first time there was anything was after we had dated a whole year, almost every night. It was just unbelievable the contact we had had. One night we were at home after a date, sitting on the sofa, listening to a Joan Baez album. He had his arm around me, which was okay. I could handle that. But he took his thumb and he rubbed my breast. I thought maybe it was an accident. That's how it was; it must have been an accident. But when it happened a second time, it was no accident. So I slapped him in the face and left him sitting there, and went to bed. Just left him there. He stayed about twenty minutes. I guess he didn't know if I was coming back or not. I didn't plan to come back. That was it. We dated a whole year and all he did was he took one thumb and brushed up against my chest. I was really uptight about it, because I had felt very safe with him, since he had made no advance at all. Then all of the sudden he was violating me and I felt very much in danger, and I didn't want to be part of this relationship any more. So I just walked out of it. I was seventeen at the time.

He wrote me a letter saying he wouldn't call me again till I called him, that he didn't know what he had done that was wrong. So I wrote him a letter and it was at that point that I realized that this was absurd. I confided in him and told him what the problem was, and that I was really uptight because of the relationship with my father. I told him everything that had happened. He immediately got very angry at my father. He had thought my father was the greatest man in the world. He had met my father and respected my father, so he was very angry at my father. He said he wanted to pursue my father, and I said, "It's senseless; don't even bother."

Things progressed very slowly after that in a sexual way, sort of on a program I could handle. He was understanding and I could handle it, but still it was very, very slow. So that was definitely a problem. I guess I didn't realize it before, but when I was in therapy my therapist said he must have been pretty strange too if he could handle a program like that. But that was something I needed then. I don't think I could have tolerated it in any other way. I had to have somebody who was extremely low key. I don't think I could have had anything else.

Once I began to realize that this wasn't all bad, I really enjoyed the relationship I had with Bob. It was comfortable enough that I could handle it. It got to the point that I was so comfortable that I was looking for more than he was going to give. That's when the problem started in our marriage. The sexual thing had great bearing because, first of all, it was too much and then it was not enough. I never really had the right introduction, I guess. But early in our relationship there were so many problems with changing and dressing, and even after I was married I had to change in the bathroom and wore my robe to bed. It was really crazy.

Also I think I tried to protect myself by wearing clothes. I used to wear underpants, and then I would wear panty stockings and I never needed a girdle, but I always wore a girdle. I always said I wore it to keep the stockings up but I didn't really need it to keep the stockings up. I always wore all this armor. My husband said, "My God, if someone was going to rape you, they would never be able to because of all the clothes you have on." I don't think I'm worried about going out on the streets and being violated at this point. I just think it's a kind of habit.

The end of the story on my father and stepmother is interesting. He left her. In fact that was the most ironic thing I'd ever heard of. She called one night and told me. I don't know how many years ago it was, probably five or six. He just came home one night and said that he had had it. He was leaving her. He walked out and that was it. He just had had it. I think she was relieved in some respects. But she was also at a loss as to what was going to happen to her financially, worried about that and disappointed for the kids' sake, because there were still several young children who were attached to him. But I didn't get the feeling from her that she was terribly upset about losing him. I remember that my feeling was, "Great!" When she called me and told me, I said it was the best thing that ever happened. I said it's too bad he didn't do it years ago.

I don't think she ever would have left him, ever. I think she would have just stayed until he killed her. She was very passive. She didn't know how to get herself out of the situation she was in.

In the end, I resented her and blamed her much more than my father for what was wrong. As I went through therapy I think I learned to appreciate the things she could do and not resent the things that she didn't do. I tried to look at her in a different light. My therapist said she just was a very passive kind of person and she just did not have it to get up and move herself out of it. She just wasn't like that. Of course, I know the kind of person she was referring to, because we treated them all the time in the clinic. Very passive, dependent people, who could just not do anything for themselves, could not realize that they had the power to get up and move off a rock, you know. They just couldn't.

I was angry at her because she didn't protect me. When I got older I realized that she really didn't have it or couldn't have, but I'm still not sure. I think I started feeling angry after I confided in her and told her what was going on. She didn't say anything. From then on I just hated her. I hated her as a child, hated everything about her.

I just think it goes back to the basics of expecting your mother to protect you from harm when you were feeling violated or harmed and there was no one to turn to. If you are hurt or crying as a child you usually always turn to your mother. If your mother is not there, then maybe your father. But if your father is the one who is rendering the hurt, then the only other place to go is your mother, and if your mother is not going to respond to that hurt and she's going to turn you off time and time again, that's going to make you very angry and I think it's just as basic as that.

Had it not been for therapy, I still would have had it misproportioned. The one thing I learned from therapy was that it was my father who caused the hurt. He was the one I should be angry at and I believe that now. I think if I didn't believe it I wouldn't feel the way I do. But he beat her down as much as he did anyone else. And I saw him do harm to her and I'm sure she felt it.

My brother recently spent a few months with us here. He's twenty-three. I thought I had been the only victim of sexual abuse in the family. But then I found out that my sister next to me was and so was my brother Eddie. We were the three oldest down the line. I don't know about the others because I've not talked to them.

For a while I'm sure I was the only recipient of my father's attentions. But then as I got older and more aggressive and more difficult to approach because I realized it was wrong and started to fight him off, then it was easier for him to go to one of the younger children. I think that's probably what happened.

When my brother was here we talked about it. He told me that my father forced him to masturbate him and forced him to have fellatio. Eddie was mortified. I think it's much more traumatic for a boy because you're breaking more taboos than just the family. He had the same experience with my mother too. She knew what was going on and didn't do anything to stop it. He said that she stood there one night and watched my father make advances to him and she did nothing to prevent it.

It's hard to say what kind of effect it had on Eddie, but he was a rebel. He went out and got into a lot of antisocial behavior for a while, drugs, stealing, things like that. He's straightened out at this point, though.

Then about two years ago, when I was in New York, I got a call from my sister Annie who is now sixteen. Annie told me that he had made advances to her. This was on a visit. Since they separated, my father had visiting rights for the children. He would come get the girls and take them out to the country. Then he would send Betty out of the room and start doing the same thing with Annie that he did with me, putting his hands in her pants and so forth. She's a pretty sharp kid and she was little older than I was so she knew that it was wrong. So she told me and I explained to her what kind of person he is and told her not to ever go with him because he's never going to change.

Then I called my mother up and threatened her. I said, "Don't you ever let those children go out with him again, ever! You know what he's like. You know what he did to me and what he did to Chris [other sister]. Don't ever let those girls go out with him again because if you do I'm going to put you in jail as well as him." I don't think she ever had it put to her quite like that. I think she thought that to protect her child support she had to let him have them. I said, "Don't you dare." And she hasn't ever since.

When I was fifteen I had thought about reporting him, but I didn't really know how to go about it. What I feared the most then was that no one was going to believe me. My father was going to deny it. My mother was going to deny it. And where would I be? So I just never pursued it.

Now I don't feel so helpless. Through therapy and through all of my contacts, there would certainly be enough verification. My therapist gave me the name of an official in North Carolina. She really wanted me to do something about it. She said, "Why wait until next time?" I guess I kept hoping that maybe there wouldn't be a next time. But there was a next time. But there hasn't been a next time since then and I really feel very strong at this point that I wouldn't hesitate to take the next plane home and do something about it. My therapist says how do I know that he's not in the schoolyards or lurking around like Chester the Molester? How do I know he's not going to attack some innocent person that I would never know about? I guess I don't know that. My sympathies go out to those people, but not enough so that I'd just go on the attack. Really he's a pathetic man. Maybe it wouldn't be an attack. Maybe it would be a help. But I just don't know at this point.

My brother asked me recently, "What would you do if your father died?" It's a question that I haven't really answered. I know that when I was in therapy the biggest thing I was to accomplish was to wish that he should be dead. I should consider him dead and that would be it. But I know that I had difficulty writing him off because, despite all the terrible things he had done to me, I still felt the closest bond with him. I got nothing from my mother. My fear was that if I wrote him off, I had no one. My rationalization was, well, if I ever needed anything he was always there. But I think at this point I have enough insight to know that he really isn't there when I need him. He's only there when he needs me.

I've gotten calls from his current wife. She called once and said "Your father's really in trouble. I think you should come." I said, "No. I'm not coming." I don't know what she knows, but she does know there was some special relationship between us because she says, "He really cares about you and talks about you." That's really bullshit because he never does anything for me. He never remembers my birthday. He never sends me a Christmas card. He calls me up about every three years on *his* birthday and says, "Do you know what day this is?"

I had a fear a couple of years ago that he would just show up on my doorstep one day and say, "Look, I need your help. I'm down and out, and I have nowhere to go." I would say, "Well, you're absolutely not going to stay here. I'll find you a place but it won't be here." I would extend myself so far as to find him a place in a state hospital or an alcoholic unit, but it would not be in my home. I know enough about the history of alcoholics to know that if he ever came to my doorstep, he would die on my doorstep. He'd be there forever to be taken care of, and I just couldn't be bothered. But I wouldn't be surprised if some day he showed up.

As for what I would do if he died, I'm probably not going to make a decision until the phone rings and someone says he died last night. I've thought of it many times, and I think I would almost have to go to the funeral, not out of any love, but just to have the satisfaction of knowing that he's actually dead and buried and that I'm finally safe. I have this fear that if I don't actually see him dead, I won't believe he's dead.

Commentary

WHOSE CHILD?

An eight-year-old tracks down clues to her own parentage. The child's cleverness is breathtaking! But is it any wonder: for Barbara this sleuthing was a matter of survival. To whom did she belong? Where was her real family? These people she was living with obviously did not give her a sense of security or a sense of belonging.

Such a climate is not uncommon among incestuous families, whose members are often not sure about who is "in" and who is "out." They doubt whether family members will be loyal to them. There may be a high level of what some writers have called "abandonment anxiety," the fear among some family members that they may be abandoned or betrayed by others (Henderson, 1972; Kaufman *et al.,* 1954).

Such fears arise when family ties are loose. In compound families, for example, made up of the offspring of multiple marriages, and sometimes including extended family and adopted children, ties of loyalty and belonging may be unclear. In families where members have died, left suddenly, or been removed, there may be a simliar climate. In some incestuous families, it has been reported, a history of abandonment dates back several generations (as in Barbara's father's family).

Incest may be an outgrowth of this kind of family climate in two ways. First, the obligations and responsibilities of family members toward one another may be very vague, and the understanding that exists in most families that kinspeople do not take sexual advantage of one another may not exist. Second, incest may be a way of trying to stave off abandonment. A child plagued with fantasies of being left alone may readily accept a sexual relationship with a father or brother in preference to no relationship at all. Sex may be the "glue" that desperate people in such families use to ward off their worst fears.

PORTRAIT OF AN INCESTUOUS FATHER

Could a psychologist or a novelist give us a better portrait of Barbara's father? For all the havoc he wreaked on her life, she can see him with amazing clarity and objectivity: a man with no friends, no family, alone, frustrated and alcoholic, and yet, capable, handsome, powerful, and full of pride.

Barbara's father is typical in several ways of many incestuous fathers. Of course, they cut across all molds, and most people knowledgeable in this field justifiably scoff at requests for a portrait of the "typical" incestuous father. But certain features of Barbara's father's history are recognizable in the histories of other incestuous fathers.

One telling characteristic is the alcoholism. Again and again in accounts of incestuous fathers one hears about drinking problems. Available statistics from large studies confirm the impression from case histories: between 30 to 50 percent of offenders would appear to be chronic alcoholics (Maisch, 1972; Virkkunen, 1974).

However, no one familiar with the problem thinks that alcoholism causes incest. It is seen rather as another symptom of underlying deviance in the offender. Yet alcohol does seem to facilitate the occurrence of the crime, at least when a predisposition to incest already exists. Barbara remembers that it was only when he had been drinking that her father ever molested her. He obviously had some inhibitions about his incestuous behavior, and only under the influence of alcohol did he "allow" himself to overcome them (McCaghy 1968).

Barbara's father was also a man who considered himself a failure. Here he was, someone with social class and educational credentials, stuck among people he felt to be his inferiors, trapped in jobs that were below his capacities, never recognized by his superiors.

Only in the past few years, therapists have become aware of a large amount of incest in respectable middle-class families. In many cases the respectable fathers in these respectable families display this same sense of frustration and failure (My husband 1977).

In our society, it is not unusual for men to try to make up in sexual conquest for things they feel are lacking in other spheres of their life. Men seem to use sex and sexual domination of women as an equalizer for true and imagined insults they feel they have suffered. In this way, incest may be a kind of stealing, the revenge of men (of any class) who feel frustrated and underprivileged (Meiselman 1978). The fact that they "steal" from members of their own family may only be an indication of their desperation to take something they feel is owed them.

Another common pattern among incestuous fathers is for a rather low level of competence in external matters to be accompanied by rampaging authoritarianism in family matters. They are often labeled family tyrants (Lustig *et al.,* 1966; Weinberg, 1955). This was certainly the case for Barbara's father, who kept his wife and children in terror by his physical outbursts and his exacting expectations of obedience. Such tyrants show, in an exaggerated form, the belief—implicit in our society's family arrangements—that a man's family is his property to be disposed of as he wishes. It is not an enormous leap of imagination for such men to think that sexual access to their children is included in their parental prerogatives. Their children, like Barbara, conditioned to obedience, are rarely resistant to such demands.

Finally, one of the most interesting features of Barbara's father's history is the story of his family. Essentially he was a man without a family. He had been abandoned, passed around; he had no siblings and virtually no parents. It is easy to understand how a man with no experience of family would have a hard time acting like a parent toward his own offspring.

The incest taboo is one aspect of family role relationships that all of us learn in our families of origin. That learning may be defective for one reason or another, as it is in many incestuous fathers (Meiselman, 1978). The taboo simply may not have been modeled in some families and thus not learned. Or the families themselves may have been so tenuous, as in the case of Barbara's father, that one never had a model. In both cases, the result could be an incest-prone individual.

THE ISOLATED FAMILY

According to Barbara, her family always lived way out in the country. Growing up, she rarely had other children to play with, because they lived too far away. In addition, there were the frequent moves which further cut off her contacts. Moreover, the family had no relatives with whom they were in close contact. All in all, it was an isolated, lonely existence.

This kind of isolation is fairly common in incestuous families (Bagley, 1969). Sometimes it is an isolation associated with rural living (Riemer, 1940); the backwoods and rustic family incest is not purely a prejudiced stereotype. Farm families have been shown, for example, to have an unusually high incest rate (See Chapter 8). But incest also occurs in urban settings. In fact, the kind of isolation associated with incest is more a matter of life style than geography. A deviant life style and set of values often go along with social and geographic isolation (Weinberg, 1955). Barbara's family seems to well illustrate the interplay of deviance, isolation, and incest.

There were two parts of her family's isolation. Obviously their economic straits made it hard for them to settle into a middle-class permanence. But although she doesn't say so explicitly, one suspects that there was a voluntary aspect to their isolation too. Her father, a loner, no doubt sought out living situations that put them at a distance from the community. That isolation kept the family out of the eye of neighbors and gave him the freedom to pursue his unconventional life style. It both reflected his deviant values and gave him increased opportunity to act as he pleased. As the story of the sanitary conditions shows, unusual sexual behavior was not his only area of irresponsibility.

THE FAMILY DYNAMICS OF INCEST

Barbara conveys well to us some of the full complexity of the incestuous family. She has introduced us earlier to her authoritarian, highly sexed, promiscuous father. She reveals to us that the sexual relationship between him and his wife was highly unsatisfying. But it is unlikely that these two factors alone created an incestuous situation. Notice other features of the family dynamics that conspire in the incest.

We meet her passive and ineffectual mother, whom she describes with less objectivity, perhaps, than her father. She admits that for years it was her mother she blamed for all that had happened.

However, since she has been groomed from an early age by her father to be her mother's rival, is it surprising that she views her in such a critical way? What a heady and yet frightening position for a child to be in, possessing such power. Barbara runs the family and holds it together in many ways, and much as she dislikes it, it is easy to see how the immense sense of strength Barbara conveys as an adult must have its origins in those responsibilities she managed so well as a child. Moreover, she enjoys all the seeming privileges of being her father's favored one, more favored even than her mother: the special praise, the attention, and exemption from the beatings. It is not hard to see how such a relationship might become sexual and how Barbara might at first mistake the sex for an expression of love and specialness.

What makes Barbara so vulnerable is that she has hardly any rapport with her mother. It is not only that her mother is weak and preoccupied with her own problems with her husband; but as a rival, and her father's vehicle for belittling his wife, Barbara can hardly turn to her mother for advice and protection. Thus Barbara lacks a model and protector who in other families might have deterred the father's advances or helped Barbara cope with them.

Is it now in vogue to blame the mothers for the incest rather than the fathers (Rush, 1974)? Although we, along with Barbara, wish that her mother had protected her, we can see (from the story she tells) how erroneous it is to hold the mother responsible for the incest. Barbara's mother was nothing but a second victim in this family (Zaphiris, 1978). She was physically beaten and intimidated by her husband and continually belittled not just by him but also by his ally, Barbara. Trapped in a marriage with six children and meagre economic resources, it is clear that she hardly had the power to stand up for her own protection, let alone the children's.

SEXUAL AWARENESS IN THE YOUNG CHILD

Barbara tells of being sexually fondled for several years before she had an inkling of what was going on, so much was it an integral part of her affectionate relationship with her father. This story raises an interesting question: Are many children molested at such an early age that they carry no recollection of it into adulthood? If Barbara's father had stopped his activities before the incident with her mother, would Barbara ever have been aware it had happened?

Compared to the accounts of other victims, Barbara's experience seems somewhat unusual in this matter. Most other victims, even those who have been molested very early in life, say that they knew something strange was going on, even if they did not know exactly what. They are usually alerted by two things. They know that touching the genitals is suspicious. Once children are toilet-trained in our culture, adults just never have contact with their genitals, and children certainly never have contact with those of the adults. So when an act involves the genitals of either party, they know something strange is happening. Moreover, children are also alerted by the behavior of the adult. "He was acting sneaky" or "rough" or "scared," they say in describing the behavior of their adult partners. They knew it was wrong because the adult was acting strange.

In Barbara's case, however, she did not become suspicious until much later. As she got instruction in sexual modesty from her mother and housekeeper, her sexual activity with her father took on another character. Other instances of this kind of revelation have been documented. Just as when children learn about sexual intercourse, they sometimes suddenly "remember" an earlier incident in which they discovered their parents doing something strange, so too, when children learn about sexual modesty they may remember an incident in which they were molested at a time when they did not know what was happening.

INTERCOURSE IN INCEST

Barbara's father never tried to have intercourse with her even though he obviously had plenty of opportunity. Although this may surprise some people, it is fairly typical of incest. Much father-daughter incest does not involve actual intercourse (Gebhard et al., 1965).

There seem to be three main reasons why intercourse is not the predominant sexual act in encounters between adults and children. First, intercourse between an adult and a *prepubertal* child is physically difficult. A child's vagina is too small, and intercourse cannot take place without great pain and injury to the child. It does happen, but many offenders are unwilling to subject the child to such pain.

Second, adults who are sexually interested in children are often seeking a more childish form of sexual gratification than that provided by intercourse. They are often men who are fearful of adult forms of sexuality, and they appear to prefer fondling and masturbation.

Finally, by shying away from intercourse, many sex offenders against children try to relieve themselves of some amount of guilt over what they are doing. Without intercourse, they think, they are not technically violating the child. It may be a way for them to help deny the seriousness of the taboo they are violating. "After all, it was only . . ." they may say to themselves. It may have been this factor that was paramount for Barbara's father.

"ENJOYING" INCEST

Barbara explains something in a few paragraphs that is enormously difficult for many people to understand. "It felt good," she said, to be manually stimulated. Other victims report similar feelings: of being sexually aroused, of being comforted, of feeling needed. Some people find such statements tantamount to an admission of guilt. How can one expect people to be morally outraged about the victimization of a child, they think, when here is the child admitting to pleasure in the act? For some people such admissions reinforce their belief that the child really asked for it, wanted it, enjoyed it, and helped it to continue.

What Barbara also explains so graphically is that it was a horrifying experience. She was brutalized, dominated, and physically coerced, all the while feeling totally helpless to rescue herself. She lived in constant fear, and yet mixed in were moments of physical pleasure. As logically contradictory as that may sound, emotionally it was all a part of the same experience.

As other victims with similar reactions explain it, in fact, the moments of physical pleasure often made the experience all the more horrible. Not only did they feel totally at the mercy of the adult, but in addition they felt out of control of their own body and their own emotions. They were having reactions that felt inappropiate, that they did not understand, and that made it all the more difficult to deal with what they were going through.

FORCE AND INCEST

Instances of childhood sexual victimization, unlike rape, do not always start under circumstances of force and coercion. Barbara's story makes it easy to see why. The offender is usually someone of great emotional importance to the child, someone whom the child trusts. He may be charming and playful. He offers the child affection which may otherwise be missing in the child's life. The child may cooperate in anticipation of some promised reward. In some cases, the offender may just outrightly misrepresent the acceptability of the moral standards involved, as when a father tells his daughter that this is something all fathers and daughters do. Under such circumstances children often cooperate in the sexual encounter or at least passively consent at first.

Force more often comes into play in the continuation of the sexual relationship. A child rarely wishes to continue the relationship as long or as often as does the adult. He or she soon finds it an unpleasant or painful game and becomes alarmed by the strange, preoccupied behavior of the adult. Or the child begins to realize that what they are doing is wrong and is overcome by guilt and fear. Then the child starts to resist or complain.

However the adult is rarely of a mind to give up his easy pleasure. When the child starts to resist, the adult begins to compel him or her to cooperate, which is when the coercion starts. Sometimes the adult must use physical force to gain his satisfaction. Sometimes he will threaten punishment or the witholding of privileges. It is not unusual for the adult to become frightened himself and threaten dire consequences if the child reveals the activity to someone else.

BLAMING THE MOTHER

Barbara's mother knew what was going on. She knew her husband was having affairs, she knew he was going to Barbara because Barbara had told her, and apparently she had witnessed firsthand the father's sexual advances to Barbara's younger brother. Yet she did nothing. Barbara, like so many other victims of incest, for a long time blamed her mother for what had happened. Following their lead, it has become popular for many other observers, therapists, and researchers to blame the mother, too (Rush, 1974).

It seems paradoxical to some people that the mother should be the one to be blamed by the victims, but Barbara helps us understand why. The mother is supposed to be the help of last resort, she points out. When she abandons you, that is the last straw. Also, mothers in incestuous families are natural scapegoats. They are often helpless, passive, and opposed by the father. Almost like a lightning rod, they are natural receptors of blame. Moreover, the daughters in these families are raised to discount their mothers. Thus it is not surprising that even in accounting for their victimization at the hands of the fathers, they should blame their mothers.

However, as we said earlier, these women are better visualized as victims themselves than as culprits. They are often, as in the case of Barbara's mother, physically beaten or otherwise intimidated by their husbands. More importantly, like so many women in our society, they are trapped by their economic and social position. How much leverage can a woman with six children and no economic resources bring to bear against the breadwinner? As Barbara says, her mother was concerned about her children's welfare, even if in a misguided way. She knew that without her husband she would never be able to support her family, and so she made a choice that her children would have to tolerate the sexual abuse as a price of having a father and a meal.

VICTIMS COPING

Barbara gives quite a graphic account of her life between the ages of nine and fifteen. The nightmarish quality of those years is all too clear. Two particular themes stand out in her story and in the stories of other victims—two themes describing what seemed the most traumatic about the whole experience.

One is the feeling of being trapped. Here Barbara was imprisoned in the household of a monster of almost fairytale proportions. His demands were unpredictable, but inevitable and inescapable. She never knew when to expect him or what new trick might lie around the corner. She had no place to go, nowhere to turn.

The other theme is the one of being alone. She was living through these horrible experiences and she could confide them to no one. Most victims, like Barbara, believe that no one could possibly understand them and telling would only bring down on themselves blame, ridicule, and disbelief (Armstrong, 1978). Thus they suffer in silence.

Nonetheless, these victims go on coping, struggling for a way out of their predicament. What no doubt determines the ultimate psychic cost of the experience is how resourceful they are. Barbara coped with her predicament in ways common to other victims. Fortunately, she was more successful than many, which probably accounts for much of her strength today.

Many victims talk about dissociating themselves from what was happening, trying to block it out of their minds. During the day, they tried not to think about it; during the night, they tried to sleep through the assaults. Victims tell of trying to melt into the wall, trying to think they were someone else or somewhere else. Barbara tried some of this behavior, but it was not her best resource.

As another alternative, many victims try to run away. Only recently have community agencies begun to consider runaways from the point of view of incest. The number of victims now being discovered among runaways is very large (Weber, 1977).

In addition to trying both of these strategies, Barbara coped by turning her energies to other things. She worked hard in school; she stayed late; she performed well and was successful. As a result she was able to conserve some self-esteem in a situation that was potentially devastating.

Moreover, she was able to overcome the isolation. Perhaps as a result of happenstance, she found an opportunity to tell a friend about the terrible events without risk of being ridiculed or contradicted. In that confidence she found a source of strength and solace.

Finally and most importantly, Barbara fought back. She resisted her father, tried to outsmart him, and in the end she won. "My voice was more powerful than his hand," she proclaims in triumphant eloquence. This fact more than any other may be the source of her self-esteem, counteracting whatever devastation it must have suffered thoughout those years. Although there was pain, she ultimately came out on top, and as a result of her own inner strength. Coping with such adversity in a way that makes one feel powerful must certainly be an important ingredient that distinguishes the survirors from the casualties of an experience like incest.

THE JEALOUS FATHER

When a daughter reaches the dating age, it usually marks the beginning of the end of the incestuous relationship. The father recognizes the threat to his sexual monopoly and reacts accordingly. He becomes very jealous. He tries to restrict his daughter's contacts. He suspects her every activity and flies into a rage over them. This is a common pattern. The affront of these new restrictions in the context of their growing sense of power as adolescents is usually the last straw for the victims. Some decide to blow the whistle; others run away. Still others grab the first available marriage partner as a way out of their hellish family life (Meiselman, 1978).

Barbara's situation was a curious variation on the theme of jealousy and possessiveness. Although her father demonstrated all the jealousy of the incestuous parent, in the end he did allow her to date, and he took the bizzare course of finding a husband for her. As she later discovered, however, he had transferred his sexual attentions to her younger brother and sister. This victimization of other siblings helps to explain why he yielded sexual control over Barbara more easily than many incestuous fathers.

THE CONSEQUENCES OF INCEST

The experience of incest leaves many kinds of imprints on its victims. For some the nightmare doesn't stop. They end up in institutions, addicted to drugs, or married to men like their fathers who abuse them and their children. But others find resources in themselves and friends and establish a sense of control over their lives, control they often felt was lacking during the incestuous episode.

Incest usually has some impact on a woman's sexual development (Meiselman, 1978). One possible outcome is promiscuity. The unfortunate lesson that some children take away from the sexual abuse is that it is only through offering sex that they can capture any love and attention, and they carry that fruitless quest on into their adulthood. It is not surprising that studies of prostitutes, for example, show that a large number were sexually abused as children.

Others, more like Barbara, find that the incestuous experience leaves them frightened and rejecting of sexual behavior. Sexual contact conjures up detested memories of the father's advances, and for them, it can never be fun, comforting, playful, or adventuresome.

However, victims report that the lasting trauma of incest is not so much sexual as emotional. The scar that stays the longest is a deep inability to trust others, particularly men. They find themselves suspecting other motives, feeling that they are being used. They have a hard time opening up or getting close, because they fear that all men want from them is sex.

Victims also talk about the long-term toll the experience takes on their self-esteem. It is common for them to have spent many years feeling ugly, sinful, and irreparably different. They often blame themselves for the incest, believing that if there hadn't been something wrong with them, it never would have happened.

Barbara went through both of these reactions. Fortunately she found a relationship that was a good therapeutic environment for her. She was able to control the rediscovery of her own sexuality in a situation of little threat. She was able to regain self-esteem in the company of someone who cared for her in a nonexploitative way.

REFERENCES

AMIR, M. *Patterns in forcible rape*. Chicago: University of Chicago, 1971.

ANDERSON, L. M. Personal communication. April 1977.

ARIES, P. *Centuries of childhood*. New York: Basic Books, 1962.

ARMSTRONG, L. *Kiss daddy goodnight*. New York: Hawthorn, 1978.

ASTIN, A., KING, M. R., LIGHT, J. M. and RICHARDSON, G. T. *American freshman: National norms for fall 1973*. American Council on Education, n.d.

BAGLEY, C. Incest behavior and incest taboo. *Social Problems,* 1969, *16,* 505–519.

BAKAN, D. The test of significance in psychological research. In D. E. Morrison and R. E. Henkel (Eds.), *The significance test controversy: A reader*. Chicago: Aldine, 1970.

BANE, M. J. *Here to stay: American families in the twentieth century*. New York: Basic Books, 1976.

BARKER, W. J., and PERLMAN, D. Volunteer bias and personality traits in sexual standards research. *Archives of Sexual Behavior,* 1975, *4,* 161–171.

BENDER, L., and BLAU, A. The reaction of children to sexual relations with adults. *American Journal of Orthopsychiatry,* 1937, *7,* 500–518.

BENDER, L., and GRUGETT, A. A follow up report on children who had atypical sexual experiences. *American Journal of Orthopsychiatry,* 1952, *22,* 825–837.

BENWARD, J., and DENSEN-GERBER, J. *Incest as a causative factor in anti-social behavior: an exploratory study*. Paper presented at the American Academy of Forensic Sciences, February 1975.

BRADBURN, N., SUDMAN, S., BLAIR E., and STOCKING, C. Question threat and response bias. Article submitted to *Public Opinion Quarterly,* January 1978.

BROWNING, D. and BOATMAN, B. Incest: Children at risk. *American Journal of Psychiatry,* 1977, *134,* 69–72.

BROWNMILLER, S. *Against our will: Men, women and rape*. New York: Simon and Schuster, 1975.

BURGESS, A. W., GROTH, A. N., HOLMSTROM, L. L., and SGROI, S. M. *Sexual assault of children and adolescents*. Lexington, Mass.: Lexington Books, 1978.

BURGESS, A. W., and HOLMSTROM, L. L. *Rape: Victims of crisis*. Bowie, Md.: Robert Brady, 1974.

BURTON, L. *Vulnerable children*. London: Routledge and Kegan Paul, 1968.

CARTER, H., and GLICK, P. *Marriage and divorce*. Cambridge, Mass.: Harvard, 1976.

215

CHAPMAN, J. R., AND GATES, M. *The victimization of women.* Beverly Hills, Cal.: Sage, 1978.

CLARK, J. P. and TIFFT, L. Interview validation of self-reported deviant behavior. *American Sociological Review,* 1966, *31,* 516–523.

COHEN, M. L. and BOUCHER, R. Misunderstandings about sex criminals. *Sexual Behavior,* 1972, pp. 57–62.

CONSTANTINE, L. and CONSTANTINE, J. M. *Group marriage.* New York: Macmillan, 1973.

CORMIER, B., KENNEDY, M., and SANGOWICZ, J. Psychodynamics of father-daughter incest. *Canadian Psychiatric Association Journal, 1962, 7,* 207–217.

Crime in California. *Time,* March 2, 1953.

CURRIER, R. L. Debunking the doublethink on juvenile sexuality. *Human Behavior,* September 1977, p. 16.

CURTIS, L. Present and future measures of victimization in forcible rape. In M. Walker and S. Brodsky (Eds.), *Sexual assault: The victim and the rapist.* Lexington, Mass.: D. C. Health, 1976.

DE BEAUVOIR, S. *The second sex.* New York: Bantam, 1953.

DE FRANCIS, V. *Protecting the child victim of sex crimes committed by adults.* Denver, Col.: American Humane Assn., 1969.

DELAMETER, J. and MACCORQUODALE, D. Effects of interview schedule variables on reported sex behavior. *Sociological Methods and Research,* 1975, *4,* 215–236.

DE MAUSE, L. *The history of childhood.* New York: Harper and Row, 1974.

DENSEN-GERBER, J. *Legislative responses and treatment challenges.* Paper presented at the meeting of the Second International Congress of Child Abuse and Neglect, London, September 1978.

DEVROYE, A. L'inceste; revue de données bibliographiques. *Acta Psychiatrica Belgica, 1973, 73 (6) ,* 661–712.

DUDAR, H. America discovers pornography. *Ms.,* August 1977, p. 47.

ELIAS, J., and GEBHARD, P. Sexuality and sexual learning in childhood. In *Phi Delta Kappan,* 1969, *50* (7), 401–405. Also in D. Taylor (Ed.), *Human sexual development.* Philadelphia: F. A. Davis, 1970.

FORD, C. S. and BEACH, F. *Patterns of sexual behavior.* New York: Harper and Row, 1951.

FOX, J. R. Sibling incest. *British Journal of Sociology,* 1962, *13,* 128–150.

FREUD, S. *Three essays on the theory of sexuality.* New York: Basic Books, 1962.

GAGNON, J. Female child victims of sex offenses. *Social Problems,* 1965, *13,* 176–192.

———. *Human sexualities.* Glenview, Ill.: Scott, Foresman, 1977.

GAGNON, J., and SIMON, W. *Sexual conduct.* Chicago: Aldine, 1973.

GEBHARD, P., GAGNON, J., POMEROY, W., and CHRISTENSON, C. *Sex offenders: An analysis of types.* New York: Harper and Row, 1965.

GEISER, R. L. and NORBERTA, M. Sexual disturbance in young children. *American Journal of Maternal and Child Nursing,* 1976, *1,* 187–194.

GIARETTO, H. Humanistic treatment of father–daughter incest. In R. E. Helfer and

C. H. Kempe (Eds.), *Child abuse and neglect: The family and the community.* Cambridge, Mass.: Ballinger, 1976.

GIL, D. *Violence against children.* Cambridge, Mass.: Harvard, 1973.

GLIGOR, A. M. Incest and sexual delinquency; A comparative analysis of two forms of sexual behavior in minor females. Doctoral dissertation, Western Reserve University, 1967. *Dissertation Abstracts International,* 1967, 27B. University Microfilms No. 67-04588, 3671.

GLUECK, B. C., JR. Psychodynamic patterns in sex offenders. *Psychiatric Quarterly,* 1954, *28,* 1-21.

GOLDSEN, R. Letter to the editors of *Human Behavior,* February 1978, pp. 7-8.

GREELEY, A. *That most distressful nation.* Chicago: Quadrangle, 1972.

GREEN, F. Quoted in Sexual abuse among children common, says hospital study. *Bath-Brunswick Times Record,* November 13, 1977, p. 3.

GREENE, N. B. A view of family pathology involving child molest—from juvenile probation perspective. *Juvenile Justice,* 1977, pp. 29-34.

GROTH, N. Guidelines for assessment and management of the offender. In Burgess *et al.* (Eds.), *Sexual assualt of children and adolescents.* Lexington, Mass.: Lexington Books, 1978.

HAMMER, E. F., and GLUECK, B. C., JR. Psychodynamic patterns in sex offense: A four factor theory. *Psychiatric Quarterly,* 1957, *3,* 325-345.

HENDERSON, J. Incest: A synthesis of data. *Canadian Psychiatric Association Journal,* 1972, *17,* 299-313.

HERMAN J., and HIRSCHMAN, L. Father-daughter incest. *Signs,* 1977, *2,* 1-22.

HILBERMAN, E. *The rape victim.* New York: Basic Books, 1976.

HOOVER, J. E. How safe is your daughter? *American Magazine,* July 1947, p. 32.

Horror Week. *Newsweek,* November 28, 1949.

HUNT, M. *Sexual behavior in the 1970's.* Chicago: Playboy Press, 1974.

JAMES, J., and MEYERDING, J. Early sexual experiences as a factor in prostitution. *Archives of Sexual Behavior,* 1977, *7* (1), 31-42.

JESSOR, S., and JESSOR, R. Transition from virginity to nonvirginity among youth: A social psychological study over time. *Developmental Psychology,* 1975, *11* (4), 473-484.

KANIN, E. and PARCELL, S. Sexual aggression: A second look at the offended female. *Archives of Sexual Behavior,* 1977, *6,* 67-76.

KAUFMAN, I., PECK, A., and TAGIURI, C. K. The family constellation and overt incestuous relations between father and daughter. *American Journal of Orthopsychiatry,* 1954, *24,* 266-279.

KINSEY, A., *et al. Sexual behavior in the human male.* Philadelphia: Saunders, 1948.

———. *Sexual behavior in the human female.* Philadelphia: Saunders, 1953.

KRAFFT-EBING, R. von. *Psychopathia sexualis.* New York: Physicians and Surgeons Book Co., 1935.

KUTCHINSKY, B. The effect of easy availability of pornography on the incidence of sex crimes: The Danish experience. *Journal of Social Issues,* 1973, *29,* 163-181.

LANDIS, J. Experiences of 500 children with adult sexual deviants. *Psychiatric Quarterly Supplement,* 1956, *30,* 91–109.

LANGNER, T. *Life stress and mental health.* New York: McGraw-Hill, 1962.

LANGSLEY, D. G., SCHWARTZ, M. N., and FAIRBAIRN, R. H. Father-son incest. *Comprehensive Psychiatry,* 1968, *9*(3), 218–226.

LASCH, C. *Haven in a heartless world.* New York: Basic Books, 1977.

LEGMAN, G. *The limerick.* New York: Bell Publishing, 1964.

LESTER, D. Incest. *Journal of Sex Research,* 1972, *8*(4), 268–285.

LITIN, E., GIFFIN, M., and JOHNSON, A. Parental influence in unusual sexual behavior in children. *Psychoanalytic Quarterly,* 1956, *25,* 37–55.

LLOYD, R., *For money or love: Boy prostitution in America.* New York: Vanguard, 1976.

LUSTIG, N., DRESSER, J. W., SPELLMAN, S. W., and MURRAY, T. B. Incest: A family group survival pattern. *Archives of General Psychiatry,* 1966, *14,* 31–40.

McCAGHY, C. Child molesters: A study of their careers as deviants. In M. B. Clinard and R. Quinney (Eds.), *Criminal behavior systems: A typology.* New York: Holt, Rinehart, 1967.

———. Drinking and deviance disavowal: The case of child molesters. *Journal of Social Problems,* 1968, *16,* 43–49.

———. Child molesting. *Sexual Behavior,* 1971, *1,* 16–24.

McCORMACK, A. H. New York's present problem. *Mental Hygiene,* 1938, *20,* 4–5.

McDONALD, H. C. *Playtime with Patty and Wilbur.* Culver City, Cal.: Murray and Gee, 1952.

MACDONALD, J., *Indecent exposure.* Springfield, Ill.: C. C. Thomas, 1973.

McFARLANE, K. Sexual abuse of children. In J. R. Chapman and M. Gates (Eds.), *The victimization of women.* Beverly Hills, Cal.: Sage, 1978.

McGUIRE, R. J., CARLISLE, J. M., and YOUNG, B. G. Sexual deviations as conditioned behavior: A hypothesis. *Behavior Research and Therapy,* 1965, *2,* 185–190.

MACHOTKA, P., PITTMAN, F. S., and FLOMENHAFT, K. Incest as a family affair. *Family Process,* 1966, *6,* 98–116.

MADEN, M., and WRENCH, D. Significant findings in child abuse research. *Victimology,* 1977, *2,* 196–224.

MAISCH, H. *Incest.* New York: Stein and Day, 1972.

MARSHALL, W. A. Growth and sexual maturation in normal puberty. *Clinics in Endocrinology and Metabolism,* 1975, *4,* 3–25.

MARTINSON, F. M. *Infant and child sexuality.* St. Peter, Minn.: The Book Mark, 1973.

MEAD, M. *Coming of age in Samoa.* New York: William Morrow, 1928.

———. *Sex and temperament in primitive societies.* New York: Dell, 1968.

MEISELMAN, K. *Incest: A psychological study of causes and effects with treatment recommendations.* San Francisco: Jossey-Bass, 1978.

MILLER, P. Blaming the victim of child molestation: An empirical analysis. Doctoral dissertation, Northwestern University, 1976. *Dissertation Abstracts International,* 1976. University Microfilms No. 77–10069.

MINUCHIN, S. *Families and family therapy.* Cambridge, Mass.: Harvard, 1974.

MOHR, J. W., TURNER, R. E., and JERRY, M. B. *Pedophilia and exhibitionism.* Toronto: University of Toronto, 1964.

MOLNAR, B., and CAMERON, P. Incest syndromes: Observations in a General Hospital Psychiatric Unit. *Canadian Psychiatric Association Journal,* 1975, *20,* 1–24.

MONEY, J., and TUCKER, P. *Sexual signatures.* Boston: Little Brown, 1975.

MULVIHILL, D. J., and TUMIN, M. *Crimes of violence: A staff report to the National Commission on the Causes and Prevention of Violence.* Washington, D.C.: U.S. Government Printing Office, 1969.

MURDOCK, G. P. *Social structure.* New York: Macmillan, 1949.

"My husband broke the ultimate taboo." *Family Circle,* March 8, 1977.

NABOKOV, V. *Lolita.* New York: Putnam's Sons, 1955.

NEWSON, J., AND NEWSON, E. *Four years old in an urban community.* Chicago: Aldine, 1968.

NOBILE, P. Incest: The last taboo. *Penthouse,* January 1978, p. 117.

OREMLAND, E., and OREMLAND, J. *The sexual and gender development of young children: The role of education.* Cambridge, Mass.: Ballinger, 1977.

PARSONS, T. Social structure of the family. In R. N. Anshen (Ed.), *The family: Its function and destiny.* New York: Harper, 1949.

PETERS, J. J. Children who were victims of sexual assault and the psychology of offenders. *American Journal of Psychotherapy,* 1976, *30,* 398–412.

———. [Commentary] In C. H. McCaghy, Child molesting. *Sexual Behavior,* 1971, *1,* 16–24.

PFOHL, S. J. The discovery of child abuse. *Social Problems,* 1977, *24,* 310–323.

PILINOW, A. Czynniki rozktadu i technika rozbijania podstowowych wiezi spotec-zych. In A. Podgorecki (Ed.), *Socjotechnika.* Ksiazka i Wiedza, 1970.

POMEROY, W. *Dr. Kinsey and the Institute for Sex Research.* New York: Harper and Row, 1972.

———. *Your child and sex.* New York: Delacorte, 1974.

———. A new look at incest. *The Best of Forum,* 1978, pp. 92–97.

POPE, H., and MUELLER, C. W. Intergenerational transmission of marital instability; Comparisons by race and sex. *Journal of Social Issues,* 1976, *32*(1), 49–66.

POZNANSKI, E., and BLOS, P. Incest. *Medical Aspects of Human Sexuality,* October 1975, pp. 46–77.

PRESCOTT, J. W. Body pleasure and the origins of violence. *The Futurist,* 1975, pp. 64–74.

QUEEN'S BENCH FOUNDATION. *Sexual abuse of children.* San Francisco: Queen's Bench Foundation, 1976.

RAMER, L. *Your sexual bill of rights.* New York: Exposition Press, 1973.

RANDOLPH, V. *Pissing in the snow and other Ozark folktales.* Urbana: University of Illinois, 1976.

"Readers discuss family sex." *Forum,* July 1977, pp. 89–94.

REISS, I. L. *The social context of premarital permissiveness.* New York: Holt, Rhinehart, 1967.

RHINEHART, J. W. Genesis of overt incest. *Comprehensive Psychiatry,* 1961, *2,* 338–349.

RIEMER, S. A research note on incest. *American Journal of Sociology,* 1940, *45,* 566.

ROSENFELD, A. Sexual misuse of children. Unpublished paper. Stanford University, 1977.

———. Incest: The victim-perpetrator model. Unpublished paper. Stanford University, 1978.

RUSH, F. The sexual abuse of children: A feminist point of view. In N. Connell and C. Wilson (Eds.), *Rape: The first sourcebook for women.* New York: NAL Plume, 1974.

———. The Freudian cover-up. *Chrysalis,* 1977, *1,* 31–45.

SCHECHTER, M. D., and ROBERGE, L. Sexual exploitation. In R. E. Helfer and C. H. Kempe (Eds.), *Child abuse and neglect: the family and the community.* Cambridge, Mass.: Ballinger, 1976.

SCHERRER, P. La sexualité criminelle en milieu rural. L'inceste. In P. Lassa (Ed.), *Congres de psychiatrie et de neurologie de langue française.* Paris: Masson, 1959.

SCHULTZ, L. G. The child as sex victim: Socio-legal perspectives. In *Rape Victimology.* Springfield, Ill.: C. C. Thomas, 1975.

———. Sexual victims. In H. L. Gochros and G. S. Gochros (Eds.), *The sexually oppressed.* New York: Association Press, 1977.

SEARS, R. Antecedents of gender development. In F. Beach (Ed.), *Sex and Behavior.* New York: Wiley, 1965.

SEARS, R., MACCOBY, E., and LEVIN, H. *Patterns of child rearing.* Evanston, Ill.: Row, Peterson and Co., 1957.

Sex Rampage. *Newsweek,* February 13, 1950.

SGROI, S. Sexual molestation of children: The last frontier of child abuse. *Children Today,* May-June 1975, *44,* 18–21.

SHEPHER, J. Mate selection among second generation kibbutz adolescents and adults—incest avoidance and negative imprinting. *Archives of Sexual Behavior,* 1971, *1,* 293–307.

SHEPPARD, D., GIACINTI, T., and TJADEN, C. Rape re-education: A citywide program. In M. Walker and S. Brodsky (Eds.), *Sexual assault.* Lexington, Mass.: Lexington Books, 1976.

SILVERMAN, R. Victim precipitation: An examination of the concept. In I. Drapkin and E. Viano (Eds.), *Victimology: A new focus,* Vol. I. Lexington, Mass.: Lexington Books, 1974.

SLATER, P. *Pursuit of Loneliness.* Boston: Beacon, 1968.

SLOANE, P., and KARPINSKY, F. Effects of incest on participants. *American Journal of Orthopsychiatry,* 1942, *12,* 666–673.

STEINEM, G. Pornography—not sex but the obscene use of power. *Ms.,* August 1977, pp. 43–44.

STEINMETZ, S. K., and STRAUS, M. A. (EDS.) *Violence in the family*. New York: Harper and Row, 1974.

STOLLER, R. *Perversion: The erotic form of hatred*. New York: Pantheon, 1975.

STONE, L. *Family, sex and marriage in England, 1550–1800*. New York: Harper and Row, 1977.

SUMMIT, R., and KRYSO, J. Sexual abuse of children: a clinical spectrum. *American Journal of Orthopsychiatry*, 1978, *48*, 237–251.

SUTHERLAND, E. H. The diffusion of sexual psychopath laws. *American Journal of Sociology*, 1950, *56*, 142–146.

SWANSON, D. W. Adult sexual abuse of children. *Diseases of the Nervous System*, 1968, *29*, 677–683.

SWIFT, C. Sexual victimization of children: An urban mental health center survey. *Victimology*, 1977, *2*, 322–327.

SZABO, D. L'inceste en milieu urbain. *L'annee sociologique*, 1958 (3eme serie).

TORMES, Y. *Child victims of incest*. Denver: American Humane Association, n.d.

TRANKELL, A. Was Lars sexually assaulted? A study in the reliability of witnesses and of experts. *Journal of Abnormal and Social Psychology*, 1958, *56*, 385–395.

VAN STOLK, M. *The sexually abused child*. Paper presented at the Meeting of the Second World Conference of the International Society on Family Law, Montreal, June 1977.

VIRKKUNEN, M. Incest offenses and alcoholism. *Medicine, Science and Law*, April 1974, *14*, 124–128.

WALTERS, D. *Physical and sexual abuse of children: Causes and treatment*. Bloomington: Indiana University, 1975.

WEBER, E. Sexual abuse begins at home. *Ms.*, April 1977, pp. 64–67.

WEINBERG, S. K. *Incest behavior*. New York: Citadel, 1955.

WEINER, I. Father–daughter incest: A clinical report. *Psychiatric Quarterly*, 1962, *36*, 607.

WEISS, J., ROGERS, E., DARWIN, M., and DUTTON, C. A study of girl sex victims. *Psychiatric Quarterly*, 1955, *29*(1), 1–27.

WESTERMARCK, E. *The history of human marriage*. London: Macmillan, 1894.

YORUKOCLU, A., and KEMPH, J. Children not severely damaged by incest. *Journal of the Academy of Child Psychiatry*, 1969, *8*, 606.

ZAPHIRIS, A. *Assessment and treatment for sexually abused families*. Workshop presented at the meeting of the National Conference on Child Abuse and Neglect, April 1978.

INDEX